AUTISM IN CHILDHOOD AND
AUTISTIC FEATURES IN ADULTS

p. 210 – Identifying
autistic from narcisstic
phenomena Through
c. tranf.

Autism in Childhood and Autistic Features in Adults is one of a series of low-cost books under the title **PSYCHOANALYTIC ideas** which brings together the best of Public Lectures and other writings given by analysts of the British Psychoanalytical Society on important psychoanalytic subjects.

The books can be ordered from:
Karnac Books
www.karnacbooks.com
Tel. +(0)20 7431 1075
Fax: +(0)20 7435 9076
E-mail: shop@karnacbooks.com

AUTISM IN CHILDHOOD AND AUTISTIC FEATURES IN ADULTS

A Psychoanalytic Perspective

Editor

Kate Barrows

Series Editors

Inge Wise and *Paul Williams*

KARNAC

First published in 2008 by
the Institute of Psychoanalysis, London
Karnac Books Ltd
118 Finchley Road
London NW3 5HT

British Library Cataloguing in Publication Data

A C.I.P. for this book is available from the British Library

ISBN: 978–1–85575–424–9

Designed, typeset and produced by
Florence Production Ltd, Stoodleigh, Devon
www.florenceproduction.co.uk

Printed in Great Britain by the MPG Books Group,
Bodmin and King's Lynn

www.karnacbooks.com

CONTENTS

ACKNOWLEDGEMENTS

I would like to thank Maria Rhode for her unfailing generosity and availability to discuss issues concerning childhood autism in relation to this book. Countless interesting and informative conversations have added greatly to my enjoyment of this enterprise and understanding of the field, as well as to the quality of the book itself. Heartfelt thanks also to Paul Barrows for his patient and steadfast support and inimitable editorial skills where my own writing is concerned. I am grateful to Frances Tustin and to Sydney Klein, from whom I learned so much, and whose contributions have formed the bedrock of subsequent developments in the field of work with autism in children and adults. Last but not least, many thanks to all the contributors to this volume and to their patients.

ABOUT THE EDITOR AND CONTRIBUTORS

Anne Alvarez, PhD, MACP, trained as a clinical psychologist in Canada and the USA before training as a child and adolescent psychotherapist in the UK. She is an honorary consultant child and adolescent psychotherapist (and retired Co-Convener of the Autism Workshop) in the Child and Family Department of the Tavistock Clinic, London. She is author of *Live Company: Psychotherapy with Autistic, Borderline, Deprived and Abused Children*, and has co-edited with Susan Reid *Autism and Personality: Findings from the Tavistock Autism Workshop*. A book in her honour, edited by Judith Edwards, entitled *Being Alive: Building on the Work of Anne Alvarez* was published in 2002. She was Visiting Professor at the San Francisco Psychoanalytic Society in November 2005.

Kate Barrows is a training analyst with the British Psychoanalytical Society and works in private practice in Bristol. She is also a Tavistock-trained child psychotherapist and currently works as a staff member of the Child and Family Service at the Bridge Foundation for Psychotherapy and the Arts. She writes and lectures in England and abroad. Her interest in autism is evident from this book, and she has written several papers about the relationship between literature and psychoanalysis. Her publications include *Envy* (Icon Books).

Paul Barrows works as a consultant child and adolescent psycho-therapist in the NHS in Bristol. He was winner of the Frances Tustin Memorial Prize and Lectureship for his paper "The Use of Stories as Autistic Objects". He was also previously Editor of the *Journal of Child Psychotherapy*.

Velleda Cecchi, MD, is a psychiatrist and a child and adolescent analyst, and she has been a lecturer at the Angel Garma Institute in the Argentine Psychoanalytical Association since 1987. From 1991 to 1996, she co-ordinated a research group into Music and Psycho-analysis. Since 1998, she has co-ordinated an interdisciplinary team for the study and care of child and adolescent psychoses. She is the author of several papers on childhood autism. Her latest book, *Los Otros Creen que no Estoy. Autismo y Otras Psicosis Infantiles [The Others Think I Don't Exist. Autism and Other Childhood Psychoses]*, was published in 2005 (Lumen, Buenos Aires). She is the co-author of *Argentina: Psicoanálisis: Represión Política [Argentina: Psycho-analysis: Political Repression]* (Kargieman, Buenos Aires, 1986) and of *Clínica psicoanalítica de niños y adolescentes [Child and Adolescent Psychoanalysis]* (Lumen, Buenos Aires, 1998).

Mario Gomberoff, MD, is Senior Professor of Psychiatry in the Faculty of Medicine at the University of Chile. He is a Master of Chilean Psychiatry and Director of Graduate Studies (Diplomas, Master and Doctor Programmes in Psychoanalysis) at the School of Psychology, Andrés Bello University. Former President of the Chilean Psychoanalytic Association, he is a training psychoanalyst at the Institute of Psychoanalysis, Chilean Psychoanalytic Associa-tion.

Liliana Pualuan de Gomberoff is a training psychoanalyst at the Institute of Psychoanalysis, Chilean Psychoanalytic Association. She is also a Professor with the Graduate Studies Programme in Psychoanalysis at Andrés Bello University. In addition, she has a Master of Arts in Hispano-American and Chilean Literature from the Literature Department, University of Chile. She is former Professor of Infant and Adolescent Clinical Psychology at the Catholic University of Chile.

Didier Houzel, PhD (Medicine, Paris, 1972), was Professor of Child and Adolescent Psychiatry at the University of Caen (Basse Normandie, France). He is a Full Member of the Association Psychanalytique de France and a Member of the European Federation for Psychoanalytic Psychotherapy in the Public Sector. He is especially interested in the psychoanalytic treatment of autistic and psychotic children. He was trained in that field by Donald Meltzer and Frances Tustin in London. He was also trained in Infant Observation. He has used an application of Esther Bick's method to treat very young children under three, particularly infants with autistic features.

H. Sydney Klein (1918–2005) was a Founder Fellow of the Royal College of Psychiatrists. He qualified as a psychoanalyst with the British Psychoanalytical Society in 1953 and as a child analyst in 1957, and subsequently as a training analyst. He held numerous roles within the Institute of Psychoanalysis, including that of Director of the Children's Department of the London Clinic. He supervised Frances Tustin with one of her first autistic child patients at the Belgrave Hospital, which she described as a formative experience at the start of her specialisation in work with autistic children. Klein worked in the NHS for many years and believed strongly that psychoanalysis should be available nationwide to children and adults.

Judith Mitrani, PhD, trained as a psychoanalyst in Los Angeles. She is a member of the Senior Faculty of the Psychoanalytic Center of California and the Guest Faculty at the Los Angeles Society and Institute for Psychoanalytic Studies, as well as the Southern California Psychoanalytic Institute. She works in private practice with adults and children. In her professional development she was profoundly influenced by the work of Frances Tustin. She founded the Frances Tustin Memorial Society, which runs conferences and promotes developments in the psychoanalytic study of autism.

Carmen Noemi Callejas studied medicine at the University of Chile and then specialised in child psychiatry in the Calvo Mackenna Hospital, directed by the psychoanalyst Dr Guillermo Altamarino.

She studied adult psychiatry and subsequently became a training psychoanalyst with the Chilean Institute of Psychoanalysis.

Thomas H. Ogden is Director of the Center for the Advanced Study of the Psychoses, a supervising and personal analyst at the Psychoanalytic Institute of Northern California, and a member of the International Psychoanalytical Association. He has published seven books, the most recent of which are *This Art of Psychoanalysis: Dreaming Undreamt Dreams and Interrupted Cries*; *Conversations at the Frontier of Dreaming*; *Reverie and Interpretation: Sensing Something Human*; and *Subjects of Analysis*. He was awarded the 2004 *International Journal of Psychoanalysis* Award for the Most Important Paper of the Year.

Caroline Polmear is a training analyst of the British Psychoanalytical Society. She works in private practice in North London. She takes an active role in the organisation of psychoanalytic training at the Institute of Psychoanalysis.

Maria Rhode is Professor of Child Psychotherapy at the Tavistock Clinic/University of East London. She has co-edited *Psychotic States in Children* (Duckworth, 1997), *The Many Faces of Asperger's Syndrome* (Karnac: Tavistock Clinic Book Series), and *Invisible Boundaries: Psychosis and Autism in Children and Adolescents* (Karnac: EFPP Series). She co-convenes the Tavistock Autism Workshop.

David Simpson is a Consultant Child and Adolescent Psychiatrist at the Tavistock Clinc and a Member of the British Psychoanalytical Society. He is Joint Head of the Tavistock Clinic Learning and Complex Disabilities Service and Joint Chair of the Autism Workshop. He also works in private practice as a psychoanalyst.

Frances Tustin (1913–93) trained at the Tavistock Clinic as a child psychotherapist, qualifying in 1953. She worked in the NHS until 1978 and concurrently in private practice, where she specialised in work with autistic children. She wrote four books and numerous articles about autism, and lectured and taught widely in this country and abroad. She was appointed Honorary Affiliate of the British Psychoanalytical Society in 1984 and Honorary Member of the Association of Child Psychotherapists in 1986.

Introduction

Kate Barrows

This collection draws together papers which are central to today's psychoanalytic understanding of childhood autism and of autistic aspects of adult patients. Some of these papers are classics in the field while others describe more recent advances in understanding and technique. They show a broad range of psychoanalytic ideas and a variety of views. Many relevant and important authors could not be included in this attempt to cover an area which is paradoxically rich despite the fact that it focuses on such barren and unthinking states of mind. I shall mention some of these authors in this account, to give the wider picture and to offer readers the possibility of following up the ideas that interest them.

Since Leo Kanner (1943) first described a small group of autistic children and focused attention upon the condition, there has been an enormous growth of interest in autism, and there are of course many theoretical approaches to it: psychiatry, neurology, experimental psychology and psychoanalysis, to name but a few. David Simpson in his chapter discusses some of these approaches. Autism is now generally agreed to comprise a "triad of impairments", as described by Wing and Gould (1979). They are "impairment of

1

social interaction, repetitive activities in place of imaginative symbolic interests, and impairment of language development".

The many different approaches to autism can at times seem to be mutually exclusive and to represent rival camps. However, over the last twenty years or so, some of these diverse approaches have come together in the minds of child psychotherapists and child psychoanalysts to account for different facets of a condition whose aetiology and presentation can vary enormously and can be particularly enigmatic. For instance, Frances Tustin, a Tavistock-trained child psychotherapist, described (1994a) how she came to discard her original idea of a state of "normal primary autism" in the light of the researches of the developmental psychologists Stern (1983, 1985) and Trevarthen (1979). They demonstrated that there is no stage of primary fusion with the mother and that on the contrary the infant has some considerable capacity to relate to the mother as a separate person from birth. Autistic anxieties and defences may, however, stultify this innate capacity and prevent it from developing.

The last few decades have seen a burgeoning of interest in autistic spectrum disorders which cause enormous suffering to individuals and families and pose extremely serious problems in terms of treatment, education and care. Susan Reid (Alvarez & Reid, 1999, pp. 13–32) has described some of the difficulties of living with an autistic child and the momentous effects that this can have on the whole family. However, the growth of interest in autism may also be due to the intriguing nature of autistic children. While not all such children are attractive, some of them are, and can be beautiful in a way that is characteristically ethereal and enigmatic. They have been compared to sleeping beauties, giving an impression of locked up potential, though this can sometimes cause huge frustration and despair. They can seem to offer tantalising hope that their potential can be set free, though the realisation of that hope may turn out to be unattainable; this can cause those who work with them immeasurable disappointment and grief about unrealised possibilities. Tustin remarked that they can break the hearts of those who try to help them. It takes courage and strength to work with autistic children over time, in whatever capacity.

The growth of widespread interest in autism has led to the recognition that many people employ autistic defences and that even fairly well functioning neurotic adults can be held back from progress in their lives if the autistic levels of the personality are not addressed. Impasses in adult analysis can be due to autistic functioning which has not been recognised (see Klein, this volume, Chapter Eight). The increased psychoanalytic understanding of childhood autism has expanded our understanding of primitive levels of the human psyche. The fears of bodily and mental catastrophe which can underlie autistic defences are described in the chapters on work with neurotic adults as well as in those chapters which focus on autistic children.

There are by now several psychoanalytic books and many papers on the subject of childhood autism. However, comparatively little has been written on autistic aspects of adult patients. Severely autistic adults, who are likely to live in institutions, do not find their way to psychoanalysis and are not discussed in these pages. The need for early intervention in childhood is usually critical if the autistic state is not to become permanently entrenched. Yet the understanding of childhood autism has a lot to contribute to work with those adult patients who employ autistic defences in order to cope with their anxieties.

A wide range of such adult patients is described in this book. They may be highly articulate, successful people who have nonetheless an encapsulated autistic area which blocks communication and keeps them at one remove from their emotions and contact with others. Sydney Klein and Mario Gomberoff *et al* describe such patients. Caroline Polmear tells us about two patients with pronounced autistic features who were nonetheless able to use their high intelligence to manage demanding professional lives. Others who have been less able to cope with normal life may exist in a more extreme state of withdrawal which prevents engagement in work or human relationships. Thomas Ogden and Kate Barrows describe patients of this kind, while Judith Mitrani discusses a variety of cases. Frances Tustin writes about a young woman who had originally come to her as a child. I hope that the juxtaposition of child and adult work within the same volume will prove enriching for people who work with either age group.

Before going further, I shall briefly mention the relationship between Asperger's syndrome and autism, an area which has been much debated in recent years. Hans Asperger (1944) described a small group of boys with particular characteristics, who had good

linguistic and cognitive skills but poor capacity for social relationships. They tended to develop interests in particular areas, such as
science or mathematics, or to collect information in an obsessive way,
such as timetables or information about cars. They would try to
communicate by deluging the listener with information in a way that
seemed compulsive and was hard to listen to. They tended to be
clumsy. Asperger saw them as having autistic features, particularly
in their inability to make emotional contact. His paper was not known
in this country until reviewed by Lorna Wing in 1981, and since then
Asperger's syndrome has been widely recognised and has become
a condition which has attracted much interest and considerable
resources. It was thought by Tustin (1994b, p. 114) to derive, like
autism, from a catastrophic experience of separateness, but at a later
stage of development, after the acquisition of language. Polmear's
patients (Chapter Fourteen) were variously described as having
autistic features or Asperger's syndrome, and there would seem
to be considerable overlap between the two. However, this view is
not universally held, as discussed in Simpson's chapter in *The Many
Faces of Asperger's Syndrome* (Rhode & Klauber, 2004, pp. 25–38).
I do not attempt in the present volume to discuss in detail the
similarities and differences between the two conditions, but would
refer the reader to that chapter.

It is certainly the case that the earlier autistic spectrum disorders
can be diagnosed and treated, the more hopeful the outcome.
Colleagues in Caen in Normandy have for twenty years been utilising
Infant Observation as a method to treat dysfunctional interactions
between mother and infant, including some early cases of infantile
autism (Houzel, 1999). Specialist paediatric nurses are trained in
Infant Observation, as developed by psychoanalyst Esther Bick,
and visit families identified as being at risk to observe the mother
or father and infant in the home setting. (This form of observation
is well known by now and there are many examples of its application in the *International Journal of Infant Observation*.) The observations
entail one or two visits a week, and these are written up and discussed in a seminar group. The visits offer "one hour of close
attention in a state of mind that is open and receptive to all that might
be expressed by those family members present, whether verbally or
non-verbally ... At times the therapists experience extremely
powerful feelings, even to the extent of somatic responses ... it is of

vital importance to consider the reactions which have been prompted and which are, very often, of profound significance" (Houzel, 1999, p. 43). The family is also visited once a month by the child psychiatrist, and psychotherapy may be offered when the infant reaches two years of age. Through this experience mothers are helped to contain and work through some of their anxieties in relation to the child, and to develop their capacity to give the child a quality of attention which helps the child to move forward: in cases of early autism the infant may be enabled to come out of a state of autistic withdrawal and be freed to develop. Similar home observations of infants at risk have more recently been started at the Tavistock Clinic in London. (For further studies of early characteristics of infants who develop autism and of early intervention, see Acquarone, 2007.)

The first account of the psychoanalytic treatment of an autistic child is Melanie Klein's paper "The Importance of Symbol Formation in the Development of the Ego" (1930). She describes the analysis of a four-year-old boy who presented with symptoms which would now be taken to indicate a strong likelihood of autism.

> Adaptation to reality and emotional relations to his environment were almost entirely lacking. This child, Dick, was largely devoid of affects, and he was indifferent to the presence or absence of his mother or nurse. From the beginning he only rarely displayed anxiety, and that in an abnormally small degree ... He had almost no interests, did not play and had no contact with his environment. For the most part, he simply strung sounds together in a meaningless way, and constantly repeated certain noises ... When he was hurt, he displayed very considerable insensitivity to pain, and felt nothing of the desire, so universal with little children, to be comforted and petted ... he also ran round me, just as if I were a piece of furniture, but he showed no interest in any of the objects in the room. [pp. 219–220]

In six months Klein helped Dick to make considerable progress, in particular to regain his curiosity and his wish to communicate, both essential building blocks for development. She was puzzled as to a diagnosis, finding that Dick did not entirely fit the description of childhood schizophrenia (p. 231).

As Tustin (1983) was to point out in her discussion of this paper, Klein anticipates Kanner's description of childhood autism. Klein's paper is also a landmark in the understanding of the importance of symbol formation for ego development. She suggests that Dick's inhibition was due to his fears of aggressive feelings towards his mother, her body and its phantasied contents. She contends that phantasies about the contents of the mother's body underpin mental and emotional development, and that where fears of damaging the mother and her contents are too powerful, inhibition in emotional and intellectual development sets in to protect the mother from damage and the child from fears of retaliation or feelings of unbearable guilt. Symbol formation occurs in response to anxiety about ambivalence towards the mother and her contents, the child seeking new objects to represent the original relationship with the mother at the same time as diluting the anxiety about damage. However, where the anxiety is too great, the child cannot form symbols but lives in a state where the only option is avoidance of a world which is equated with a dangerous version of the mother's body and felt to be too terrifying to approach. This avoidance, and the seeming lack of anxiety of some autistic children, thinly masks their anxiety about their objects. Klein identifies a premature concern for the object, and a difficulty in establishing the necessary "ruthlessness" which Winnicott (1965, pp. 21–23) was later to describe as crucial for development. Paradoxically, then, autistic children have retreated to a position of treating others as if they were furniture, and themselves as though they could feel no pain, as a response to an early hypersensitivity to damage.

An adolescent patient of Frances Tustin found a poem—a song by Paul Simon—which eloquently expressed this position:

I've built walls,
A fortress steep and mighty
That none may penetrate.
I have no need of friendship.
Friendship causes pain.
It's laughter and it's loving I disdain
I am a rock,
I am an island . . .
And a rock feels no pain,
And an island never cries.

Klein describes how, in the normal development of the child, an internal world is built up, mediated through the emotional quality of the relationship to his parents (see, for example, 1940, pp. 345–353). Klein suggests that at first the infant experiences the mother in terms of extreme contrasts between herself (or her breast) as idealised or persecutory: the mother who satisfies the baby's needs as ideally good, the absent mother as persecutory or bad. Gradually a more balanced view emerges, and the infant realises that his feelings of love and hate colour the picture, that the mother with whom he is angry is also the mother whom he loves. He begins to recognise the part played by his own ambivalent feelings.

Wilfred Bion significantly developed psychoanalytic under-standing of how these developments come about, describing how the infant communicates unbearable feelings to his mother, who is able to "contain" them—to take them in, digest them and modify them so that they can be handed back to the baby in a form that is now bearable (1967, p. 114). The same idea of containment is applied to the psychoanalytic setting, the analyst or child psychotherapist taking in the feelings that their patients project into them and gradually, through being able to bear these feelings and think about them, transforming them into communications which the patients can manage to take in and think about. This is no easy process, and it takes thorough training and the support of insightful colleagues to maintain. Autistic manoeuvres prove particularly difficult to bear, since the therapist has to contend with feeling very isolated and shut out by the patient, as well as the pull towards mindlessness, towards the autistic state.

Tustin refers in Chapter Two to her autistic patient John, aged three years and seven months when he started twice weekly psycho-therapy, and aged five years (and in five times weekly psychother-apy) at the time of the material which she discusses. John was initially mute, though he understood a few words. He began to speak, and in his sessions it emerged that in phantasy he created a breast for himself to which he was joined up, as if he had the nipple permanently in his mouth. She states that this situation arose from a lack of clear differentiation of his mouth from the breast. She adds: "It is difficult for us, as differentiated individuals, to get in touch with such undifferentiated modes of operation. In these states objects which, in sensuous terms, have a rough-and-ready 'clang' similarity with each other are grouped together and treated as if they were the same." He felt that he could lose the "red button" from his mouth, that he and the breast could become broken asunder. The absent breast became in his mind a "black hole with a nasty prick", or "broken". It was after these feelings were expressed by him and understood by his therapist that he became aware that "the red button *grows* on the breast". This realisation led to his also understanding that he had "a good head on my shoulders! Can't fall off! *Grows* on my shoulders!" He became much more able to use his mind. In three years he recovered sufficiently to attend school, and subsequently went on to do well at university.

This work showed Tustin how the child felt that his mother was part of his body, and how separation was experienced as a bodily catastrophe. Whilst, like Klein, she was aware of the child's fears of damaging the mother, she felt that the autistic defences of mindlessness and illusions of being physically joined up to the mother protected him from more primitive terrors based in bodily experiences—fears, for instance, of having a bit torn out of his mouth, fears of liquefaction, or of falling into nothingness. Tustin suggests that these anxieties are lived mainly in terms of unbearable physical sensations which are kept at bay by defensive sensation-manoeuvres: hard autistic objects, soft autistic shapes and other protections. The hard "autistic sensation object", as Tustin called it (Chapter Two), is an object with which the autistic child feels equated. This may be an actual object, such as a hard toy, or a part of the child's body used to block out anxiety. The bodily sensation of hardness fortifies the child against his fears, and the objects are used not in terms of their objective functions but in terms of the hard sensations they engender. "Autistic sensation shapes" (Tustin 1986, Chapter 7), on the other hand, are soft sensations experienced on the surface of the body. They are not associated with appropriate objects but remain as idiosyncratic bodily sensations. This impairs the development of percept and concept formation and hence prevents cognitive development, so that the autistic child may appear to be mentally defective. No shared perceptions can develop, for instance those that would involve proto-declarative pointing at objects to express a shared interest in them.

Donald Meltzer and his colleagues (1975) offered a somewhat different account of the basis of the lack of cognitive and emotional development. They came to the conclusion that the autistic children whom they studied had dismantled their perceptual apparatus, separating the senses of sight, touch, hearing and smell so that they could not come together to form a realistic picture of the world. "Common-sense", or the working together of the different sensory modalities towards integration and perceptual development, is replaced with isolated sense impressions and mindlessness. "Dismantling occurs by a passive device of allowing the various senses . . . to attach themselves to the most stimulating object of the moment . . . This scattering seems to bring about the dismantling of the self as a mental apparatus, but in a very passive, falling-to-bits kind of way" (ibid., p. 12). Meltzer talks of an initial sensual intensity and possessiveness in the child which makes unbearable the integration of the senses, the bringing together of the infant and mother or her breast; the child fears that the intensity of his feelings may be too damaging, particularly if the mother is fragile in some way. This view of the characteristics of autistic children is in agreement with Tustin's observations that they are highly sensitive, possessive and afraid of damage, and that they experience objects and people in physical or sensual terms. However, Tustin places greater emphasis on the physically experienced primitive terrors of separation and annihilation from which the child's sensuality protects him.

Genevieve Haag, a psychiatrist and psychoanalyst from Paris, has continued both Meltzer's and Tustin's work on the bodily experiences of autistic children. Through infant observation and her work with autistic children, she has come to the conclusion that it is through the medium of the physical and emotional relationship to his caregiver that the baby acquires a detailed sense of the integrity of his own body. She sees the gradual development of control over the joints in the body—the neck, arms, back and legs—as crucial to the developing sense of self. Where this development has not been successful, the infant will not develop a bodily and emotional sense of identity, will not feel that his body and mind are properly connected, but will live in fear of being disjointed or of loss of parts of the body (Haag, 2000).

Tustin found that she had to adapt the psychoanalytic technique used in child psychotherapy to reach her autistic child patients. When she felt they were ready, she would stop them perseverating with repetitive habits and would speak to them with more obvious liveliness and emphasis than would be needed by a neurotic, functioning child. Here her resilient personality undoubtedly helped;

indeed, it takes a robust individual, with a deep conviction about the possibility of rescuing the child from his autism, to stand up to its deadening and discouraging impact. She also spoke candidly about how bearing the child's autistic fears entailed being able to bear her own.

Other contributors to this volume have also found that modifications in technique have helped them to reach the autistic child, though this is not a recipe for "anything goes", and the modifications are carefully thought out and take place in a consistent and rigorous psychoanalytic setting. The times of the sessions are regular, each child has a box of toys which is kept for them, and above all the therapist is there to attend to the child's communications, thinking both about the child's behaviour and about the feelings which are communicated in the session. In this way, the availability of the therapist and her mind as a tool for containing and understanding are the same as they are in the setting of the analysis of an adult patient. However, an imaginative use of technique may sometimes help the therapist to get through the child's habitual and chronic defences.

Velleda Cecchi describes how she used song to gradually make contact with a little girl whose parents had been violently abducted in front of her eyes. Cecchi gradually built up contact from singing one note, through tunes without words, to songs with meaningful lyrics. She gives a moving account of how she intuitively came upon this means of communication and then discovered from the little girl's grandmother that her parents had been amateur musicians. She had got in tune with a way to connect to her young patient in a modality which could reach her. She shares with us the anxiety entailed in adapting her technique. As she puts it, "With these deeply disturbed patients, we often feel we are transgressors on account of alleged deviations from the technical guidelines. But in fact the transgression implies only trying to penetrate into that strange defensive world, the psychotic creation."

Paul Barrows describes carefully introducing an aggressive element into the play with his young patient, who had been traumatised through early illness and separation. The sensitive inclusion of a more vigorous and challenging element into the play had the effect of helping the child feel safer to be aware of and to express his own aggressive feelings.

Anne Alvarez has studied ways of talking to her autistic patients, which she describes as "motherese" and "fatherese". Her carefully timed use of these ways of talking to the child can provide a means to enliven the relationship and demonstrate the possibility of a constructive combination of softness and firmness. These qualities can be brought together by the therapist rather than being split into irreconcilable opposites, as is so often the case with the autistic polarisation of sensual experience.

Didier Houzel also addresses the issue of bringing together maternal and paternal elements, developing Tustin's idea of the autistic child's intense rivalry with a "nest of babies" who he feels occupy the mother. Houzel notes the need for the sense of a firm and understanding paternal figure to mediate the child's extreme possessiveness and the persecutory anxieties which can result from it.

Maria Rhode describes in a different way the need for the child to feel that he or she can find a place in relation to the parental couple and other children, real or imaginary. She discusses the importance of the infant's relationship to the mother's eyes in developing the sense of there being a human family within the mother's mind. She suggests that this is a part of normal development which is usually taken for granted, but has not been possible for many children on the autistic spectrum. It seems to me that this may also be the case with some relatively well functioning adults, as for instance with the patient whom I discuss in Chapter Thirteen, who declared after two years in psychoanalysis that she felt she had become a member of the human race.

The sense of a human family within the mother's mind may sometimes be impeded by an experience which she has not been able to overcome. This may in some instances be a death or trauma which remains lodged in her mind and blocks access (see also Fraiberg *et al*, 1975). I describe work with a young woman whose autistic symptoms and retreat from life seemed linked to unmourned losses in the lives of her parents. This area has also been written about by Bianca Lechevalier, a child psychiatrist and psychoanalyst from Caen, who has described how she found that intergenerational trauma led to pockets of autistic functioning in her patients (2003). Through the dreams of her adult patients and the play of her child patients, as well as through work with mothers and infants, she managed to identify these areas of autistic functioning and to help her patients free themselves from the paralysing hold of the family traumas upon their emotional lives.

Autistic conditions may be attributed to constitutional vulnerability in the child, to emotional factors in the family, or to some combination of the two. In the treatment of any childhood mental disturbance, this is a balance that needs to be considered if appropriate treatment and support are to be provided. The picture is always complex and may never be completely possible to clarify. David Simpson, in his chapter on psychiatric approaches, discusses the balance between nature and nurture and the way in which this should be given careful consideration in each individual case.

Whatever the balance between the child's constitution and environmental factors, child psychotherapists and child psychoanalysts have found addressing the concrete fears of the child to be essential in helping him to emerge from his autistic state. Some of the chapters in this book show how these physically experienced fears can also operate in adults, and that awareness of this concreteness and mindlessness may help the analyst to understand the patient and prevent an impasse.

As well as developing psychoanalytic understanding of childhood autism, Tustin also went on to explore the autistic aspects of adult patients (1986, 1990), and her chapter in the second section of this volume discusses a young adult who had first come to her for psychotherapy as a child and returned for twice weekly psychotherapy in her mid-twenties. She describes how the young woman's need for an illusion of bodily continuity gave way to an experience of a "rhythm of safety" based on a reciprocal interaction with her therapist and with her own deeper feelings, and how this in turn enabled her to feel that she could leave her therapy and move forward on her own. Tustin also describes a more active technique than that which is generally practiced by psychoanalysts who work with adults. She tells the young woman that she should break her habit of chewing on the insides of her mouth, explaining to her in depth how she is using the habit to protect herself from powerful anxieties about bodily separateness. The young woman agrees to stop this habit, and the therapy takes a step forward. Tustin developed this active technique in her work with children; its use with adults has been controversial and has been met with questions: did the instruction to the patient deprive her of the possibility of gaining more insight into the feelings underlying her habit, or did it help her to internalise a firm but kind aspect of her therapist and move on in her development? The reader may be interested to think further about these questions.

In his seminal paper, reprinted here, Sydney Klein (1980) showed how encysted autistic areas of the personality could lie behind impasses in the psychoanalyses of highly intelligent, articulate and successful patients. An absence of direct contact, a use of words to avoid emotions rather than to express them, a lack of depth, and a clinging tenacity which revealed profound insecurity could all stem from an encapsulated autistic area of the mind. Klein found that fears of death and disintegration underlay the autistic defences, and that analysis of this area could free these patients to make more contact both with their analyst and with their own deeper feelings, ultimately to feel more alive. Klein also described how language itself can be used as a barrier to prevent communication. This is a theme which has been developed by Mario Gomberoff, Carmen Noemi and Liliana P. de Gomberoff, who describe in detail in their chapter how the analyst can be subtly pulled into using words as a screen rather than to deepen emotional contact. They describe the pressure on the analyst to be drawn into a relationship of mutual idealisation in which separateness is denied.

Thomas Ogden also found that awareness of autistic functioning led to greater understanding of primitive states in his patients. He writes in terms of an "autistic-contiguous position" which, he suggests, "involves a sensation-dominated way of organising experi-ence. One might think of it as a psychic perspective or vantage point from which earliest experience is viewed by the infant and which continues as a dimension of all subsequent experience at every stage of life." He views this position as the most primitive form of psychic organisation. This is in contrast to the view that Tustin reached when she abandoned her earlier idea of normal primary autism and came to see autism as a defence against anxiety. These two approaches— the idea of autistic manoeuvres as defensive on the one hand or as based on normal early sensory experience on the other—have been much debated.

Ogden makes it clear that recognising the autistic aspects of his patients makes it more possible for him to maintain sympathy for them in difficult circumstances: for instance, he describes a blind patient who did not wash and brought a pervasive body odour into the room; of course the analyst felt intruded upon by this aspect, which lingered long after the patient had left the room. Ogden gradually came to realise that the smell created a comforting shape with which the patient surrounded and protected himself.

Caroline Polmear, in her detailed paper on work with two women with autistic features, likewise describes how understanding the autistic nature of her patients' experiences enabled her to develop an understanding approach to negative aspects of their communication: "The experience of others' feelings as if they were in one's own body is so strong, so overwhelming that it must be evacuated or dissociated if the patient is not to be assaulted by feelings which cannot be moderated or contained. So for 'mindlessness' I would say 'mind over-fullness' or perhaps more accurately 'mind body over-fullness'." Polmear goes on to say that she believes this has important implications for technique and for the analyst's capacity to empathise with the patient: "This shift in thinking is important because it allows the analyst to be ready to catch the wish to make contact, or to recognise the need for the retreats for a recovery period at a particular moment in the session; to realise when language and action are being used not simply as a barrier, but as a communication too. Without this state of mind in the analyst, communication could be experienced and understood simply as destructive attacks." She describes the intense feelings evoked by her patients, as well as the analyst's struggle to stay emotionally alive and to understand the patients' oscillations between extreme emotions and withdrawal and retreat.

Judith Mitrani also found that an awareness of the autistic aspects of her adult patients gave her a framework for understanding the physicality of their anxieties, and she talks in terms of "unmentalised" experiences which the patients have never felt that they could translate into feelings and thoughts. Mitrani suggests that it is clinically important to be precise about the nature of the autistic retreat as compared to other kinds of retreats, such as triumphant manic retreats from persecutory or depressive states. She emphasises the importance of the analyst being open to some very uncomfortable states of mind which the patient induces in her as a central way of communicating his difficulties. This communication of almost unbearable feelings is an involuntary or unconscious manoeuvre, and the analyst's capacity to bear the emotions and communicate her thoughts about them makes it possible for them to be brought into the patient's conscious domain.

There is still work to be done to elucidate the connections between autistic functioning and other constellations which have been more widely written about in the mainstream of psychoanalytic literature. I shall take as one example the concept of pathological narcissistic organisations in adult patients. Herbert Rosenfeld (1971) and Donald Meltzer (1966) described how the patient as it were hands over his mental capacities to an idealised bad figure, such as a mafia leader, invested with seemingly protective power. The patient aims to feel tough and invulnerable. The powerful but corrupt figure and its values control the personality and prevent the real distinction between good and bad, positive and negative, which could lead to emotional development. Tender feelings, curiosity and concern are all looked down on as pathetic or weak, to be despised or feared. Separateness is denied, along with the desires, anger and vulnerability that accompany it. But this ambiguous organisation can also serve to protect the individual from intense anxiety. John Steiner describes how the whole personality may be "invaded by anxiety, which can result in an intolerable state". He suggests that this "may be so unbearable that defensive organisations are needed to create some kind of order out of chaos" (1993, p. 30).

There is a striking similarity between the accounts of this type of narcissism in adults and descriptions of childhood autism: for instance, one might see the defensive turning to an organisation with a "hard" gang leader as being similar to the way that the autistic child will cling to a hard toy for protection, as though it has the power to prevent annihilation by anxiety. In both instances, the individual attempts to deny the possible loss of someone or something which is experienced as an extension of the self rather than as a separate person or thing to be valued in their own right. The more sophisticated, highly symbolised narcissistic retreat could be seen to be based on sensory experiences involving such polarities as hard-soft or powerful-helpless. (Freud, after all, wrote that "the ego is first and foremost a bodily ego" [1923, p. 26].) The threatened loss of the object as if it were part of the self exposes the child or adult to catastrophic anxieties experienced in a concrete way, described vividly in various ways by the authors of this volume.

With autism, as with other conditions, the heart and the sustaining interest of psychoanalytic work lies in the relationship between the individual's symptoms and his personality and creative capacities. There may be a danger that the similarity of some of the presenting features and major anxieties shown by children on the autistic spectrum can obscure the fact of each child being different, having his own identity, and of the autism being interwoven with the individual personality in a unique way in every case (Alvarez & Reid, 1999). Psychoanalytic work with autistic children, or adults with autistic features, is a way of understanding their need to retreat from inner and external reality. When their fears can be faced, this can free them, to some extent and to varying degrees, to join the human family: to develop their own personalities, emotional lives and capacities for thought, imagination and relationships with other human beings.

References

Acquarone, S. (2007). *Signs of Autism in Infants: Recognition and Early Intervention*. London: Karnac.

Alvarez, A. & Reid, S. (Eds.) (1999). *Autism and Personality: Findings from the Tavistock Autism Workshop*. London: Routledge.

Asperger, H. (1944). *Autistic Psychopathy in Childhood* (Trans. Uta Frith). In: U. Frith (Ed.), *Autism and Asperger's Syndrome*. Cambridge University Press, 1991.

Bion, W.R. (1967). A Theory of Thinking. In: *Second Thoughts*. London: Karnac, 1984.

Fraiberg, S., Adelson, E. & Shapiro, V. (1975). Ghosts in the Nursery: a Psychoanalytic Approach to the Problems of Impaired Infant-Mother Relationships. In: *Clinical Studies in Infant Mental Health*. London: Tavistock, 1980.

Freud, S. (1923). The Ego and the Id. *SE 19*.

Haag, G. (2000). In the Footsteps of Frances Tustin: Further Reflections on the Construction of the Body-Ego. *Infant Observation*, 3: 7–22.

Houzel, D. (1999). A Therapeutic Application of Infant Observation in Child Psychiatry. *Infant Observation*, 2: 42–53.

Kanner, L. (1943). Autistic Disturbance of Affective Contact. *Nervous Child*, 2: 217–250. Reprinted in *Childhood Psychosis: Initial Studies and New Insights*. New York: Wiley, 1973.

Klein, M. (1930). The Importance of Symbol-Formation in the Development of the Ego. In: *Love, Guilt and Reparation and Other Works* (pp. 219–232). London: Hogarth, 1975.

Klein, M. (1940). Mourning and its Relation to Manic Depressive States. In: *Love, Guilt and Reparation and Other Works* (pp. 344–369). London: Hogarth, 1975.

Lechevalier, B. (2003). Autistic Enclaves in the Dynamics of Adult Psychoanalysis. Unpublished paper.

Lechevalier, B. (2004). *Traitement Psychanalytique Mère-Enfant: une Approche au Long Cours des Psychoses de l'Enfant*. Paris: Editions In Press.

Meltzer, D. (1966). The Relation of Anal Masturbation to Projective Identification. *Int. J. Psychoanal. 47*: 335–342.

Meltzer, D., Bremner, J., Hoxter, S., Weddell, D. & Wittenberg, I. (1975). *Explorations in Autism: A Psycho-Analytical Study*. Strathtay: Clunie Press.

Rhode, M. & Klauber, T. (2004). *The Many Faces of Asperger's Syndrome*. London: Karnac.

Rosenfeld, H. (1971). A Clinical Approach to the Psycho-Analytical Theory of the Life and Death Instincts: an Investigation into the Aggressive Aspects of Narcissism. *Int. J. Psychoanal, 65*: 169–78.

Steiner, J. (1993). *Psychic Retreats*. London: Routledge.

Stern, D. (1983). Implications of Infant Research for Psychoanalytic Theory and Practice. *Psychiatric Update, 2*: 8–21.

Stern, D. (1985). *The Interpersonal World of the Infant: a View from Psychoanalysis and Developmental Psychology*. New York: Basic Books.

Trevarthen, C. (1979). Instincts for Human Understanding and for Cultural Co-Operation: their Development in Infancy. In *Human Ethology: Claims and Limits of the New Discipline*. London: Cambridge University Press.

Tustin, F. (1972). *Autism and Childhood Psychosis*. London: Hogarth.

Tustin, F. (1981). *Autistic States in Children*. London: Routledge & Kegan Paul.

Tustin, F. (1983). Thoughts on Autism with Special Reference to a Paper by Melanie Klein. *Journal of Child Psychotherapy, 9*: 119–132.

Tustin, F. (1986). *Autistic Barriers in Neurotic Patients*. London: Karnac.

Tustin, F. (1990). *The Protective Shell in Children and Adults*. London: Karnac.

Tustin, F. (1994a). The Perpetuation of an Error. *J. Child Psychotherapy, 20*: 3–23.

Tustin, F. (1994b). Autistic Children who are Assessed as Not Brain Damaged. *J. Child Psychotherapy, 20*: 103–121.

Wing, L. & Gould, J. (1979). Severe Impairments of Social Interaction and Associated Abnormalities in Children: Epidemiology and Classification. *Journal of Autism and Developmental Disorders, 9*: 11–29.

Winnicott, D. (1965). *The Maturational Processes and the Facilitating Environment.* London: Hogarth Press and the Institute of Psychoanalysis.

PART I

AUTISM IN CHILDREN

A psychiatric approach to autism and its relationship to a psychoanalytic perspective

David Simpson

Introduction

In 1943, Leo Kanner, an American child psychiatrist who worked at John's Hopkins University Hospital in Baltimore, lucidly described "eleven children with fascinating peculiarities". In his paper "Autistic Disturbances of Affective Contact" (Kanner, 1943) he sets out for the first time a psychiatric description of a syndrome he called "Early Infantile Autism".

Before this time, children with features of this syndrome were usually described as suffering from schizophrenia, a serious form of mental illness or psychosis which is more usually seen in adults. The term "autism", which simply means "withdrawn", was taken from the original description of schizophrenia, where it was considered to be a fundamental feature (Bleuler, 1911). Although Kanner originally considered autism to be a childhood form of schizophrenia, he distinguished it clearly from schizophrenia, and from the 1970s onwards it has been considered by most psychiatrists to be a different disorder.

Childhood autism, as it is now known, or simply "autism", is now usually grouped together with a number of related disorders, including Asperger's syndrome, and referred to as either one of the

21

pervasive developmental disorders or one of the "autistic spectrum disorders". Autism is considered to be the core syndrome, which displays the core features of the group. There is little argument about the features of this core syndrome. However, where the boundaries of the wider group lie at the less extreme end, and to what extent other syndromes such as Asperger's syndrome are fundamentally different from autism, remains controversial.

Autistic disorders are not common. The prevalence of autism has risen in recent years due to a number of factors, including increased awareness, early detection and the use of wider definitions. A recent estimate of the prevalence of autism in the general population is 10 cases per 10,000 children (Fombonne, 2003). The estimates for the prevalence of broader definitions of autistic spectrum disorder are much higher, rising to 20 per 10,000 (Wing & Gould, 1979) or even 80 per 10,000. There is always preponderance of boys over girls. The sex ratio is believed to be about 3 or 4:1. The reason for this sex difference is unknown, although a number of ideas have been proposed. One of these relates to the idea that autism is an extreme expression of a normal male trait towards being objective and systematising rather than subjective and empathic. This is called extreme male brain theory (Baron-Cohen, 2002). This links with the idea that in females the second X chromosome inherited from the father acts as a protection against autism by activating a gene on the maternal X chromosome which is responsible for the development of the social skills which are lacking in autism. It is suggested that the incidence for autism is higher in males because, not having an X chromosome derived from their father, they lack this protection (Skuse, 2000).

Characteristic features of autism

Kanner (1943) described three characteristic features seen in children with autism.

1. They show a profound lack of social engagement from or shortly after birth. He considered their *extreme autistic aloneness* to be the first of two cardinal features of the disorder.
2. They show characteristic communication and speech difficulties.

3. They show an *anxiously obsessive desire for sameness*. This is the second cardinal feature.

These characteristic features have remained stable since that time, and are the basis of the categories used to define autism in both of the two main current international systems of psychiatric classification, the International Classification of Diseases (ICD) of the World Health Organisation and the Diagnostic Statistical Manual (DSM) of the American Psychiatric Association. The two systems have converged over the years, such that the recent versions, ICD 10 and DSM IV, are very similar. In defining autism both systems include three categories based upon the three clinical features listed above, and both include a separate fourth category which is "early onset". I will now consider each characteristic feature in turn and describe the typical patterns of symptoms and behaviour, seen in children with autism, which determine the presence of each feature. These patterns change as the child grows older and develops.

1. Specific social impairment

I agree with the views of those, including Kanner, who believe that the fundamental problem in children with autism lies in their specific type of social impairment. Kanner described the problem as an "inborn autistic disturbance of affective contact" which results in "extreme autistic aloneness" and an "inability to relate themselves in an ordinary way to people and situations". Although he acknowledged the role of environment, he believed that the problem was present from the beginning of life and did not result from a withdrawal from existing relationships. He described these children as from the start showing self-sufficiency and acting as if "people were not there" and as if "hypnotised". Although many theories have been put forward to explain autism, modern thinking, spurred on by developments in psychological and brain research, is beginning to place the emphasis again on Kanner's hypothesis of reduced affective contact. I believe this makes sense from a clinical perspective.

The essential difficulty that autistic children display is a deficit in the capacity for reciprocity in their relations with other people. "Reciprocity" is the capacity for an interactive "give and take" in which a "productive communication" takes place between people. I use the term "productive communication" in the sense of there being a growth of common knowledge between the participants. This process involves sharing between people while acknowledging each other's separate existence, psychologically speaking.

Autism is suggested in young children by the presence of a variety of social behaviours, many of which are symptomatic of this difficulty in reciprocity. However, the picture is variable, so that deficits may not be present in all areas, and no behaviour on its own necessarily means that autism is present.

The mothers of babies who develop autism sometimes report that they knew that "something was wrong" with their baby from the beginning. They may report that their baby showed a lack of responsiveness, was slow to begin smiling, or didn't "catch their eye" to lead them. They may be clingy, or indiscriminately cuddly, or dislike being held so that they do not raise their hands or adjust their bodies in anticipation of being lifted (Le Couteur *et al*, 1989). This last feature was reported by the mothers of all of Kanner's cases.

Toddlers may be more clearly socially withdrawn and prefer solitary activity, showing little interest or spontaneous affect towards other people, and lacking the ability to imitate. Although children with autism are often reported to avoid the gaze of others, a more characteristic difficulty is an inability to use eye contact to regulate their communication with other people in the way that other children do. Facial expression is usually similarly restricted.

In autism, the quality of attachment the child displays to its parents is unusual. Most older children with autism display separation anxiety which may be excessive, with extremes of rage. However, sometimes their reaction to separation may be very limited, the child appearing to ignore the parent's presence or absence. In these situations, they do not appear to use their parents as points of security, sometimes called a "secure base", in the way that normal children do. They tend not to follow if their parents leave the room, nor to greet them when they return. Children with autism also appear to lack empathy and the capacity to see situations, particularly emotional situations, from another's perspective, so that they tend not to offer comfort when another is distressed, nor to share enjoyment with others. If they do engage socially, they prefer to do this on their own terms. In older children and young people with autism, peer relationships and close friendships are understandably usually very restricted.

2. Specific communication and language impairment

The characteristic difficulties in communication and language seen in autism can be viewed as largely following from the underlying deficits in social reciprocity. It was said that fifty per cent of children with autism never develop useful language (Rutter, 1978); however, with wider definitions and increased recognition, the percentage of children without speech has decreased. Alongside the delay in speech, development of all aspects of communication is affected, including gesture, spoken language and understanding.

As babies and toddlers, they may be unresponsive and can appear to be deaf. (It is important to remember that children who are deaf may also, although rarely, show autism.) They may babble less and tend to avoid babbling in communication or gesturing to express emotions; the expression of interest is usually restricted. Autistic children characteristically take peoples' hands directly to what they want rather than communicating their needs. If they point, they do so to indicate their wishes rather than to show interest to others. When speech develops, it is not used appropriately by the child to communicate with others, and it shows characteristic abnormalities. It very often sounds stilted, with the child speaking in a monotonous drone or in an odd "sing-song" manner. The impression on others is commonly that of being "talked at" rather than being engaged by the child. The child may, for example, only speak to indicate its wishes or to repeatedly question the listener about its preoccupations, without regard to whether the listener is interested. Autistic children sometimes reverse pronouns such as "I" and "You" (pronominal reversal), giving the impression of confusion about their identity. They may repeat words or phrases (echolalia), either immediately or after a pause. They may also make up words (neologisms) and repeat words or phrases in unusual manners.

3. Obsessive desire for sameness—restricted interests and repetitive behaviours

Kanner considered this to be the second cardinal feature of autism. He described the autistic child's world as made up of elements which, once they have been experienced in a certain setting or sequence, cannot be tolerated in other settings or sequences or in any other spatial or chronological order. He believed that the obsessive repetitiveness, phenomenal memory, and even the desire to reverse pronouns seen in autistic children might follow from this.

Autistic children generally lack a capacity for imaginative play. They tend to use toys in restrictive and repetitive ways and not for the purpose intended: for example, they may endlessly line up toy cars in patterns, or watch their wheels spin, or repeatedly let them fall to make a noise. They tend to be interested in the physical and sensory aspects of objects, for instance their colour, reflection, texture, shape or smell. They may, for example, repeatedly open and close a door, seemingly fascinated by the change of view, or they might squint out of the side of their eye at the patterns of shadows made by the movement of their fingers in front of a light. Sometimes they may display habitual movements, such as twisting their bodies and flapping their hands. It is not uncommon for them to display an obsessive attraction to unusual objects like keys or bottle tops.

A very common problem is the way they can frequently demand fixed routines in regard to feeding, toileting, bedtime, and virtually any aspect of life. Older children with autism may typically make obsessive demands, e.g. to watch a particular DVD film repeatedly. Any change in routine, which may sometimes be of a very minor degree and often unpredictable, e.g. a slight change in the parent's position when offering food, can lead to extreme reactions of rage. These behaviours place a considerable burden on their parents.

4. Early onset

In over half the cases of childhood autism, some difficulties are noticed in the first year of life, although it is not clear whether this is a sign of autism or a predisposition to it. In about 20% of cases parents report normal development until twelve or eighteen months of age before signs of regression and autism develop (Volkmar, Stier & Cohen, 1985). To make a diagnosis of autism, abnormalities must be present before three years of age, although this cut-off is arbitrary and in practice it is often very hard to date onset in autism. Early detection is clearly beneficial, and much effort is being put into developing reliable screening methods e.g. CHAT (Baird et al, 2000).

Asperger's syndrome

In 1944, Hans Asperger (1944/1991), a Viennese paediatrician, described a clinical picture of four boys between the ages of six and eleven who showed marked problems in social expression and interaction but maintained linguistic and cognitive skills. Unaware of Kanner's 1943 paper, he described the fundamental problem as a form of autism using Bleuler's term. He did not, however, consider these children to be psychotic, but rather that they had a disorder of personality development.

This is the basis of modern definitions. Asperger's syndrome is distinguished from autism on the basis of normal intellectual abilities alongside characteristic difficulties in social interaction and reciprocity, and the presence of unusual circumscribed interests. There remains a debate as to whether Asperger's syndrome is fundamentally different from autism. Many people consider it to be a milder form, and place it on a spectrum with autism, following Wing (1981), who described Asperger's syndrome in children with language and intellectual delay. Although there appears to be a genetic link, with the two conditions running together in families, Asperger's syndrome can be distinguished from autism in a number of other ways (Volkmar & Klin, 2000).

Firstly, children with Asperger's syndrome are more frequently clumsy, with delayed motor skills development. Secondly, those with Asperger's syndrome tend to have a higher verbal than performance IQ on testing, while the reverse is true of autism. Thirdly, compared with autism, the obsessive circumstantial interests seen in Asperger's syndrome are more complex and involve amassing unusual information, e.g. types of spacecraft. Fourthly, the quality of social and communication difficulties in Asperger's syndrome appears different from that in autism in that these children tend to seek interaction with others, and are sometimes very verbose, but are unable to comprehend the rules of social discourse that would allow them to do this.

This would support the idea that Asperger's and autism are distinct conditions which, being disorders of socialisation, have common clinical features, psychological mechanisms and genetic contributions to their causation.

Other developmental disorders

Atypical autism refers to a condition in children which is like autism, in which the age of onset or the symptomatology does not meet the criteria for making a diagnosis. *Disintegrative psychosis and Rett's syndrome* are rare conditions in which children show developmental regression and loss of skills after a period of normal development. Disintegrative psychosis usually starts after the age of two years while Rett's syndrome, which occurs in girls, usually starts in the first year and is clearly a genetically determined (X-linked dominant) progressive disease.

What causes autism and how does it happen?

There are many ideas but no definitive comprehensive answer which accounts for the condition. Autism is considered by many to be a neuro-psychiatric disorder of organic origin. There are a number of different sources of support for this idea.

Firstly, autism is associated with medical conditions. A wide variety of diagnoses have been reported in about 10–15% of cases of autism, although there are only a small number of clearly significant associations. The strongest association is with epilepsy, which occurs in about 16% of cases (Fombonne, 2003), and which more frequently starts in adolescence and in those with generalised learning disabilities. Generalised learning disabilities are also very commonly associated with autism and were estimated to be present in about 75% of cases. However, with broader definitions, the estimate of the percentage with generalised learning disabilities has reduced to less than half the children affected (Chakrabarti & Fombonne, 2001). Isolated good cognitive skills are not uncommon in autism, and occasionally there are those with unusual abilities, e.g. in music or mathematics. Autism appears more commonly in certain conditions causing learning disabilities, notably tuberous sclerosis and fragile X syndrome (genetic conditions with physical and behavioural disorder); it is, however, rare in others, such as cerebral palsy or Down's syndrome. This suggests that autism is not simply a non-specific result of having learning disabilities. The suggested links between autism and measles vaccination or mercury are highly suspect (Fombonne & Chakrabarti 2001; Wilson, Mills, Ross, McGowen & Jadad, 2003).

Secondly, there is now very strong evidence to support the importance of genetic inheritance in autism. Surveys show a much higher correspondence, or concordance, between the rates of autism seen in pairs of identical (monozygotic) twins, who have the same genetic constitution, when compared with the concordance seen in non-identical (dizygotic) twins, whose genetic make-up is as variable as that of ordinary siblings. In family studies, siblings of children with autism are more likely to develop autism, with a recurrence rate of about 3% for strictly defined autism and 10–20% for a broader range of communication and social abnormalities (Bolton *et al*, 1994). Modern genetic approaches suggest that a broad clinical picture of autism, including milder variants, results from the interaction of multiple separate genes. Environmental influences are not ruled out, and inheritance may be less important where there are autistic features in the presence of severe learning disabilities.

A third area from which support has been sought for organic causes comes from studies of the structure of the brain in those with autism. The association of autism with generalised learning disabilities makes it difficult to interpret what is specific to autism, but it is clear that the brain is involved.

These studies, however, raise more questions than they provide answers. Although a wider variety of abnormalities of structure and function have been reported in autism using a variety of approaches, including autopsy and functional magnetic resonance imagery (MRI), no single focal deficit has emerged; rather, every system in the brain appears to be implicated. A significant minority of children with autism have larger heads than normal and increased brain volume. It has been suggested that in the first months of life, when the core symptoms of autism develop, there may be an abnormality in the growth of the brain, leading to an overgrowth in some areas and an undergrowth in others, including the connecting fibres. This results in reduced connectivity and disorganised function in the brain (Courchesne *et al*, 2001; Courchesne *et al*, 2003). In autism there may be specifically disorganised integration and under-functioning in those brain mechanisms which mediate the capacity to relate affectively with other people (see Volkmar *et al*, 2004).

This is a more complicated picture than one of autism being due to a simple organic deficit. It implicates difficulties in specific psychological process and does not rule out environmental or social influences.

Cognitive psychology has provided three main theories, each of which proposes a primary deficit in psychological mechanisms. The first of these suggests a deficit in Theory of Mind, in the capacity to conceive of one's own and others' minds, and to attribute to them mental states, points of view, beliefs or intentions (Baron-Cohen *et al*, 1995). This defect in mentalising prevents the person with autism constructing a social world. The second theory, Weak Central Coherence (Happe & Frith, 1996), is suggested by the tendency of autistic children to focus on details of a situation rather than to integrate meaningful wholes, which results in a lack of coherence in the social domain. The third theory, which is similar to Weak Central Coherence, is the Executive Dysfunction Hypothesis, and suggests that people with autism lack the ability to abstract the rules and to generate the goals required for problem solving and executing tasks (Pennington & Ozenoff, 1996).

Can these perspectives be integrated with each other?

These perspectives can by no means be completely integrated with each other, although there are some important connections. Modern research is now concentrating on the development of young children with autism, and has identified difficulties in several key aspects of their early social development which might underpin the later emergence of deficits in Theory of Mind, Central Coherence and Executive Functioning. These include deficiencies in the ability to share common attention, the capacity to imitate others, and the motivation for social engagement and preference for orientating to other people. At the same time, functional brain imaging studies are concentrating on and suggesting deficiencies in those areas of the brain which correlate with the human infant's emerging capacities for social relatedness. What is emerging is a common research focus on early deficits in the motivation for engagement with other people and emotional relationships. There has thus been a return to Kanner's original hypothesis of "reduced affective contact" in autism (see Volkmar *et al*, 2004).

This has also been the focus of the work of Hobson (1993, 2002), who provides another lead, having further developed the idea of a core impairment in social relatedness in autism (see Hodges in Rhode & Klauber, 2004). He has proposed that autism may arise when psychological processes involved in the development of social relatedness are disturbed. In his view, this development takes place in the context of shared experience between an infant and its mother. The infant's sense of self and understanding of its subjective states develops by relating to its mother's subjective emotional state communicated through her bodily expression. Hobson believes that human infants are born with a pre-wired capacity for this development to take place, and the psychological manifestations of autism, including cognitive difficulties like impaired theory of mind, result when this pre-wiring is missing. This is supported by studies which show that children with autism can show deficiencies in recognising and understanding emotional states (for example, from facial expression) when compared with children without autism (Weeks & Hobson, 1987) and when compared with their capacity to recognise non-emotional characteristics (Hobson, Ouston & Lee, 1988). Hobson's ideas stress the intersubjective nature of autism and emphasise the need to look at what develops between people. His views are informed by psychoanalytic ideas.

Psychoanalytic perspectives

Although the evidence is limited, with outcome research being at a rudimentary stage, from my clinical experience of working in services where this approach is used, it is clear that many children with autism can benefit from psychoanalytic psychotherapy, and that some benefit considerably in terms of their development, diminution of their symptomatic difficulties and improvement in their general well-being. Despite this, psychoanalytic approaches to autism remain controversial. It is very unfortunate that many people believe erroneously that psychoanalysts and those who apply psychoanalytic methods blame parents for their child's autism.

Psychoanalysis has been associated with the notion of the "refrigerator mother". This is an idea which developed during the 1940s and 50s that autism in children is a result of their parents' emotional coldness. Kanner (1943, p. 42) reported on a tendency to coldness in the attitude of the parents of his cases, although he also stressed the innate nature of the problem. This observation has not been verified in further research. Bettleheim, who was Head of the Orthogenic School in Chicago and a psychoanalyst, described the damaging effect of the parents on the autistic children he had treated. However, his sample was very limited, and general conclusions should not be drawn from this. These descriptions and associations, which can easily lead to parents feeling criticised for causing their children's autism, have been very harmful to the reputation of psychoanalytic approaches. The parents of children with autism have to struggle to cope with an extremely painful trauma for which they can very easily feel responsible and blamed. What they require is professional help which can understand their predicament and particularly their tendency to blame themselves. It is very unfortunate that a psychoanalytic approach has been viewed as adding blame, because in fact a psychoanalytic approach, in addition to being helpful to these children, can be very useful in helping their parents bear the unwarranted sense of guilt and other painful feelings that are often engendered when their child receives a diagnosis of autism. By means of psychoanalytically informed parental psychotherapy and counselling which aims to clarify their beliefs about their children's disorders, parents can be helped to come to terms with their feelings and to face the situation.

Contributing to this difficulty has been the commonly held misunderstanding that from a psychoanalytic perspective all psychological difficulties, in children or adults, are a result of the influence of their parental upbringing rather than their biological inheritance. There is a common misapprehension that psychoanalysis exclusively supports nurture over nature. In fact, when considered overall, psychoanalytic theories of development are quite balanced in regard to the relative contribution they ascribe to nature and nurture. Although the influence of childhood experience, including the quality of the child's relationship with its parents and other significant figures, plays an important part in psychoanalytic theories, the role of the individual's inherited nature has also been fundamental to psychoanalytic thinking, from Freud's original conceptions through to the models used by contemporary psychoanalysts. It has been consistently argued that the inherited human instincts—the sexual (life) and destructive (death) drives—as well as biological differences both play a very important role in determining mental conflict.

From this perspective, in psychoanalytic theory inherited constitution is as important as environment in determining psychic development and abnormality. However, when considering a particular psychological condition like autism, it is true to say that the balance between nature and nurture is often very subtle and hard to pin down. There are many psychoanalytic theories of autism, some of which are referred to in other chapters in this book. Some of these stress the influence of the child's inherited nature, some their nurture, and most attempt to address the complexity of the interaction between the two. I shall outline a particular psychoanalytic concept to demonstrate the connection to the psychiatric and psychological approaches described in this chapter.

Psychoanalysts have given much attention to the developmental task of the infant developing a sense of self and an awareness of its mother as a separate person and establishing her internal representation in its mind. Frances Tustin proposes that the clinical syndrome of autism occurs when this process is disturbed. In her view, if for a variety of reasons the infant is exposed to bodily separateness when it is unprepared and hypersensitive, then this will be traumatic and intolerable, and will set in train defences to block out awareness of the "not me". These defences, particularly withdrawal, and their effects account for the clinical manifestations of autism. Tustin does not believe that children who become autistic are innately unresponsive, nor that they are "snubbed" by cold, unresponsive mothers; rather that the normal process of development in the relationship between the infant and its mother becomes upset. This relationship depends upon a subtle balance of interacting factors.

One of the factors that Tustin considers to be very important is the child's hypersensitivity to "not self", to bodily separation from its mother. She implies that this hypersensitivity is a constitutional variable and that the infant reacts by sensitisation to the "not self" environment. This is the mode of action of a somatic allergic response. Tustin's idea that there is a psychic immune response or "allergy" to others or "not self" in autism (which follows suggestions by Stein [1967] and Fordham [1976]) is very similar to the concept of "psychic atopia" developed by Britton (1998, p. 58). Working with adult patients who display a "thin-skinned" intolerance to difference and objectivity, Britton has used this term to describe their antipathy for knowing anything that is different from themselves. In his view psychic atopia is a constitutionally determined, psychic counterpart to the intolerance to "non body" shown by the body's immune system. It is simultaneously constitutionally determined and environmentally reactive. Tustin's view is that for the autistic child these experiences are located in the body.

When discussing "thin-skinned" patients, Britton makes the important point that it is not just the difference of "not me" that cannot be tolerated but also the relationship between the "not me" or "the other" and somebody or something else. It is this relationship of the other with "another or a third" which causes discomfort and fear and is a source of allergy in psychic atopia. I believe this is also vividly illustrated by some autistic children who cannot bear any sign of their mother's difference from them, and particularly their mother's relationship with anything or anybody else. Their intolerance is to an oedipal triangle, and could be described as an allergy to "mother's relationship with father" or to anything that symbolises her relationship with father. This includes her capacity to think independently, including her ability to have an objective view of her child. If the child cannot tolerate this last aspect, which could be described as the mother's relationship with her own mind, it cannot identify and develop its own capacity to think independently and to see itself objectively; to develop what Britton has called "a third position" in its mind. I suspect that many of the difficulties in self and cognitive development (such as theory of mind deficits) which are characteristic of autism result from the failure to develop a third position as a consequence of the child's psychic atopia, which I would call the child's "allergy to the other's relationship with a third". The autistic child's difficulty in showing curiosity to the world around him and towards other people in particular may also be connected to this aversion to difference.

This is just one example of a theory which embraces constitutional and environmental influences, nature and nurture. The relationship of the autistic child to the oedipal couple and siblings has also been discussed in this volume, in particular by Didier Houzel and by Maria Rhode. The relevance of this perspective to adult patients with autistic features is also apparent, where problems in relating to the world and developing their own capacity for thought may stem from this early difficulty.

References

Anthony, J. (1958). An Experimental Approach to the Psychopathology of Childhood Autism. *Brit. J. Med.Psychol. 31*: Nos. 3 & 4.

Asperger, H. (1944). *Autistic Psychopathy in Childhood* (Trans. Uta Frith). In: U. Frith (Ed.), *Autism and Asperger's Syndrome.* Cambridge University Press, 1991.

Baird, G., Charman, T., Baron-Cohen, S., Cox, A., Swettenham, J., Wheelwright, S., & Drew, A. (2000). A Screening Instrument for Autism at 18 Months of Age: A 6-Year Follow-Up Study. *Journal of the American Academy of Child and Psychiatry, 39*: 694–702.

Baron-Cohen, S. (1995). *Mind Blindness.* Cambridge, MA: MIT Press.

Baron-Cohen. S. (2002). The Extreme Male Brain Theory of Autism. *Trends in Cognitive Sciences, 6*: 1–7.

Bion, W.R. (1962). *Learning from Experience.* London: Heinemann. Reprinted London: Karnac, 1984.

Bleuler, E. (1911). *Dementia Praecox oder Gruppe der Schizophrenien* (Trans. J. Zinkin). New York: International Universities Press, 1950.

Bolton, P., Macdonald, H., Pickles, A.., Rios, P., Goode, S., Crowson, M., Bailey, A. & Rutter, M. (1994). A Case-Control Family History Study of Autism. *Journal of Child Psychology and Psychiatry, 35*: 877–900.

Britton, R. (1998). *Belief and Imagination: Explorations in Psychoanalysis.* London: Routledge.

Chakrabarti, S. & Fombonne, E. (2001). Pervasive Developmental Disorders in Pre-School Children. *Journal of the American Medical Association, 285*: 3093–3099.

Courchesne, E., Carper, R. & Akshoomoff, N. (2003). Evidence of Brain Overgrowth in the First Year of Life in Autism. *Journal of the American Medical Association, 290*: 337–344.

Courchesne, E., Karns, C.M., Davis, H.R., Ziccardi, R., Carper, R.A., Tigue, Z.D., Chisum, H.J., Moses, P., Pierce, K., Lord, C., Lincoln, A.J., Pizzo, S, Schreibman, L., Haas, R.H., Akshoomoff, N.A. & Courchesne, R.Y. (2001). Unusual Brain Growth Patterns in Early Life in Patients with Autistic Disorder. An MRI Study. *Neurology, 57*: 245–254.

Fombonne, E. & Chakrabarti, S. (2001). No Evidence for a New Variant of Measles-Mumps-Rubella-Induced Autism *Pediatrics, 108*: E58.

Fombonne, E. (2003). The Prevalence of Autism. *Journal of the American Medical Association, 289*: 87–89.

Fordham, M. (1976). *The Self and Autism.* London: Heinemann Medical.

Freud, S. (1905). Three Essays on the Theory of Sexuality. *SE 7.*

Frith, U. (1989). *Autism: Explaining the Enigma.* Oxford: Blackwell.

Happe, F.T. & Frith, U. (1996). The Neuropsychology of Autism. *Brain,* 119: 1377–1400.

Hobson, R.P. (1993). *Autism and the Development of Mind.* Hove: Psychology Press.

Hobson, R.P. (2002). *The Cradle of Thought.* Basingstoke: Macmillan.

Hobson, R.P., Ousten, J. & Lee, A. (1988). What's in a Face? The Case of Autism. *British Journal of Psychology,* 79: 441–553.

Hodges, S. (2004). Asperger's Syndrome. In: Rhode & Klauber (Eds.), *The Many Faces of Asperger's Sydrome.* London: Karnac.

Kanner, L. (1943). Autistic Disturbance of Affective Contact. *Nervous Child,* 2: 217–250. Reprinted in *Childhood Psychosis: Initial Studies and New Insights.* New York: Whiley, 1973.

Le Couter, A., Rutter, M., Lord, C., Rios, P., Robertson, S., Holdgrafer, M. & Mclennan, J. (1989). Autism Diagnostic Interview: Semi-Structured Interview for Parents and Caregivers of Autistic Persons. *Journal of Autism and Developmental Disorders,* 19: 363–387.

Mahler, M (1968). *On Human Symbiosis and the Vicissitudes of Individuation.* New York: International Universities Press.

Pennington, B.F. & Ozonoff, S. (1996). Executive Functions and Developmental Psychotherapy. *Journal of Child Psychology and Psychiatry,* 37: 51–87.

Rutter, M. (1978). Language Disorder and Infantile Autism. In: M. Rutter & E. Schopler (Eds.), *Autism: A Reappraisal of Concepts and Treatment* (pp. 85–104). New York: Plenheim Press.

Simpson, D. (2004). Asperger's Syndrome and Autism: Distinct Syndromes with Important Similarities. In: M. Rhode & T. Klauber (Eds.), *The Many Faces of Asperger's Syndrome.* London: Karnac.

Skuse, D.H. (2000). Imprinting the X-Chromosome and the Male Brain: Explaining Sex Differences in the Liability to Autism. *Pediatric Research,* 47: 9–16.

Stein, L. (1967). Introducing Not Self. *J. Anal Psychcol.* 12: No. 2.

Tustin, F. (1981). *Autistic States in Children.* London: Routledge & Kegan Paul.

Volkmar, F.R. & Klin, A. (2000). Diagnostic Issues in Asperger's Syndrome. In: A. Klin, F.R. Volkmar & S. Sparrow (Eds.), *Asperger's Syndrome.* New York and London: Guildford Press.

Volkmar, F.R., Steir, D. & Cohen, D.J. (1985). Age of Recognition of Pervasive Developmental Disorder. *American Journal of Psychiatry* 1942: 1450–1452.

Volkmar, F.R. *et al* (2004). Autism and Pervasive Developmental Disorders. *Journal of Child Psychology and Psychiatry, 45*: 135–170.

Weeks, S.J. & Hobson, R.P. (1987). The Salience of Facial Expression for Autistic Children. *Journal of Child Psychology and Psychiatry, 28*: 137–152.

Wilson, K., Mills, E., Ross, R.C., McGowan, J. & Jadad, A. (2003). Association of Autistic Spectrum Disorder and the Measles, Mumps and Rubella Vaccine: a Systemic Review of Current Epidemiological Evidence. (Comment). (Review) (28 refs.) Comment in: *Archives in Pediatric and Adolescent Medicine*: 123–147, 2003, 1571, 619–21, PMID: 12860780. *Archives of Pediatrics and Adolescent Medicine, 157*: 628–634.

Wing, L. & Gould, J. (1979). Severe Impairments of Social Interaction and Associated Abnormalities in Children: Epidemiology and Classification. *Journal of Autism and Developmental Disorders 9*: 11–29.

Wing, L. (1981). Asperger's Syndrome: A Clinical Account. *Psychological Medicine, 11*: 115–129.

CHAPTER TWO

A significant element in the development of psychogenic autism[1]

Frances Tustin

> Black was the without eye
> Black the within tongue [. . .]
> Black too the muscles
> Striving to pull out into the light
> Black the nerves, black the brain
> With its tombed visions
> Black also the soul, the huge stammer
> Of the cry that, swelling, could not
> Pronounce its sun.
>
> Ted Hughes, *Crow*: "Two legends"

This chapter, which is a considerably revised version of a paper published in the *Journal of Child Psychology and Psychiatry* (1966, pp. 53–67), concerns a particular type of elemental depression manifested by autistic children. Rank and Putnam (1953) used Edward Bibring's term "primal depression" (1953) for this type of depression. Winnicott (1958) has called it "psychotic depression"; Margaret Mahler (1961) has written of such children's "grief". My own work has confirmed that this elemental depression has been crucial in the massive arrest of emotional and cognitive development

39

which afflicts psychogenic autistic children. Clinical material will now be presented which illustrates the specific characteristics of such autistic children's grief, and demonstrates why it has been so damaging to their psychic development.

Clinical material

John's parents became worried by his lack of speech and the fact that he seemed different from and slower in mental development than other children of his age. When aged 2 years 6 months, he was seen by a psychiatrist who feared mental defect. However, on being seen again six months later, John was found to have made a small, hopeful development in that he now put toy motor cars the right way up. (Previously, he had kept them upside down all the time in order to spin their wheels.) On the basis of this, John was referred for a second opinion to Dr Mildred Creak, at Great Ormond Street Children's Hospital, who had an international reputation as a diagnostician in the field of childhood psychosis. She gave a diagnosis of autism, and then referred John, now 3 years 7 months, to me for intensive psychotherapy with the following report:

> There has been a failure almost from birth to take his milestones in his stride, as if there were a reluctance and drag back at each stage. He now shows so many of the attitudes we associate with autism. His chief interest seems to be to tap different surfaces, or to spin round objects. He is fascinated by mechanical moving parts, and has always been quite clever at learning to move his body. Although he is surefooted he still does not feed himself; not that he cannot—it seems as if he will not. This is what I mean by jibbing at milestones. He shows excessive anxiety at times, with days of screaming, but this aspect is much less evident. He has no useful speech, and only communicates very tentatively by trying to use your hand. Nevertheless, I felt sure he was capable of making a primitive contact at this sort of level, and an attempt at therapy. My deepest anxiety is as to whether the basic determinant of all this may be an inherent degree of mental retardation.

A "bad family history on the paternal side" was reported. The father's only sister was a hospitalised schizophrenic, and there were other eccentric and psychotic relatives. It was also reported that there had been "tremendous strain" between the child's mother and an aunt who had been mainly responsible for the care of the father during infancy and childhood. John was a first baby; on the physical side pregnancy and birth were normal, but the mother, who came from a remote village in Europe, had been upset by what she felt to be the foreign procedures of an English maternity hospital.

She also felt that the nurses prevented her and the baby from getting together in a good feeding relationship. She had a great deal of milk, and was very disappointed when breastfeeding could not be established. The baby seems to have been a poor sucker, and the mother reported that for one week after birth he did not open his eyes. When mother and baby left hospital, they went to live with the paternal aunt. Again, the mother felt she was prevented from getting together with her baby, this time by the interference of the aunt. The father was working in another town for the first few months of the baby's life, and the mother was insecure and unhappy during this time, but her depression was not such that she had to have treatment.

When I saw the parents, they reported that John had had no traumatic experiences such as separations or serious illnesses. He had shown little reaction to the birth of his sister when he was eighteen months old, and had always been a quiet baby. They could give no details about the time at which he first held up his head or sat up, but in the locomotor sphere his development seems to have been quite normal. They began to worry when he failed to learn to talk, and by the strange nature of his play. Bizarre hand movements were reported; he moved his fingers in front of his face in a queer, stiff way. He could not be persuaded to put pencil or crayon to paper. Soft foods would be eaten but he rejected hard lumps. He seemed to confuse his mother's mouth with his own. Bowel and bladder control had not been achieved. I had the impression that the mother had had special difficulty with this aspect of childcare. Remembering her own childhood in which she had experienced, on the death of her father, the deprivation of living mostly away from home in an institution, she spoke of her impatience at being a child and her longing to be grown up.

The referring psychiatrist gave intermittent but important supportive help to the parents (although, sadly, this was no longer available when the psychiatrist retired). They needed this support, because when the treatment "holding situation" (Winnicott, 1958) was ruptured on various unfortunate occasions, John had screaming attacks and sleeping difficulties which they found very difficult to bear. The parents were sensitive, intelligent people, and it says much for their concern for John that they maintained support for the treatment during these times and brought him regularly. Without this, the present relatively satisfactory result could not have been achieved.

Course of treatment

John was aged 3 years 7 months when he began treatment. At first he came once a week, later three times, and finally five times a week. On his first visit he was expressionless. He went past me as if I did not exist. The one moment when this was not so occurred in the consulting room, when he pulled my hand towards the humming top which I spun for him. At this, he became very flushed, and leaned forward to watch it spin. As he did so, he rotated his penis through his trousers whilst his other hand played around his mouth in circular spinning movements. This suggested to me that he made little differentiation between the movements of the top and those of his own body. He exuded a quality of passionate, sensuous excitement. It convinced me of the importance of maintaining the analytic setting and interpretative procedure if I was to be gradually distinguished from his primitive illusions, and to do my work as a therapist who would help him to come to terms with his sensuous excitements and disillusionments. From now on, I kept to a bare minimum my compliance with the actions he pressed me to do. I made simple interpretations, interspersing them with the few words the parents had told me he might understand. These were "John, Mummy, Daddy, Nina [his sister], pee-pee, baby, potty, spin, spinning". I repeated the interpretations in several different ways, and occasionally used actions to supplement my meaning—although I kept these to a minimum when I sensed that they were interpreted by him as seductive or threatening approaches.

The following are extracts from detailed notes which illustrate John's responses to interpretations. The first reported session is one in which he used his first word with me. It occurred after the Christmas holiday (he had begun treatment in November 1951). John had no pronouns, so that this, and his limited vocabulary, restricted what could be said in the interpretations, although I had the impression that he understood much more than was implied by the restricted vocabulary he was reported as knowing.

Friday 10 January 1952: Session 9

John now came three times a week. This was his last session of the week. I quote verbatim from my notes: "As he had done since his second session, he began by playing with the humming top. On the basis of previous material, as well as the manner of his play in this session, I interpreted that he was using his hand to spin the Tustin top so that he could feel that John was Tustin and Tustin was John. Thus he could feel that we were always together."

Immediately following this, he took out the mother doll and handled the bead that joined the handbag to her hand with the same circular movement with which he had handled his penis in the incident with the humming top. After tapping the mother doll he threw her to the ground, saying very plainly "Gone". (I interpreted that John was spinning the mummy's bead as if it were his pee-pee to feel he could go right inside the mummy bag, but then he felt it made her into "gone" mummy.) He immediately picked up the little girl doll, turned her round and round and ground his teeth loudly. (I interpreted that John was spinning into the mummy's bag to bite the girl baby, but then he felt he made the girl "gone" and the mummy "gone".)

He now took the baby doll and put it in the cot which he turned upside down so that the baby fell out. (I interpreted that he was spinning into the Tustin mummy bag to upset her babies because he wanted to be her only baby.) Following this, he worked the top inside the suitcase provided for his toys, pressing the point into some soft plasticine strips in the bottom of it. Once he touched the baby doll and said "Baby" or "Pee-pee", I could not tell which. (I interpreted that John felt that his spinning made a soft mummy who let him spin inside her to make her babies gone, and this made her into a "gone" mummy.)

(During such material, I found my thoughts wandering, so that I was in danger of complying with some unspoken request and thus behaving as if I were a part of his body of a toy instead of a mature, thinking person who was trying to help him come to terms with his feelings. Other workers have found that this is a not infrequent occurrence with such "atmospheric" children. Later, I found it helpful to interpret to him that he felt he spun inside my head to make my "brain children" "gone", so that he could feel that I was a "softie" with whom he could have all his own way.)

In the above material, we see the beginning of his disillusionment arising from the fact that I can be "gone", both in the sense of not attending to him, and in the actual bodily sense of being separated from him. This meant that I was not under his control. This was developed further four weeks later when he spoke two more words. Again it was in the last session of the week.

Friday 9 February 1952: Session 23

Mother and John had rung several times before I could manage to get to the door to open it. As they stood on the step they looked cold and frozen. John had stopped rattling the letterbox; on previous occasions I had had the impression that he felt he controlled me to come to the door by doing this. He mournfully repeated "Dirty" after his mother, as she looked into the orifice of his ear. In the consulting-room he tried to spin the top on the soft carpet. It would not spin. Violently thrusting his hand into mine, he tried to use it as an append-age to his own hand to make it do so. It did not. Spitting with rage and breathing heavily, he threw the offending top to the ceiling. It just missed the electric light. With a crash it fell to the ground and broke into two halves. The inside fell out. Shocked, he went to it and said "Broken!" and "Oh dear!" in a grief-stricken way. He spent the rest of the session hopelessly trying to mend it. It seemed that depressing realities were penetrating the autism.

There now followed a confused period in the analysis (February–April 1952). During this there was the attempt to make people and things behave in a way which ran counter to their real nature, as in the incident with the humming top. The toys and myself seemed to be manipulated as if they were his excreta or parts of his own body. During this time he spent most of the sessions lying on the couch playing with his penis, and with his own faeces and occasional bits of plasticine, which hardly seemed to be differentiated from faeces. There was also nose-picking and spitting.

This ceased after the three-week Easter holiday in April. This was his second long break in treatment. He now developed an obsessional habit of tapping a button on a cushion and saying "Daddy! Daddy!" (his father was away from home during this time). This, and the toy he called "the red daddy bus", played a large part in the analysis during this period. There were tantrums when he realised that they were not part of him and so could go away and leave him. Following this, he would say "Broken!" "Gone!" "Oh dear!" very dolefully (May–June 1952). His first use of the personal pronoun came after he had broken the "red daddy bus" in such a tantrum. He said, "I mend it! I mend it!" (Session 118).

Monday 26 November 1952: Session 130

One day, after changes in the routine of bringing him, he was distressed when his father, who had now returned home, nearly missed his footing on the front steps as he was waving goodbye to John after leaving him for his session. During this session, John seemed to be trying to maintain that the movements of his body could keep his father alive. (For example, he jumped up and down on the couch, saying "Daddy mended! Daddy mended!") At the end of the session, when he found that his mother, not his father, was waiting for him, he screamed "Daddy! Daddy gone! Daddy broken!" Following this incident he had a severe nocturnal screaming fit. It was reported to me that in it he had said such things as "I don't want it! Fell down! Button broken! Don't let it bite! Don't let it bump!"

With hindsight, I realised that these nightmare screams expressed infantile terrors which had been active in relation to the father, the red toy bus, and the button on the cushion, all of which had been felt to be identical with each other. They were not symbols for the father; they were felt *to be* the father, who was undifferentiated from his bodily parts (Hanna Segal [1957] has written of such *symbolic equations*). But as long as the terrors were scattered in this way, I could not sufficiently understand them to help him come to terms with them.

A session which occurred fifteen months after treatment began will now be reported in detail. In this session terrors which had been adumbrated in previous sessions were brought together, and John was able to use representations by means of words and toys to tell me about them. He could do this because people were now being distinguished as people instead of being used like inanimate objects such as toy buses, buttons and the like. Thus the autism was much diminished and representational activities were beginning.

25 January 1953: Session 153

(Before giving this session, I should say that in December John had seen a baby feeding at the breast and had shown great interest. I had not used the word "breast", not knowing whether he knew it. It now came into his material.) He carefully arranged four pencil crayons in the form of a cross and said "Breast!" Touching his own mouth, he said "Button in the middle!" (I interpreted Baby John's desire to make up a breast for himself out of his own body.) He then put out more pencils in a hasty, careless fashion to make a ramshackle extension to the cross. To this he said "Make a bigger breast! Make a bigger breast!" (These children feel called upon to be extraordinary, and so they feel they need an extraordinary breast. In the session I interpreted baby John's desire to have a bigger breast than really existed.)

He angrily knocked all the pencils so that they spread in a higgledy-piggledy fashion over the table. He said "Broken breast!" (I interpreted his baby anger that he could not have a breast as big as he wanted.) He said "I fix it! I fix it! Hole gone! Button gone! Hole gone! Button gone!" (I interpreted his baby desire to have a breast he could make or break as he pleased. He again angrily pushed the pencils all over the table and said "Broken!" He then opened and shut a wooden box with ear-splitting bangs. (I interpreted his baby anger that he couldn't have a breast with which he could do as he liked.)

He said "Broken" again and went to the umbrella stand which is in the consulting-room; he put his hand into the glove cavity which is in dark shadow. He shuddered and said "No good breast! Button gone!" (I interpreted that he felt that his anger with the breast which would not behave exactly as he wanted it to do made him feel he had a "no-good breast" with a hole instead of a button.) He went to the case and fetched a piece of dirty grey cardboard and a crocodile. He put them on the chest he had banged. He pointed to the Sellotape round the edge of the cardboard and said "Icy! Icy!" Then he said "No good breast! Button broken!" He slid the crocodile around the cardboard as if it were slithering on ice. His face went cold and pinched. (I took up his feeling that breaking the breast made an icy no-good breast which was no comfort to him when he was on his own.)

Now that the infantile transference was well established and the anxieties were "contained" in the analysis, his behaviour outside showed great improvement. He was eager to come to analysis and made good progress in spite of family illness, changes in the routine of bringing him, and family bereavements. He began to admit his dependence and helplessness, and would say of things that were beyond his powers: "I can't do it! Please help me!" This progress was maintained when his mother and younger sister went abroad and he was left with his father. An unfortunate break now occurred in the "holding situation" (Winnicott, 1958, p. 268).

Friday 5 April 1953: Session 194

I showed him, by means of a diagram, the day he would come back to analysis after the two-week Easter holiday. Family circumstances made it impossible for his father to bring him back until one week later. In addition, he had been left for one week with the aunt with whom they lived. When he came back I was appalled. He seemed traumatized and frozen. He had a stiff-legged mechanical gait. What speech he had left was stammered. He was indeed in the grip of the "icy, no-good breast". This had provided no comfort for "poor little baby John left all alone on an island", as he put it later.

As the bodily tensions relaxed, the night-time screaming fits became such a regular occurrence that the referring psychiatrist prescribed a sleeping draught. During the screaming fits he would hallucinate birds in various parts of the bedroom, and say some of the phrases he had used in his first screaming fit. The birds threatened to peck him and were a great source of terror.

However, he gradually began to bring the infantile terrors back into the analysis. He again proceeded with the differentiations he had been making ever since his first word of "Gone!" He continued to relate to his father in a more real way, and less in terms of a "thing" like a button that could be broken. He accepted that space and time separated him from me. He put experiences into categories such as "nice" and "nasty", and people were classified as "naughty" or "sensible" according to whether they did what he wanted them to do. There was the beginning of the differentiation between fact and fantasy. He would sometimes say "It's a story", or "It's not really true". He now told me in more detail the illusory terrors that had given rise to the cryptic phrases in the screaming fits.

He began to associate the misuse of objects with their being broken. For example, of the humming top he said "It's broken! Tops don't go on the carpet." At the end of sessions he sometimes hinted that he felt I left him because he had a part missing, or because he was a "stinky little goat". Sometimes he would make as if to break off his "stinkers" (his word for the hard faeces that hurt his anus), and pretend—a significant development—to drop them down the front of my dress. Sometimes he got rid of his own feelings of silliness by calling his father "silly" and "naughty", and to his sister, Nina, as to me, were assigned all the nasty experiences he did not want himself. Thus he demonstrated clearly the fantasy of breaking off unacceptable parts of himself and thrusting them into other people.

Tuesday 28 January 1954: Session 360

The effect on his psychic development of having his projections contained by understanding was again shown by his use of the pencil crayons which he arranged to make a "breast". This was the first time he had done this since the previous occasion eight months earlier, before the unfortunate separation experiences. He pointed to the carefully arranged pencils and said "Breast!" Then, touching his own mouth, he said "Button in the middle!" Then he stood a pencil in the middle and said "Rocket!" He called the whole thing a "firework breast". This linked with the drawing of a dome-shaped object with brown and red "stinkers" coming out of it which he afterwards called "fireworks". (This had been drawn following a tantrum when I would not let him use my hand as if it were his own.) Holding his mouth as if it hurt, he said: "Prick in my mouth!" Then: "Falls down!", "Button broken!", "Nasty black hole in my mouth!" Then, in an alarmed way, he held his penis and said: "Pee-pee still there?" as if he thought it was not. (In the session which followed, he said of the broken humming top: "Broken top! Nasty peoples coming out to blow me up!")

Wednesday 29 January 1954 : Session 361

Material then came about his "stinkers" burning and piercing the button and making "a black hole in my mouth". I asked him about the black hole. He answered simply, "When naughty things are burned they go black." Following this he said sadly: "My nice dreams turn into nasty dreams", and then, brightening up: "I have my nasty dreams with Tustin." One day the screaming fits, the cryptic phrases and some of the previous fantasies all came together in one session.

Thursday 6 February 1954: Session 367

He was in a screaming tantrum when I opened the front door because he had fallen and bumped his head. There was no sign of damage, but he seemed panic-stricken as well as enraged. When he stopped crying I took him to the consulting room. Without taking anything from the case of toys, he went to the table to talk to me. He said: "Red button gone! It fell with a bump!" He then indicated both his shoulders with a semi-circular movement and said: "I've got a good head on my shoulders. Can't fall off. Grows on my shoulders." He then said: "It was the naughty pavement, it hit me." (I said I thought that he was trying to tell me about his fears when he fell down just now.) Touching his own mouth, he said, "Nina's got a black hole. She had a prick in her mouth. Button broken! Nasty black hole!" (I should have interpreted here that these were his own nasty experiences of which he was ridding himself by attributing them to Nina, but I birked it.)

He took the plastic tractor, which was a toy he had attacked remorselessly. He touched the plastic axle, which is not in reality sharp. However, he touched it, gave a huge shudder and said: "Nasty hard tractor, it pricks." He spat as though spitting out something that was repugnant. He then screwed himself up and screamed loudly. (I reproached myself for not having attempted to put his feelings into words, and so possibly spared him from having to express them in violent action.) In his screaming he pushed away flying beaks. I was afraid that he would fall off his chair, so I took him on my knee and interpreted through the shrieks. The interpretations concerned his feeling that the button was part of his mouth and the destructive feelings he had when he found that this was not so. He then felt he had a "black hole" and a "nasty prick" instead of a nice button. He felt he spat the nasty thing into the girl baby who he felt had taken the button away from him. But then he felt that she tried to spit it back at him and her nasty mouth seemed like flying birds. (We had had material where he had equated the flying birds with mouths.) Without the "button" he felt that they could hurt him. He was afraid that he might lose his head or his penis, as he felt he had lost his button.

For two sessions after this he was afraid of certain objects in the consulting room: one was the dark glove cavity, another was a penis-like pipe near the ceiling, a third was the "dirty water bucket". (This room had no water plumbed in, so there was a jug of water and a bucket for dirty water.) After these sessions the night-time screaming stopped. (It came back after a particularly worrying holiday, and when the question of ending treatment was being discussed.) The hallucinations subsided and did not, so far as I know, trouble him after this.

Closure note

Treatment came to an end when John was aged 6 years 5 months. This was earlier and more sudden than I would have liked, but the parents were urging that he finish, particularly as his need for psychotherapy was not now so obvious. He attended a school for normal children. He was making friends, enjoyed school, and was learning avidly. He had a vocabulary beyond that of most children his age, but this was not surprising since his parents were both intelligent people.

He was still a "finicky" eater. In times of stress he was inclined to stammer and to have sleeping difficulties. These remaining symptoms made me want to continue, but since there were signs that he was moving into latency, and since I felt that the parents very much wanted to have John to themselves, I agreed to the cessation of treatment, with the proviso that it might be advisable to seek further help in adolescence.

Follow-up

It has only been possible to get information about John in a somewhat roundabout way. The parents of encapsulated autistic children seem to want to forget the whole experience once it is over. This is in marked contrast to the attitude of parents of symbiotic (entangled) children, who keep contact with the therapist. John's parents did not seek further help. I have heard that John attended public day school at the normal age and did well. Later he obtained a good university degree. He has developed into a sensitive young man who is very musical.

Discussion

John's experience of grief

Such a young child's descriptions are probably the closest we can get to crucial, panic-stricken experiences concerned with grief about the loss of a vital object which John called the "button". This was his experience of the nipple of the breast which he had taken for granted, and indeed had not known that it existed until he discovered that it was not always there. When he became aware that it was not there, overwhelming feelings of disillusionment were aroused, the essence of this grief-provoking situation being partly expressed in his first words of "Gone!", "Broken!", "Oh dear!" These ejaculations expressed evocations from his infancy, when the loss and seeming destruction of the "button" had been felt to leave a "black hole with a nasty prick". This was John's present-day formulation for the previously undifferentiated, unformulated, insufferable experience of sensuous loss which had precipitated the autism. Seeing the baby feeding at the breast had evoked the whole system of illusion which had set John's autistic reactions in train. He was now able to get sufficiently in touch with this experience to put me in touch with it also. Being preverbal, it is difficult to discuss in words; evocative rather than theoretical language seems most appropriate to describe it.

Recalling the two sessions in which he represented the breast with coloured pencils (Sessions 156 and 360), it will be remembered that the "no-good breast" with the hole becomes the "firework breast" with "stinker" rockets discharged into it by himself. The firework, rocket-like discharges had been felt to go into a "hole"—into a nothingness—instead of being received by a human presence who responded to them in an appropriate way and helped him to manage them. These are very early infantile experiences, in which "feelings" are experienced in a bodily, tactile way as sensations of various kinds. When the "button" will not stay in John's mouth to be under his control and to be available just whenever and however he wants it, he becomes discombobulated. In panic and rage, the aggravatingly "naughty" "button" is felt to be discharged from his body like spit or faeces. It seems to leave a "hole" in the breast where the "button" had been. Since his mouth had been undifferentiated from the breast, it leaves a "hole" in his mouth also. The burning sensations of rage make it into a "black hole". (As John says, "When naughty things are burned they turn black.") Putting these preverbal experiences into words distorts their original nature, but both John and I felt that it had to be done if we were to come to terms with them. "Acting out" is often the first way in which such primal dramas find expression. But following this way of dramatizing them in psychotherapy, words are necessary if the impulsive discharges are to be contained by thinking about them. As this is done, the patient feels that a part of himself, which had previously reacted impulsively in terms of powerful illusions, is being brought within the orbit of thoughtful attention and understanding care.

Autistic patients like John have felt assailed by nameless dangers. In order to feel that these dangers were kept at bay, they have needed to feel in control of what happened to them. When they find that they are not in control but in reality are weak and helpless, they are devastated. This is well illustrated in Session 367, in which the "naughty" pavement got out of control and "hit" John. In this session it was clear that he felt he had lost a part of his body. In his relatively undifferentiated state, he was not sure which part had "gone". Was it his head? His penis? Or was it that sensuously exciting "button"? I had the impression that he experienced his screams as solid, piercing, tangible objects; his mouth emitting them as a round black hole. In later sessions (not presented here), he told me that he avoided looking at people's eyes "because of the black hole in the middle". As these agonies and terrors about the "black hole" were worked over in the analysis, John began to look at people's faces in the way a normal child will do.

The material presented implies that in the relatively undifferentiated state, phallic and anal sensations were drawn into the primary oral experience, which seemed to affect every orifice of the boy's body. His body, fretted with sore black holes, seemed to face an outside world which was pitted with similar black holes. Empathic identification with John put me in touch with the wordless elemental dramas which had provoked the psychogenic autism. These illusory dramas arose from sensations in his body, the "button" being the product of these bodily sensations.

Let me now discuss this "button" and the role it played in the development of John's psychogenic autism.

The button

It is obvious, in terms of John's early sensuous experience, that the "button" was something more that the actual nipple of the breast or teat of the bottle. Other objects which had similar shapes, or aroused similar sensations, had accreted to it. It was an illusion which could be different things at different times. The core of the sensation experience was a "teat-tongue" combination. This arose from the lack of clear differentiation of his mouth from the breast. (You will remember that in the referral notes John was reported as confusing his mother's mouth with his own.) Later his penis, his head, his "stinkers", a toy red bus, a button on a cushion and even his "Daddy" were all drawn into this "teat-tongue" combination, probably on the basis of their common sensation of hardness. It is difficult for us, as differentiated individuals, to get in touch with such undifferentiated modes of operation. In these states objects which, in sensuous terms, have a rough-and-ready "clang" similarity with each other are grouped together and treated as if they were the same.

In undifferentiated states, the tendency is to be aware of similarities rather than differences. Thus objects which, to our more differentiated awareness, seem very unlike are experienced by the relatively undifferentiated child as being the same. To a young child, a boiling kettle and a steam train may seem to be the same as each other, because the thing that is important to him is the steam. For John, I suspect *hardness* was what was important to him, because hardness could protect him from the terrible dangers by which he felt threatened. Thus the nipple, his penis, his head, his stinkers, a pipe in the therapy room, a button on a cushion, the toy red bus, and his "Daddy" all evoked the same reactions.

It is not that they are similar and so can be used to *represent* each other. They are felt *to be* the same. In John's undifferentiated state the button on the cushion and the toy red bus evoke the same sensations as Daddy does. They did not *represent* Daddy, they were felt *to be* Daddy because they evoked the same hard sensuous impression as Daddy did (Session 130), hardness being the trigger sensation. But, so far as John is concerned, these objects had another thing in common as well as hardness—they could all be broken. The fact that they were not unbreakable, in spite of being hard, fills John with grief and despair. His desperate efforts to keep himself absolutely safe have failed. None of us likes broken things, but to the hypersensitised autistic child a broken thing is not merely a mishap, it is a catastrophe.

John's behaviour is not puzzling when we realise that the primary mode of organising our experience is by means of classification. We sort things in terms of the characteristics they have in common. John's method of classification is strange to us because he sees things as being the same which, to our more differentiated awareness, are very different. For him, objects are sorted in terms of their hardness or softness. Looked at from this point of view, John's behaviour becomes more understandable. In terms of his sensuous reactions, there is logic to his seemingly strange behaviour and puzzling statements. We need to try to think as he does, if we are to begin to understand him.

This classifying of objects and experiences in terms of sensuously significant features which they have in common also seems to be responsible for the relatively undifferentiated autistic child's confusion of the configurations of nipple-in-mouth, stool-in-bottom and penis-in-vagina. In these children, due to the lack of an adequate capacity for differentiation, as well as to the precocious arousal of auto-erotism, oral, anal and phallic constellations become confused with each other in a polymorphous way. This results in the homo-sexual tendencies of untreated autistic children. An important part of psychotherapy is the sorting out of such confusions.

In studying autism we find that we are studying the beginnings of perception. The phenomenon of the "button" seems to arise from inborn nipple-seeking patterns of response which take shape again in treatment. It is obvious that such a nipple-seeking pattern will promote breast- or bottle feeding. Piaget's observations of his own babies complement and confirm inferences derived from psycho-analytic work in respect of this (Piaget, 1954). For example, when

Piaget hid a feeding bottle or a toy stork with different parts of the body left showing, he found that it was only when the teat of the bottle or the beak of the toy stork were left exposed that the young infant would search for the object; that is, nipple-like objects promoted his response. Clinical work has made me think that such inborn responses are like "feelers" which reach out into the outside world to mould and be moulded by it. In my first book *Autism and Childhood Psychosis* (1972) I suggested the term "innate forms" to describe them. The "button" is the result of such an innate form.

Innate forms

These seem to be flexible sensuous moulds into which, at an elemental level of psychic development, experience is cast, and which are modified by the experience so cast. When an innate form seems to coincide with a correspondence in the outside world, the child has the illusion that everything is synonymous and continuous with his own body stuff. In primitive states, pattern-seeking tendencies are active but, since discrimination is minimal, any one part of the subject's own body, or other people's bodies, or objects in the environment, can seem to be the same. Thus the nipple can be felt to be part of John's body because fingers can be equated with the innate form of nipple; the knob of the humming top could match this form; penis, tongue, "stinkers", and so on could all be equated with it and with each other. Such unmodified equivalents led to bodily confusions which presaged later mental ones. In this state, live and inanimate objects were treated in almost the same way: for example, the father could be a button on a cushion and the same things could happen to him. In the confused period of the material presented, it seemed that John used parts of his body—and outside objects as if they were parts of body stuff—for the manipulation of what later could become abstracted as mental concepts; much as a child uses fingers or sticks to do arithmetical processes which he later becomes able to "do in his head".

In these early days, when the fact of his separateness from me was forced upon him, words seemed to be experienced by John as solid objects. When he was told about the ends of sessions, or breaks in the treatment due to holidays, he winced as if something had been stuck into him. These separations seemed to be experienced quite concretely as broken things which pierced his body. It is difficult to know how to discuss such states, in which the singular feature is that feelings seem to be experienced as physical entities. Absence was "goneness"—"goneness" was a broken thing—"a black hole" full of a "nasty prick". The observer might speak of "depression", but for John this was a "black hole"; "persecution" was a "nasty prick"; "despair" was felt as taking into his irreparably broken body an object felt to be broken beyond repair. He did not "think" about these things; he felt he took them into his body. When the all-powerful, controlling "button" was gone, uncontrollable dangers rushed in, in an uncontrollably painful way. These dangers were experienced as tangible things. Also, the pain of preverbal, preconceptual loss was experienced as bodily rather than mental pain.

The "black hole"

This illusion was the significant element which had set John's autistic reactions in train. This was what was felt to be left when the "button", and all that it signified, was "gone". The patient can only tell us about this experience when it is over. When it is happening, he is frozen by it. It was revoked for John when he saw the baby feeding at the breast. This enabled him to work over his reactions to his breastfeeding experiences. In so doing he showed me the multiple significances of the "button". Absence of the "button" was not just the absence of "nice" things which we might intellectually expect it to be, but it was a nasty physical presence—a "black hole". When I asked John about this, he said: "When naughty things are burned they go black." The uncontrollable "button" was a "naughty" button which had been burned away and turned black by the flames of his impulsive rage, which he had never been helped to manage appropriately. These children have never become toilet-trained in either the psychological or the physiological sense.

As well as being associated with feelings that John has not been able to control, the "button" is also associated with things that will not be controlled by him, and so arouse his uncontrollable rage. It is associated with the top that will not spin, my hand that will not spin it, the "button" that will not remain part of his body. These children lack sufficient experience of hard "Daddy" discipline being married to comfortable "Mummy" softness. They have been left alone to manage their outbursts of temper aroused by frustration. In the outburst in which they unburden themselves, they feel that they explode away a vital bodily part. In their undifferentiated state they are not sure which part it is, or whether it is theirs or another's. Thus as John's fiery rage burned the "naughty" object that would not do as it was told, he felt that a bodily part was "blacked out" also. Was it his penis? Was it his head? Was it that sensuous "titbit", the "button"? Was it broken off like his "stinkers"? Was it the hard "Daddy" bit? In his hypersensitised state, in which everything was exaggerated, the results of his unheld tantrums were experienced as "catastrophe". Bion (1962) has shown the critical decision for psychic development is whether frustration is avoided, or whether the attempt is made to come to terms with it. Winnicott's transitional area of skills, "let's pretend" play, humour and aesthetic activities come into being when depression about this catastrophe is experienced, and the attempt is made to control the feelings aroused by frustration. The child learns to sustain tension and to delay action.

In the clinical material presented here, we see John's attempts to avoid frustration by explosive projection. On the other hand, his first words of "Gone!", "Broken!", "Oh dear!" show that as soon as he developed even a limited capacity to be in touch with the "black hole", he began to develop speech (Session 23). Later he was able to represent his emotional situation (Sessions 153 and 360). Such representation required that his impulsivity should be beginning to be held in check, and that he should be beginning to have some capacity to tolerate his separateness.

The "black hole" was John's experience of "primal" or "psychotic depression". Getting in touch with this depression is crucial in the amelioration of autistic states. As one adult patient expressed it, "You held me firmly so that I did not 'break out' and so my 'breakdown' became a 'breakthrough'." Work with autistic children has brought home to me that such patients need to be held in a firm but understanding "holding situation" (Winnicott, 1958, p. 268).

The "holding situation"

In earliest infancy, the coincidence of innate forms with matching correspondences in the outside world is the first "holding situation".

Winnicott expresses this when he says: "The mother places the actual breast just where the infant is ready to create and at the right moment" (Winnicott, 1958, p. 238). Bion expresses the same idea when he says: "A preconception mates with a realisation" (Bion, 1962b). Mother and baby, teat and tongue work together to produce the illusion of continuity and to confirm it. The "button" illusion seems to "button" mother and child together, and also to enable each of them to feel "all buttoned-up"; falling apart being an existential dread.

Both Winnicott (1958, p. 238) and Milner (1956, p. 100) have stressed the importance of ample opportunities for such illusion in early infancy, and the dangers of a disastrous impingement of awareness of bodily separateness. But coincidences cannot always be exact, nor can they always be forthcoming, and Bion has increased our understanding of this early situation by delineating the role of the mother as a "container" for her infant's burning rage, which is experienced as bodily discharge. Lacking an adequate "container", the fiery passions of the autistic child have been covered by the ice-cap of autism. Such a child is like a volcano waiting to erupt. When an autistic child starts having tantrums, he is beginning to recover. How he is held through these tantrums is important if the recovery is to be sustained. He must never be left alone with them. We must "talk him through" them. Thus "held", tantrums can be the beginnings of creative responses. In the North of England, it is common for a mother to describe her child's tantrums by saying: "He *created* something terrible!" What a common-sense way to react to tantrums!

In early infancy the infant's lack of discrimination, and the mother's adaptation arising from empathic identification with him in the form of "reverie" (Bion, 1962, p. 309), serve to minimize the explosion-producing gap between primitive illusions and actuality. This empathic reciprocity at first fosters the illusion of bodily continuity, and then gradually acclimatizes the nursing couple to the dimly apprehended fact of separateness. It enables the mother to support her infant through the turbulence arising from awareness of separateness; separateness which seems to be experienced as a break in bodily continuity—as a loss of a part of the body. Changes of state, for example, from "button-in-mouth" to "button-gone", inevitably bring tensions, tensions experienced as bodily turgor, to be relieved by bodily discharges. A mother with unbearable, unformulated infantile insecurities, and little support in bearing them, finds it difficult to take such projections from her infant. In a way, both mother and child are too alike in their reactions.

Such a mother easily succumbs to attacks on her capacity to pay attention to her infant—to hold him in her awareness. Such attacks may come from her own infantile "privations", or from outside events and people, or from her infant's atmospheric reactions; it is usually a combination of these. They mean that her attention is gone, and her mind wanders just as mine tended to do in one of the reported sessions (Session 9). It seems that if a mother, through no fault of her own, is absent-minded, the "holding situation" (Winnicott, 1958, p. 268) is broken just as much as by a traumatic geographical separation between mother and baby. It is feasible that this "holding situation" is affected by the parents' relationship with each other, in that this will affect the mother's responses to the infant who is the outcome of that relationship.

A breakdown in the "holding situation" means that the naive infant is left to bear intolerable feelings alone. These seem to be discharged into a void to come back at him with renewed force. Thus stresses and strains accumulate. Continuing to use his own body as if it were another's body, and part of another's body as if it were a lifeless part of his own, means that he remains undifferentiated and cut off from alive human beings who can help him with his troubles. Instead, other people are experienced as inanimate things to be manipulated in terms of his needs and caprices. Thus John became more and more enmeshed in the terrors and sufferings associated with the illusion of the "black hole". The realistic fear of dying pales by comparison with these illusory agonies and terrors.

The autism had been a reaction to deal with John's explosive feelings in relation to loss of the "button", for which he felt that no help was forthcoming from the people around him. They seemed to be as frightened of them as he was. But John had cut himself off from such help as was there. In colloquial terms he had "cut off his nose to spite his face". This had landed him in serious trouble. As his autism broke down, these impetuous outbursts, experienced as bodily discharges, were released from their autistic wraps. As they were released, other elements in the "black hole" depressive situation were revealed. These were mourning feelings.

Mourning feelings

When I first encountered these feelings, I found it difficult to believe that they could be possible at such a primitive level of psychic development. Finally, however, the evidence was so compelling that I had to face the fact, and help John to face the fact, that he was mourning the loss of the ultra-special "button" which could never exist in reality. It was an illusion, but an important one. He felt bereft of a very vital thing. It was like a bereavement. When I was introduced to Margaret Mahler's paper "On sadness and grief in infancy and childhood: loss and restoration of the symbiotic love object" (1961), I was reassured that I was not reading feelings into the child that were not there. I realised that the "button" was John's "symbiotic love object", the loss of which had rendered him numb and dumb. As we worked this over together, we realised that his "crow-black" sulk about this loss had prevented him from working over the disillusionment that the "button", conceived in his terms, was not available in the outside world. Another type of baby would have reacted differently. As he relinquished his unrealistic hopes of finding the superlatively perfect "button" in the outside world, it became established as a psychic construct in his mind. This seemed to be the basis for a more trusting relationship with me, based on more realistic expectations. The therapeutic "holding situation" seemed to provide a "cradle", in which John's baby self could go over early unresolved psychic situations, and modify his unrealistic, perfectionist, exacting demands, both of himself and other people.

Conclusion

On superficial observation, organic and psychogenic autistic disorders can look the same. However, on careful investigation, it becomes clear that organic autism arises from gross damage to the brain, whereas in the present state of our knowledge, psychogenic autism seems to arise mainly from damage to the psyche. In my view, psychic damage needs to be investigated as meticulously as the neurophysiologists are investigating brain damage. Global understandings in terms of unresponsive mothers and unresponsive babies just will not do. If we are to be able to help children with the handicap of psychogenic autism, we need to have detailed insight into its nature.

In studying this, we find that we are studying the elemental emotions associated with the beginnings of perception, and of the ways in which perception can become blocked and distorted. John's revelations give us some insight into this.

Psychotherapy with psychogenic autism

An understanding of psychogenic autism is complicated by the fact that in the elemental, relatively undifferentiated state in which psychic damage occurred, such psychic damage is experienced as bodily damage. Since subject and object are scarcely differentiated from each other, the damage seems to happen to both child and object. Both mother and child are felt to lose the vital "Daddy button" which holds them together. John, a young child suffering from psychogenic autism, showed us the details of this psychic damage. Such a child is in shock. He feels damaged, weak and helpless. His reaction, to counteract this, has been to develop practices which give him the illusion that he is impenetrable, invulnerable and in absolute control. Although they look so passive, such children are little tyrants. In colloquial terms, they are "too big for their boots". They need firm but understanding "containment", mixed with compassion and common sense. They welcome this, for they are as unhappy about their state as are the concerned people around them.

From what she told me, I had the impression that John's mother was stunned by the beautiful baby whom she felt she had lost, as part of herself, by giving birth to him. He was not a real live baby to her, but a precious piece of Dresden china. How hurting it would have been to her, and how far from the truth, if she had been told by an "expert" that she had a "death wish" towards her child, and that this was the cause of his troubles. Some of the psychodynamicists have made grave mistakes in their approach to autism. This chapter has been an attempt to bring in evidence which corrects some of these mistaken notions.

It has also been an attempt to get in touch with the elemental feelings which have provoked the psychogenic autism. In reality, what happened to the children was in the nature of a sensuous mishap, but in the hypersensitised, illusion-dominated state of early infancy, it had become exaggerated to seem like a catastrophe. But the feelings associated with this illusion had been traumatizing.

As one patient said to me, "I know it's an illusion, but the terror is real." I have found that this early, seemingly catastrophic damage can be healed by a form of psychotherapy which is realistic about the nature of the disorder being treated. I have also found that insights gathered from such psychotherapy have thrown light on the autistic barriers encountered in certain neurotic patients.

Note

1. This chapter also appeared in *Autistic Barriers in Neurotic Patients* (Karnac, 1986).

References

Bibring, E. (1953). The Mechanism of Depression. In: Greenacre (ed.), *Affective Disorders*. New York: International Universities Press.

Bion, W.R. (1962). *Learning from Experience*. London: Heinemann. Reprinted London: Karnac, 1984.

Mahler, M. (1958). Autism and Symbiosis—Two Extreme Disturbances of Identity. *Int. J. Psychoanal. 39*: 77–83.

Mahler, M. (1961). On Sadness and Grief in Infancy and Childhood: Loss and Restoration of the Symbiotic Love Object. *Psychoanalytic Study of the Child 16*: 332–51.

Rank, B. & Putnam, M. (1953). James Jackson Putnam Children's Center. Unpublished research report.

Tustin, F. (1972). *Autism and Childhood Psychosis*. London: Hogarth.

Winniciott, D.W. (1958). *Collected Papers: Through Paediatrics to Psychoanalysis*. London: Tavistock.

CHAPTER THREE

Finding the wavelength: tools in communication with children with autism[1]

Anne Alvarez

L istening is a complex art. A few years ago, there was a series of letters in *The Times* on the subject of blackbirds and their song. Here is one from 14 June 2000.

> Sir – Blackbirds are joyful in May and sing in A major. In July, they are content and sing in F major. I've waited 68 years to say this, Beethoven's Seventh and Sixth Symphonies supporting my theory.
> Sincerely, D.F. Clarke.

The writer is clearly a good listener and seems to like listening. Here is a rather different attitude to listening, this one by Fernando Pessoa (1981).

> Cease your song!
> Cease, for along with
> It I have heard
> Another voice
> Coming (it seemed) in
> Interstices
> Of the charm, softly strong
> Brought by your song as
> Far as us.

The last stanza reads:

> No more song! Must
> Now have silence,
> To sleep clear
> Some remembrance
> Of the voice heard,
> Not understood,
> Which was lost
> For me to hear.

Note the insistence that what he needs in order to listen is silence, not song. Children with autism are notoriously poor listeners: indeed, they are often thought to be deaf. The established triad of symptoms includes, as well as impairments in social relatedness and the use of the imagination, impairments in communication and language development. It is important to identify symptoms, yet a nosology which relies too exclusively on a one-person psychology—that is, which sticks to describing attributes of the child's self—may tell only a part of the story. I think a fuller descriptive psychology of autism is provided by a two- and eventually three-person psychology. Such an approach involves a study of intra-personal relations: in a model of the mind which involves a two-person psychology, the mind contains not just a self with particular qualities and orientations and possible deficits; it also contains a relation to, and relationship with, what are called "internal objects" (Klein, 1959) or "representational models" (Bowlby, 1988), and these too may contain deficits. A more personal, intra-personal view of autism carries the implication that the self is in an emotional, dynamic relationship with its internal representations, figures, objects—no matter how skewed, deficient, or odd this relationship may be. (There is no aetiological implication here: it is the child's inner world of figures and representations that is at issue. Many psychoanalysts use the term "internal object" rather than "representation", as the latter may sometimes be taken to imply an exact copy of external figures, whereas the former carries no such implication. Internal objects are thought to be amalgams of both inner and outer factors.) If the child treats us as a piece of furniture, he may be seeing us as something like a piece of furniture, and he may also feel as though we are like a piece of furniture. If he does not listen to us, it may be in part because he does not have the habit of listening, but it may also be because he finds our talk uninteresting, or intrusive, with too few of Pessoa's silences. How, then, are we to cease our song and still be heard? And if he does not talk to us, it may be in part because he does not think we are worth the effort of speaking to, or because he feels our listening capacities are limited. Or else he may feel we want to pull his words out of him, so that in some sort of terrible way they will become ours and no longer his. His "theory of mind" (Leslie, 1987) may assert that minds are basically unmindful: this can do major damage to processes of introjection, learning and internalisation.

Yet symptomatology and pathology are not everything: each person with autism can usually be found to have an intact, non-autistic part of the personality interwoven with their autism. Bion described the importance, in psychoanalytic work with psychotic patients, of making contact with the "non-psychotic part of the personality" (1957). There is also now a growing body of research on "shared function" in autism (Hobson & Lee, 1999). For all its apparent stasis, the autistic condition is less static and more mutable than it sometimes appears. While a microsecond's interested glance by a child at a person, say, or a new toy, may be followed by an instantaneous return to old rituals, the quality of the child's glance may nevertheless offer a clue, a faint signal which can be amplified and built upon tactfully. It is important to assess what the developmental level is at which this apparently more normal part of the self may be operating. The child's chronological age may be five or ten years, but because of habitual lifelong interference from the autism, the healthy, related, object-seeking part may be functioning at ten months or even three weeks of age. Traces of early preconceptions (Bion, 1962)—of not so much a "theory of mind" (Leslie, 1987) or a sense of person (Hobson, 1993), more a proto-theory of mind or a proto-sense of person—may still be detectable. It is on this foundation that a treatment—precisely calibrated to the level of emotional communication of which the child is capable—may build.

Normal infant development, vision and proto-language

William, thirteen months old, heard his father getting up at five in the morning outside his door. William called "Ey!" The father said it sounded like, "Hey! What are you doing? Where the heck are you going?!" Dad opened the baby's bedroom door, and was greeted with another demanding "Ey!" Dad whispered, in order not to wake the mother, "I'm going to work, William, you go back to sleep now." William said "Awhhhh", and went back to sleep.

From the moment of birth, as the psychoanalyst Klein maintained and developmental psychology research has subsequently demonstrated, normal babies are now known to be extremely precocious socially (Klein, 1959, p. 249). They have all the basic equipment they require to begin to engage in face-to-face interpersonal communication—initially of a non-verbal kind. They prefer to look at face-like patterns, to listen to the sound of the human voice, and they have a remarkable capacity for finely tuned interpersonal exchanges (Stern, 1985, p. 40; Trevarthen & Aitken, 2001). Clearly, emotional communication involves a whole orchestra of "instruments" in which eye gaze (Fogel, 1977; Koulomzin et al, 2002), emotional engagement (Demos, 1986), level of attention and interest, expressive bodily gestures (Hobson, 1993), and vocalisations (Trevarthen & Aitken, 2001) all play their part. Most of these instruments are used both expressively and then communicatively, or (to put it in psychoanalytic terms) via different types of projective identification. They are also used, however, for purposes of introjection and internalisation. Vision, for example: at birth, the infant has a set of visual structures highly sensitive to those aspects of stimulation that emanate from other people's faces (Papousek & Papousek, 1975). Schore (1997, p. 10) points out that the caregiver's emotionally expressive face is by far the most potent visual stimulus in the infant's environment, and the child's intense interest in her face, especially in her eyes, her brightening and dulling gaze (Robson, 1967) leads him to track it in space and to engage in periods of intense mutual gaze. Eyes, after all, have what Robson calls immense "stimulus richness" to the newborn: their shininess and mobility, and the microsecond-by-microsecond changes in the size of the pupil attract attention, at first only fleeting, but nevertheless frequent (Fogel, 1977). After the second month, fixation on the mother's eyes increases (Maurer & Salapatak, 1976). At seventeen weeks, the eyes are a more attracting feature of the mother's face than her mouth (Uzgiris & Hunt, 1975).

Language and triadic skills involving visual regard

Towards the end of the first year of life, infants begin to extend the use of an earlier skill: the capacity for gaze monitoring. Scaife and Bruner (1975) have shown that even very young infants will turn their heads to follow the mother's line of regard. In the last quarter of the first year, following the trajectory of another's gaze and gazing at the object of the gaze is intensified, as the baby is motivated to keep track of his mother and her comings and goings. This is followed by the emergence of the more proactive activity of proto-declarative pointing between the ninth and the fourteenth month (Scaife & Bruner 1975). Bruner (1983) was one of the first to point out that language arose in the context of interactions between infant and caregiver. It was here that the infant learned to understand that there was more than one perspective, but differing perspectives could be linked (and see Urwin, 2002 for a discussion of language development as an emotional process). Burhouse (2001) has offered suggestions as to the emotional preconditions which might explain why gaze monitoring seems to precede proto-declarative pointing. She points out that the baby has learned to value the mother's return of gaze during the early months of face-to-face dyadic mutual gazing, and this interest in and valuing of her attention leads the baby to follow her gaze when it goes to someone else, such as an older sister. Eventually the baby finds active ways of getting this attention back, through communicative pointing and expressive sounds. These are emotionally laden events, and the grammar of emotional events structures language. There are huge differences in communicative intention between a "Hey there!", a "C'mon, give us a smile . . .", an "Oh, look at the lovely bright sun!", a teasing "I'm coming to catch youuuuuuu!", a "You've been a very naughty boy!", an "Oh, you really like that banana puree, don't you, oh yes, yum yum!", and an imperative "Don't touch that socket—it is VERY dangerous!" Language, as Bruner (1983) taught, emerges always in contexts and, as developmentalists have shown, is accompanied by emotion (Demos, 1986). Burhouse describes a moment when the baby seems to be thinking "She (mine) is talking to and looking at her, not me". Psychoanalytic theorists and developmentalists alike have suggested that early two-person relationships lay the foundation for the later three-person social capacities (Klein, 1945; Winnicott, 1958;

Trevarthen & Hubley, 1978). Recently Striano and Rochat (1999) have demonstrated empirically that the link between triadic social competence and earlier dyadic competence in infancy is indeed a developmental one. You don't follow the trajectory of someone's gaze unless you find his or her gaze worth having in the first place.

Therapeutic implications of impairments in communication: getting on the right developmental wavelength

The question of the psychoanalytic treatment of children with autism has been surrounded by controversy. Some psychoanalysts and psychotherapists have themselves described the need for changes in technique with these children (Meltzer, 1975; Tustin, 1981; Alvarez 1992; Alvarez & Reid, 1999). The impairments in symbolic capacity, play and language make an understanding of more ordinary explanatory interpretations very difficult for them. Where the autistic symptomatology is especially severe, and where not only the child's sense of the existence of other people but also his sense of self is weak, the concepts of transference and countertransference may seem too advanced: transference may seem to be non-existent, and a countertransference of frustration or despair in the therapist can lead to indifference. Yet close observation may begin to reveal faint or disordered signs of relatedness which can then be amplified.

The view of the Autism Workshop at the Tavistock Clinic is that regardless of aetiology, a disorder of the capacity for social interaction may benefit from a treatment which functions via the process of social interaction itself, provided this takes account both of the nature and severity of the psychopathology and of the particular developmental level at which the child is functioning. The therapeutic approach is three-pronged: it addresses the child's personality, the autistic symptomatology (disorder and sometimes deviance), and the intact or spared "non-autistic" part of the child, however developmentally delayed this may be (Alvarez & Reid, 1999). The psychotherapy is thus psychoanalytically, psychopathologically and developmentally informed.

Firstly, the psychoanalytic perspective offers the close observation of the transference and countertransference. This can alert the therapist to personality features in the child which accompany (and may act to exacerbate or reduce) his autism. (Some children with autism develop quite deviant personalities which are in no way an essential feature of the autism itself.) The psychoanalytic theory of the need and capacity of every ordinary child first to relate intensely to and gradually to identify with both of his parents contributes greatly to the understanding of normal child development. So also does the theory of the Oedipus complex, the understanding of the ordinary child's disturbance at, but also enormous interest in and stimulation by those aspects of the parental couple's relationship that exist independently of him (Houzel, 2001; Rhode, 2001).

Secondly, the psychopathological perspective helps the therapist to understand the power and pull of autistic repetitive behaviours, and the ways in which (as psychoanalysts, too, have suggested) addictive and concrete non-symbolic behaviours differ profoundly from simple neurotic mechanisms and defences (Kanner, 1944; Joseph, 1982; Tustin, 1981).

Finally, clinical intuition can be both confirmed and supplemented by the study of very young infants by the methods of naturalistic observation (Miller et al, 1989) and of developmental research. Therapists try to identify and facilitate the precursors of social relatedness: the technique draws on findings into the ways in which mothers communicate with their babies, and into how this facilitates the infant's capacity for communication and relatedness. The developmental research emphasises a number of factors: the normal baby's need for his level of stimulation and arousal to be carefully modulated (Dawson, 1989; Brazelton, 1974) and his attention channelled; the power of "motherese" (softer, higher inflections with particular adagio rhythms during pre-speech or pre-music dialogues: Snow, 1972; Trevarthen, 2001) and particular grammars (coaxing rather than imperatives: Murray, 1991); differing proximity of faces at different ages for eliciting eye contact (Papousek & Papousek, 1975); and, depending on developmental level, the child's readiness for primary intersubjectivity (face to face communication and play in a dyadic situation) versus secondary intersubjectivity (shared play with objects, where the baby glances at the caregiver, seeking moments of joint attention to a toy, for example—a triadic situation: Trevarthen, 1978).

Yet many severely autistic children have never played, nor developed a capacity for joint attention (Baron-Cohen et al, 1992). They may have no language at all; worse, they may never have babbled playfully. It may be a real achievement in the therapy when the non-speaking child begins to play with sounds, to make sounds that are more contoured than before. The technical issues for the psychotherapist are difficult: how can we reach a child with little or no language? How should we talk to such a child? I now want to describe work with a child where the use of both "motherese" and something which might be called "fatherese" combined to facilitate communication between us and to help his communicative capacities grow. In both situations I often found that I had to contain and dramatize feelings which were either unfamiliar or unmanageable for Joseph. Yet he showed growing interest in my reactions.

Joseph

Joseph was referred to me at the age of eight by his music therapist. He had been born two weeks overdue and had been induced. His older brothers were normal. Joseph was a placid baby, happy to be held by anybody, and he made eye contact until about the age of three. The parents only suspected something might be wrong when they tried to toilet train him at the age of two and he seemed not to understand. When they started trying to put pressure on him to communicate, he "closed down", and eye contact reduced. He was always content, but he cut himself off and would not play with other children. He had always been tactile and cuddly, and loved being sung to. He could sing numerous songs, but his spoken language was very limited. Joseph's mother wrote that his early pretend play was good: from the age of two years he held two dolls facing each other and made them have "conversations" with each other and dance together. Joseph did this in his sessions with me, but for much of the time the quality was very closed and shut-off, and I think by now it was no longer real pretend play. It was too real for him: he seemed to believe he really was those people talking and playing together. Most of the language I heard in the early sessions was of this private type—conversations between various video characters: lively, interested, yet very repetitive, and for much of the time impossible to understand. Occasionally a question could be heard, or an exclamation. But the only real word I heard directed to his parents or me was when we asked him if he would like to use the toilet, and he responded with an excessively light, quite disembodied

"No". It was so light and impersonal, un-aimed and unlocatable that you could easily imagine you hadn't heard it.

I saw Joseph together with his parents for three consultations. He occasionally responded to his mother's songs in the sense of joining in on the last word, but much of his positive connection with her was through cuddling. He was a big eight-year-old, and I did begin to note how easy it was to see him as younger than his age, and to want to be protective of him: he was an attractive boy, with a sweet, rather unformed face and a very loose-limbed body, which in the room was much of the time horizontally laid out on the couch, half in his mother's lap. He did examine the toys a bit, but avoided most suggestions or directives from her or me regarding any play activity. When walking, he tended to drag his arms and legs, especially his feet, after him as though they did not belong to him. I was cheered by more signs of alertness and life in a teasing game he began to play, in which he suddenly said "Night-night!" and then liked it when I did an exaggerated startle and expressed my disappointment that he was disappearing under the blanket AGAIN. He made a little fleeting eye contact after these moments. It was clear that Joseph was a much loved child, but there was also a sense in which he had never really wakened up to the world. He seemed to need to discover his bones and muscles, his verticality, his pleasure in standing and stretching up into the world, in jumping, and his capacity to move forward and explore it. There was far too much passivity in his life, and yet, as he so easily collapsed into a sort of panicky temper-tantrum when challenged or stretched, it was easy for everyone to suppose that his autism had made him far too delicate for ordinary life and ordinary demands. On the other hand, it was clear that both his parents and the school were able to be firm about certain things, as Joseph was in many respects a reasonable and easy-going child.

After two months or so of psychotherapy I got the impression that the talk between the video characters, or between the toy animals, was not always as totally absorbing to Joseph as it seemed, that in fact he was often quite aware of my attention on him as he carried out these repetitive activities. I also began to think he was enjoying my feelings of exclusion, so I began to dramatize my countertransference: "Oh, Joseph won't talk to me, it's not fair, nobody will talk to me, and they are having such a good time over there talking to each other!" I also added sometimes: "Oh please talk to ME Joseph, not to them!!" This was all quite emotional-coaxing/pleading/protesting. I was beginning to suspect that he thought of talking as something other people did together, with a third always excluded, but had no idea of the real pleasures of face-to-face talking in a twosome. I felt I needed to give the third a voice, and yet attract him back to real relationships. One day, after my coaxing, he looked straight at me and put his head up and back, starting to shake it just like a toddler, saying "No! Nonononononono!", really relishing his power to tease and thwart me. But this had at least a bit of give and take: he was, after all, looking at me, and it was a genuine "no", with some real oomph in it. Like his "Night-night", it was full of mischief and really made me laugh.

Not all of my countertransferences were so obliging, however. I sometimes found myself feeling very annoyed by his complacent assumption that only he and his shadow were interesting, or that he was not really bored silly by his unending conversations, or that he knew what was behind a particular wall in the room. Eventually I felt our relationship was strong enough for me to begin to challenge these assumptions. I began saying things like "Oh no, you DO NOT know what is in there behind that wall. You'd love to know, but you don't!" I said it strongly, but I kept it lively and fun and rhythmic, so it accompanied or responded to his sing-song style. Except that his was high and expressive, whereas I was bringing him down with my voice to a more earthbound but (I hoped) more interesting place. It was flatter and lower than his, but still quite humorous. I also persisted with the idea that his talk was NOT real, and that I knew he was dying to talk in a real way! The people in his pretend conversations seemed always to be having fun—or at least a dramatic and interesting time. But in order to become *like* someone, you also have to become aware that you cannot *be* that person.

However, you also have to feel that other people give you permission to be like them. Therefore, on occasions when he came in very wild and excited, I echoed the excited/aggressive element in his utterances. If there were sudden growls and stamping of his feet, I copied and amplified both, which delighted him. I felt he needed to discover his musculature as well as his own boy's voice. I also encouraged the toy animals to take longer journeys. They were often sitting around kissing each other most tenderly, but they never went for even a simple walk! I'm certain that even Anthony and Cleopatra went out for a breath of fresh air sometimes! I had frequently accompanied the animals' large rather assertive steps (they always remained in the same place, or moved in the tiniest of circles) with even more assertive stamps of my own feet, but eventually I began to get a bit tougher over their lack of adventurousness. I began to insist that they were not scared, they DID want to go further, that HE was holding them back. He began to climb them up the back of the sofa and, unlike the days when all I could see was their backs, he placed them to face me from the top.

As the first year progressed, Joseph took more and more pleasure in discovering his deeper voice, and a more powerful and muscular self. His parents reported that he was making more eye contact and had begun occasionally to use spontaneous speech at home. Not long after the end of the second year, he began to engage in what I think was real pretend play. He lay on the couch, shouted "Yee-ikes, 'elp, save me!" as he "fell" onto the rug. Although this scene may have come from one of his videos, it was not carried out in isolation like the doll conversations where he usually kept his back to me: here he fell off the couch right in front of me, looking at me often, and if I was too slow to call out "Help, this poor boy is falling off the cliff, we've got to rescue him, hurry, hurry!", he pulled my arm to get it to reach out to his. The sequence was repeated, but somehow it was never boring, perhaps because of Joseph's delight in the high drama. Certainly, my involvement in the game was quite intense too: lack of a capacity for pretend play and for joint attention is one of the early markers for autism, and it is moving and cheering when they begin, however immature they may be in relation to the chronological age of the child. The game seemed heavy with meaning: sometimes I told him that I agreed—he did indeed need rescuing from his self-imposed autistic isolation, and to be brought up and out onto firmer ground where there were other real people.

Discussion

The technical issues in talking to a child like Joseph are difficult. Needless to say, I have only cited parts of sessions where I think I managed to find a way of being heard and encouraging proto-speech between us. Working with these children is never easy, and the power of their autism is awesome. However, it is interesting to think about how to talk to these children, and why particular methods may be more useful than others. I think there were many different motives for Joseph's repetitive talk. Sometimes he did seem totally absorbed in it, but as I said, I began to think that at times he was definitely monitoring my response to it. And he did become less autistic when I gave urgent voice to this excluded third. This suggests that there was a communicative element in the projection at such moments. Or should we call it a proto-communication? He may not have expected a response, but he recognised it and seemed delighted by it when he got one. At other moments, when I felt his "talking" was more arrogantly self-indulgent, I challenged it. I think he needed both from me: the more receptive, coaxing "motherese", and also the more challenging "fatherese". There seem to have been two aspects to the father's voice in the room: first, a father who declines to indulge omnipotence, who makes demands on his child to learn and grow, and who makes it clear that the child is not the same as the grownups; and second, the father who invites and permits identification (with the strong voice and the potency of the stamping). Both only worked when I got the tone right. I suspect that when I challenged him too strictly, it may not have permitted the kind of identification he needed with a strong father. What seemed to work better was a firm, slightly bored tone, or a more humorous teasing. Some identification processes seemed to be beginning with his deeper growls, strong stamping and standing tall. Some identification with father certainly aids the tolerance of Oedipal rivalries, and enables omnipotent methods to be replaced by a more realistic sense of agency and potency.

I have described elsewhere the need to approach the child with autism on the right band of intensity (Alvarez, 1999), but it is interesting that Barrows (2002) has been even more specific in introducing aggressive play to a child with autism (see Chapter Five) has also found the introduction of aggressive play to a cut-off infant very helpful.

To return to the more receptive or maternal function: Bion talked about "alpha function", a function of the mind that makes thoughts thinkable and lends meaning to experience. He suggested that the mother's reverie provided the necessary emotional containment of experience that enables babies to think. He described this in terms of the mother's containment of the baby's distress which had been projected into her and then transformed there by her capacity to think about and process feelings (Bion, 1962). But as developmentalists like Stern (1985) and Trevarthen and Aitken (2001) remind us, these processes do not concern only moments of distress. Babies need to impress, to delight, to bring a light to the parents' eyes, to surprise and astonish them, to make them laugh. And they also need to be given room and space and time in which to do all this. We all may need to learn to keep our distance, know our place, wait our turn and bide our time—and, especially important, respect the child's space and the child's timing. I think it was important for this child that I could hold the experience of being left out, unwanted, helpless, and especially powerless, and give him space and time to feel that he had the power to keep me waiting. Of course the risk in such a technique is of being experienced as masochistically colluding with his omnipotence: it needed vigilant monitoring on my part, so that when it felt more self-indulgent on his part, I could be firmer.

I also want to mention another point concerning the strength of my voice when I coaxed Joseph to talk to me rather than to his imaginary (or delusional?) friends. I feel there was a kind of process of "reclamation" at such moments, possibly because Joseph didn't really believe his objects minded when he disappeared (Alvarez, 1992). Even the most loving and devoted parents, teachers and therapists can get very demoralised and give up a little under such conditions. Joseph did seem to appreciate my staying power, but only when I kept it mock-desperate, playful/needy: as soon as there was a hint of unprocessed frustration or directive pulling on my part, he retreated. (His teachers have independently developed similar non-controlling methods with him.) I also think the drama in my voice got through to the developmentally delayed proto-speaker in him. (These active elements in the technique were informed by developmental thinking and also by awareness of the powerful hold of the repetitive preoccupations. The technique was by no means strictly psychoanalytic.) We have to find ways of helping these children not only to attend to us but also to sustain their attention; and emotionally heightened interest is central to this process.

In conclusion, it is important to say that Joseph had dedicated parents, teachers, and speech and music therapists, with whom I have liaised regularly, so this has been a co-operative effort. I have simply tried to outline some techniques and concepts that seem to have been helpful in my particular part of the work. Our task continues to be enormously difficult.

Note

1. This chapter was also published in *Infant Observation: the International Journal of Infant Observation 7*: 91–106.

References

Alvarez, A. (1992). *Live Company: Psychoanalytic Psychotherapy with Autistic, Borderline, Deprived and Abused Children*. London: Tavistock/Routledge.

Alvarez, A. (1996). Addressing the Element of Deficit in Children with Autism: Psychotherapy which is both Psychoanalytically and Developmentally Informed. *Clinical Child Psychology and Psychiatry 1*: 525–537.

Alvarez, A. & Furgiuele, P. (1997). Speculations on Components in the Infant's Sense of Agency: the Sense of Abundance and the Capacity to Think in Parentheses. In: S. Reid (Ed.), *Developments in Infant Observation*. London: Routledge.

Alvarez, A. & Reid, S. (Eds.) (1999). *Autism and Personality: Findings from the Tavistock Autism Workshop*. London: Routledge.

Baron-Cohen, S., Allen, J. & Gillberg, C. (1992). Can Autism be Detected at 18 Months? The Needle, the Haystack, and the CHAT. *British Journal of Psychiatry 161*: 839–843.

Barrows, P. (2002). Becoming Verbal: Autism, Trauma and Playfulness. *Journal of Child Psychotherapy 28*: 53–72.

Bion, W.R. (1957). Differentiation of the Psychotic from the Non-Psychotic Personalities. In: *Second Thoughts*. London: Karnac, 1984.

Bion, W.R. (1962). *Learning from Experience*. London: Heinemann. Reprinted London: Karnac, 1984.

Bowlby, J. (1988). *A Secure Base: Clinical Applications of Attachment Theory*. London: Routledge.

Brazelton, T.B., Koslowski, B. & Main, M. (1974). The Origins of Reciprocity: the Early Mother-Infant Interaction. In: M. Lewis

& L.A. Rosenblum, *The Effect of the Infant on its Caregivers*. London: Wiley Interscience.

Britton, R. (1989). The Missing Link: Parental Sexuality in the Oedipus Complex. In: J. Steiner (Ed.), *The Oedipus Complex Today*. London: Karnac.

Bruner, J.S. (1968). *Processes of Cognitive Growth: Infancy*. Worcester, MA: Clark University Press.

Bruner, J.S. (1983). From Communicating to Talking. In: *Child's Talk: Learning to Use Language* (pp. 23–42). Oxford: Oxford University Press.

Burhouse, A. (2001). Now We Are Two, Going On Three: Triadic Thinking and its Link with Development in the Context of Young Child Observations. *Infant Observation* 4: 51–67.

Dawson, G. & Lewy, A. (1989). Reciprocal Subcortical-Cortical Influences in Autism: the Role of Attentional Mechanisms. In G. Dawson (Ed.), *Autism: Nature, Diagnosis and Treatment*. New York: Guilford Press.

Demos, V. (1986). Crying in Early Infancy: an Illustration of the Motivational Function of Affect. In T.B. Brazelton & M.W. Yogman (Eds.), *Affective Development in Infancy*. Norwood, NJ: Ablex.

Fogel, A. (1977). Temporal Organization in Mother-Infant Face-to-Face Interaction. In: H.R. Schaffer (Ed.), *Studies in Mother-Infant Interaction*. London: Academic Press.

Haag, G. (1985). La Mère et le Bébé dans les Deux Moitiés du Corps. *Neuropsychiatrie de l'Enfance 33*: 107–114.

Hobson, R.P. (1993). *Autism and the Development of Mind*. Hove: Psychology Press.

Hobson, R.P. & Lee, A. (1999). Imitation and Identification in Autism. *Journal of Child Psychology and Psychiatry 40*: 649–659.

Houzel, D. (2001). Bisexual Qualities of the Psychic Envelope. In J. Edwards (Ed.), *Being Alive: Building on the Work of Anne Alvarez*. Hove: Brunner-Routledge.

Joseph, B. (1982). Addiction to Near Death. In: M. Feldman, & E. Spillius (Eds.), *Psychic Equilibrium and Psychic Change*. London: Tavistock/ Routledge, 1989.

Kanner, L. (1944). Early Infantile Autism. *Journal of Paediatrics 25*: 211–17.

Klein, M. (1945). The Oedipus Complex in the Light of Early Anxieties. In: *Love, Guilt and Reparation and Other Works*. London: Hogarth, 1975.

Klein, M. (1959). Our Adult World and its Roots in Infancy. In: *Envy and Gratitude and Other Works*. London: Hogarth, 1975.

Koulomzin, M., Beebe, B., Anderson, S., Jaffe, J., Feldstein, S. & Crown, C. (2002). Infant Gaze, Head, Face and Self-Touch Differentiate Secure vs. Avoidant Attachment at 1 Year: a Microanalytic Approach. In: *Attachment and Human Development* 4: 3–24.

Leslie, A. M. (1987). Pretence and Representation: the Origins of Theory of Mind. *Psychological Review* 94: 412–426.

Maurer, D. & Salapatak, P. (1976). Developmental Changes in the Scanning of Faces by Young Infants. *Child Development* 47: 523–527.

Meltzer, D., Bremner, J., Hoxter, S., Weddell, D. & Wittenberg, I. (1975). *Explorations in Autism: A Psycho-Analytical Study.* Strathtay: Clunie Press.

Miller, L., Rustin, M., Rustin, M., & Shuttleworth, J. (1989). *Closely Observed Infants.* London: Duckworth.

Murray, L. (1991). Intersubjectivity, Object Relations Theory and Empirical Evidence from Mother-Infant Interactions. *Infant Mental Health Journal* 12: 219–232.

Papousek, H. & Papousek, M. (1975). Cognitive Aspects of Preverbal Social Interaction between Human Infants and Adults. In: *CIBA Foundation Symposium.* New York: Association of Scientific Publishers.

Pessoa, F. (1981). Cease Your Song. In: *Selected Poems.* London: Penguin.

Rey, H. (1988). That Which Patients Bring to Analysis. *International Journal of Psychoanalysis 69*: 457.

Rhode, M. (2001). The Sense of Abundance in Relation to Technique. In: J. Edwards (Ed.), *Being Alive: Building on the Work of Anne Alvarez.* Hove: Brunner-Routledge.

Robson, K. (1967). The Role of Eye-to-Eye Contact in Maternal-Infant Attachment. *Journal of Child Psychology and Psychiatry 8*: 13–25.

Scaife, M. & Bruner, J. (1975). The Capacity for Joint Visual Attention in the Infant. *Nature 253*: 265–266.

Schore, A. (1997). Interdisciplinary Developmental Research as a Source of Clinical Models. In: M.M. Moskowitz, C. Monk, C. Kaye & S. Ellman (Eds.), *The Neurobiologcal and Developmental Basis for Psychotherapeutic Intervention.* London: Aaronson.

Snow, C. (1972). Mother's Speech to Children Learning Language. *Child Development 43*: 549–565.

Stern, D. (1974). Mother and Infant at Play: the Dyadic Interaction Involving Facial, Vocal and Gaze Behaviours. In M. Lewis & L.A. Rosenblum (Eds.), *The Effect of the Infant on its Caregiver.* New York: Wiley.

Stern, D. (1985). *The Interpersonal World of the Infant: a View from Psychoanalysis and Developmental Psychology.* New York: Basic Books.

Stern, D. (2000). Putting Time Back into our Considerations of Infant Experience: A Microdiachronic View. *Infant Mental Health Journal, 21:* 21–28.

Striano, T. & Rochat, P. (1999). Developmental Links Between Dyadic and Triadic Social Competence in Infancy. *British Journal of Developmental Psychology 17:* 551–562.

Trevarthen, C. & Hubley, P. (1978). Secondary Intersubjectivity: Confidence, Confiding and Acts of Meaning in the First Year. In A. Lock (Ed.), *Action, Gesture and Symbol: the Emergence of Language.* London: Academic Press.

Trevarthen, C. & Aitken, K.J. (2001). Infant Intersubjectivity: Research, Theory and Clinical Applications. *Journal of Child Psychology and Psychiatry 42:* 3–48.

Trevarthen, C. & Marwick (1986). Signs of Motivation for Speech in Infants, and the Nature of a Mother's Support for Development of Language. In B. Lindblom & R. Zetterstrom (Eds.), *Precursors of Early Speech.* Basingstoke: Macmillan.

Trevarthen, C. (2001). Intrinsic Motives for Companionship in Understanding: Their Origin, Development, and Significance for Infant Mental Health. *Infant Mental Health Journal 22:* 95–131.

Tustin, F. (1981). *Autistic States in Children.* London: Routledge & Kegan Paul.

Urwin, C. (2002). A Psychoanalytic Approach to Language Delay: When Autistic Isn't Necessarily Autism. *Journal of Child Psychotherapy, 28:* 73–93.

Uzgiris, I.C. & Hunt, J.M.V. (1975). *Towards Ordinal Scales of Psychological Development in Infancy.* Champaign, IL: University of Illinois Press.

Winnicott, D.W. (1951). Transitional Objects and Transitional Phenomena. In: *Playing and Reality.* London: Tavistock, 1971.

CHAPTER FOUR

Analysis of a little girl with an autistic syndrome[1]

Velleda Cecchi

This paper is based on clinical material from analysis of a 28-month-old girl who developed an autistic syndrome as a reaction to a traumatic situation. I shall deal here only with three aspects: (1) the patient's peculiar way of communicating, (2) the use made of this peculiar communicating mode for the technical approach, and (3) the social context in which the therapeutic process took place and its influence on the analytic field.

Mariela was thin, graceful and fair-haired, with big blue eyes, and very pretty. She did not speak, walked slowly with rigid movements, did not fix her eyes, and looked absent—characteristics which made her look like a lifeless doll. Her maternal grandmother brought her for the first interview. She was a pleasant-looking 54-year-old woman, in a depressive state, who said that the child had not spoken for three months, that she sometimes uttered guttural cries or sounds like "sssssss", or "ta ta tata ta ta" or "sesesese". She remained quiet and absent-minded for long periods. For some time she had refused to eat, but at that moment she was eating a bit better, although mainly liquids.

Background

Mariela was the only child of a young couple. She was a wanted baby, and the pregnancy and delivery had been normal. She was breast-fed until she was eight months old and then had no difficulty in

81

passing on to solid food. Her motor development was normal, and she began to walk when she was 14 months old. Speech started when she was one year old, and a year later her vocabulary was quite rich and she was able to frame phrases. She had a good relationship with her warm, tender parents. Mariela was a cheerful, vivacious child. When she was 20 months old, her mother became pregnant under difficult circumstances. Both parents were deeply worried over the country's political situation and the possible consequences for them. The mother in particular was frightened and depressed.

Mariela began to change, and those around her noticed that she was withdrawn and sad, that she kept to herself and spoke very little, played less than before, and had no appetite: she was no longer a cheerful, vivacious child.

When Mariela was 25 months old, a group of armed men broke into her house at dawn. In the midst of deafening noise, shouting and tremendous violence, her parents were dragged away by the hair—beaten up, bleeding, half-dead. This information was provided by the only neighbour, a woman, who went into the house to help the little girl. She found her "crouching in a corner, against the wall"; she had wet and soiled herself, and was "cowering, panic on her face". When, a few hours later, her grandmother came for her, she saw the same Mariela I met in my consulting room three months later. The change had already taken place, a change that persisted and was the reason for the consultation.

In the first two interviews Mariela behaved as described, that is, she was quiet, indifferent, absent, and showed no reaction when her grandmother left the consulting room. The grandmother reported that Mariela showed the same behaviour at home, that is, she had no contact with either children or adults. As regards adults, she sometimes obeyed them passively. In the third interview she wet herself in the consulting room. The girl had no sphincter control, and I had asked her grandmother to bring her without her diapers. In view of Mariela's absence of communication, I thought that her urine and faeces might contribute a clue, some content coming out from inside this little girl who gave the impression of being behind a wall or not being there at all. She reminded me of the encapsulated children described by Frances Tustin.

In the first sessions her behaviour remained the same, and my interventions were centred upon her persecutory fantasies, her withdrawal as a defence against the persecutors and me, somebody who was outside and therefore dangerous. I will not offer a literal transcription of the interpretations, but it should be clear that they were formulated in a language adequate to the patient's age, and with accompanying gestures. Mariela did not respond in any visible way. At times, I had countertransference feelings of desolation, probably through projective counteridentification with such an isolated child, and at the same time, I was determined to keep trying to make contact with her.

In the 12th session (I saw her five times a week), the scene was the same, but I drew a little closer to her (very little) while I talked to her about her fear. Mariela wet herself, which she had not done since the third interview. I understood this as a confirmation of my interpretation that she defended herself by means of her urine and by creating a defensive space to prevent me from coming even closer, to throw me out; but at the same time this showed a recognition of my presence. When I said this, she moved a foot slightly.

The two following sessions were absolutely quiet. I drew a little closer than the previous time. Mariela remained impassive, and I interpreted that perhaps she was less afraid of me and that was why she allowed me to come closer. I added that she was testing me by accepting or rejecting my coming closer, and that she was taking her time to find out whether I was as dangerous as those who had hurt her mother and father. Since there was no response, it is difficult to know whether the interpretation was correct or merely an expression of wishful thinking.

The psychoanalyst's task is always hard and painstaking. This applies, of course, to the analysis of the neurotic adult, but even more in the case of children, where the effort to unveil the unconscious has to overcome yet another obstacle, that of having to use a language which is basically made up of play and gestures, and when not even this kind of language is available, as in Mariela's case, the difficulty increases. The theory and the clinical experience, effective allies which make up our professional identity, always appear insufficient, and the patient is always unique and different.

Freud states that for the purposes of interpretation, the analyst "must turn his own unconscious like a receptive organ towards the transmitting unconscious of the patient" (1912, p. 115). In a later work he says: "I have had good reason for asserting that everyone possesses in his own unconscious an instrument with which he can interpret the utterances of the unconscious in other people" (1913, p. 320). To use one's own unconscious as an instrument implies allowing one to "regress" to one's most primitive and hidden veins; as Tustin (1972) says, "to get in touch with our own basic depths". With Mariela it was necessary to tolerate a high degree of not understanding, to venture into the dark. Most of the time, the countertransference feeling was one of confronting something extremely painful and unknown which filled me with hopelessness.

Session 16

This session was like the previous ones: Mariela was impassive, while I interpreted on the basis of my countertransference feelings and what I knew of her history. A few minutes before the end, Mariela was still motionless and silent, and I felt utterly exhausted and discouraged. I did not speak or even look at her. Suddenly, this suffocating atmosphere was broken by a sound, the first sound uttered by Mariela since I had met her, a sound which I could recognise as the musical tone "D". When I looked at her, Mariela was motionless; then, recovering from my surprise, I sang another "D".

When the grandmother arrived to fetch the child, she told me that Mariela's parents were both musicians: the mother sang and the father played the violin. Music played an important role in the family. Her mother sang whenever she was doing something, particularly if it had to do with her daughter, with the exception of the last months, when she was depressed; but even then she had not completely given up her habit. This piece of information had not emerged in the course of the interviews because Mariela's parents did not earn their living as musicians. The grandmother and I felt an ominous kind of perplexity, particularly when I told her I was also a musician.

I had lengthy talks with the grandmother in an attempt to reconstruct or find out what songs Mariela's mother had sung most frequently. The grandmother returned to her daughter's apartment (which she had not done since her disappearance) and brought what little was left of music: records, cassettes and some scores. The rest had been destroyed or stolen during the raid.

Session 19

(In the two previous sessions, Mariela had not repeated the "D".) I uttered "D", and after a few minutes, Mariela sang another "D". My interpretation was the same as when she had uttered the sound for the first time: that she wanted to communicate with me and to that purpose she had made an effort and sung a "D"; and today, in addition, she was able to respond to my "D". I was no longer so dangerous; I was a good mummy. The child turned round slowly and, facing the toys (to which she had never paid attention before), took a doll, smelt it, took it to her mouth and sucked it. Her face had a tense expression, but at the same time showed pleasure. Then, with an abrupt gesture, she threw the doll to the floor and became indifferent again. I told her she wanted me to be her good mummy, to give her good food, but she was afraid of the bad mummy who had hurt her and feared that I might be bad too.

Despite the fact that the "D" marked the beginning of the encounter between Mariela and me and that the session I have just transcribed brought about more active work, it remained true that in the sessions Mariela was a silent, quiet, absent girl.

It was then that I implemented a technical device which, in my opinion, turned out to be positive. It consisted of using a musical way to communicate with her when she withdrew into her autistic world. Of course this did not imply leaving words aside, but the words came afterwards, once the encounter had been established. With these deeply disturbed patients, we often feel we are transgressors on account of alleged deviations from the technical guidelines. But in fact the transgression implies only trying to penetrate into that strange defensive world, the psychotic creation. "Something that should remain private is made public" (Tustin, 1972). What I noticed was that the music changed and became more complex as Mariela grew. At the beginning she could be reached only by means of sounds, melodies softly sung. As her psychic apparatus developed and became stronger, lyrics could be introduced. And in the last period of her treatment she was also able to learn new songs, adapted to the occasion, like any other person. At the beginning of the "lyrics" period it was necessary to repeat them over and over again in exactly the same way: if I happened to make a change, even the most trivial one, Mariela got terribly angry. This girl did with songs what most children do with stories. Indeed, Mariela is a musician.

I will offer a few examples of how songs were introduced and how I came to realise what I have just described.

Session 27

Mariela was indifferent and motionless, and then I sang "D". Silence; and then I sang the most popular cradle song in Argentina (I knew her mother used to sing it). There was no response. After a while, I sang the melody of Brahms' cradle song, which was among the scores the grandmother had given me. Mariela seemed to come to life: she looked at me, moved over to where the toys were, took the same doll she had chosen in the 19th session (there were two other dolls), and sucked it, now for a long time, with an expression of intense pleasure on her face.

What moved me to sing only the melody was that I myself felt that the lyrics were more disruptive. Besides, what Mariela had uttered was a sound, not a word, so what she expected was precisely that: sound (besides the "D"). Perhaps this implied a regressive recognition of her experiences, that is, starting with Mariela's last period with her mother. Considering that her mother had been depressed, she was more likely to have sung without the lyrics. Although the grandmother tended to agree with this, she could not confirm it. Her daughter did not sing as often as before, but surely she did sing, and Brahms' cradle song is sufficiently calm and comforting to be sung even by somebody who is depressed. Had we made contact with one of Mariela's experiential memories? Probably, because of the response. It seemed that most of Mariela's experiences were connected with songs. As the grandmother had said, her mother used to sing whenever she was doing something. And Mariela did the same.

In the period when Mariela uttered her first sound in the course of a session, the "D", the grandmother told me that the girl was beginning to play more actively with her voice, which she did not do in the sessions. She gurgled and crackled; the stereotyped sounds which she uttered when she first came to see me became richer and alternated with others.

The songs themselves acquired different meanings according to what Mariela needed to express. She adapted them, sang a few lines, omitted others, modified some phrases, and changed the rhythm or the speed, thus endowing the songs with different meanings. Little by little, and although the child still preferred songs, they gradually started to give way to words.

While sounds seemed to calm her, noises had a catastrophic effect on Mariela. Any noise—a scream, a knock—filled her with terror. She would crouch in a corner of the consulting room, against the wall, and remain absolutely still. This was an obvious repetition of the traumatic situation.

Later on in the treatment, the expression of hatred and sadism played an important role. For a long period, Mariela used to scream madly, violently hitting at everything, including her therapist. With the red liquid glue which I had given her in large quantities as I felt she needed it, she bathed both of us and the room in red. She turned me into the frightened, attacked child, into the attacked parents, thus revealing her identification with the aggressor and her sadistic fantasies of attacking the parental figures.

In the third year of treatment (which lasted four years) I saw Mariela and her grandmother together. The grandmother brought significant objects which had belonged to the child's parents, especially photographs. Mariela asked questions of her grandmother, who told her about her parents and about the child herself. Mariela's need to learn about herself was insatiable. Then, when she came to her own sessions, she repeated what her grandmother had told her as if I had not been there or heard anything. With my complicity, Mariela played proudly with the illusion of having experienced with her parents much more than circumstances had in fact allowed. She made her own photo album in the consulting room. She was thus reconstructing her history.

Some considerations about the sound "D" uttered by the patient and the use of sounds and songs

For Freud, the first structure of the psychic apparatus "followed the plan of a reflex apparatus, so that any sensory excitation impinging on it could be promptly discharged along a motor path. But the experiences of life interfere with this simple function . . . The exigencies of life confront it first in the form of the major somatic needs." Freud adds that "the excitations produced by internal needs seek discharge in movement, which may be described as an 'internal change' or an 'expression of emotion'. A hungry body screams or kicks helplessly" (1900, p. 565). In a previous paper, Freud had defined somatic needs as "hunger-breathing-sexuality" and internal change as "the expression of the emotions, screaming, vascular innervations" (1895, p. 317).

At this first moment, screaming is merely an attempt at expelling a painful feeling, but it does not lead to its relief for, as Freud says, "a change can only come about if in some way or other (in the case of the baby, through outside help) an 'experience of satisfaction' can be achieved which puts an end to the internal stimulus" (1900, p. 565). Only after this experience does this "path of discharge acquire a secondary function of the highest importance, that of communication" (1895, p. 318).

Sound is transformed screaming, and the difference lies in the regularity of the vibrations. The utterance of a "D" by Mariela followed by my own utterance of the same sound is an experience of this kind. An expression from the most hidden traces of Mariela's bond with her mother, that is, with the sound of her mother's voice. My ability to recognise and repeat it elicited a meaningful response. The moment when Mariela uttered the sound was of the utmost importance. I was feeling dejected; I was not speaking or even looking at her. That was the first time this had happened since I had begun to treat the child, on whom I concentrated all my attention— as she could perceive through my words and gestures—and off whom I never took my eyes. Was this a reproduction of the situation with the mother? That "good enough" mother who first felt depressed and therefore seemed absent, and then was absent forever? At that moment of abandonment, Mariela resorted to her internal good object and cried for it.

Mariela had broken her ties with the external world, which had become exceedingly dangerous. In a regressive move, she gave up communicating by gestures. In a situation of need tension, Mariela resorted to a more primitive means of communication: sound. According to Didier Anzieu, "the acquisition of prelinguistic meaning (that of cries and then of prattling) precedes that of infralinguistic meaning (that of mimicry and gestures)" (1979, p. 28).

The regularity of the sessions, the analyst's permanence, and her interpretations alleviated the patient's persecutory anxieties and made this encounter possible. "Sooner or later, after several encounters, the psychotic shows some modification of his habit which, for the analyst, is significant. Such perceptible modification is the beginning of language directed to us as a person who has been integrated into the perception field: the prelude to a possible communication . . . no word may acquire meaning for us except by going again through our memories of perceptions, through the unconscious defile of our body image" (Dolto, 1971).

Mariela's "D" found an echo in me. As a psychoanalyst, I realised how important this signal was, and I was able to recognise it thanks to my musical training. "If the signal has the same effect, manifested as pleasure or as pain in both participants, their homologous reactions may establish between them a tie of connaturality" (Dolto, 1971). And this is what happened between Mariela and me. This chance encounter facilitated things. It is obvious that if her sound had not been recognised, this girl would have found another way of making herself understood.

The "D" remained part of the sessions for a long time; it was used frequently during the first eighteen months, and afterwards not so often. Likewise, she gave it different meanings in the course of time. Instead of serving as a means of communication, it became at times a password: until the "D"-"D" was sung, Mariela remained still and expectant. If she did not sing it, then I had to (particularly at the beginning of the treatment). This need for a password was related to the situation of external danger of real persecution to which both of us felt exposed. In the course of time, the "D"-"D" gradually lost these meanings and became less important, and finally only a memory.

In the "D" period, Mariela played with air, she gurgled and crackled, just like a three- to six-month-old baby. It was auto-erotic play, without any communicational significance, with which she erogenised her buccopharyngeal region and through which she gradually recovered the audiophonic good bond she had had with her parents and began to recognise her self. This activity, in which she indulges when she is at home, by herself, is a source of intense pleasure. Her grandmother told me about it, remarking that at times she found the girl "in ecstasy". If, as Racker says (1952), "music originates in the child's traumatic experiences of separation from the mother, the basis of paranoid and melancholy anxieties, and as such, music represents an attempt at undoing that separation", Mariela's ecstasy is easy to understand. The use of sounds, and later on of songs, in the sessions often showed these elements of exclusive, narcissistic use. Some time had to pass before its use as communication finally prevailed.

We may think that even the normal adult who plays music establishes a narcissistic relationship with his instrument, and even more so if he uses his own voice. It is an activity where the body plays an important part, a sublimated autoerotic activity that produces pleasure, since if "music not only represents a means to obtain the good object, but in itself represents the good object, the object that loves and is therefore loved " (Racker, 1952), then the listener is a contingent object.

In view of the sound uttered by Mariela and of her unresponsiveness to language, I introduced melody singing (after the failure of songs with the lyrics). The therapeutic situation recreated the pleasurable relationship between the child and her parents. Mariela enjoyed again the good "sound bath" she had received while she lived with her parents. This created a "transitional" space of "illusion" which facilitated access to the painful contents of Mariela's real and psychic life.

Social context of the present case

My encounter with Mariela and our work together over four years took place within the context of the cruellest military dictatorship inflicted upon the Argentines. This dictatorship refined to a paroxysmal degree the repressive methods implemented during the preceding years. The manipulation of the mass media in order to alter the perception of reality; the creation of a terrifying atmosphere that drew people into isolation; kidnappings and tortures led society into a state of defencelessness. The protective aspect of the superego embodied in the culture was lost. The law became perverse and the same happened with its ideals.

These effects were felt by both Mariela and me. Given the family tragedy experienced by the patient, the reality of people disappearing could be neither denied nor disavowed, defence mechanisms widely used in that period. But social isolation and fear kept increasing.

Fantasy was mistaken for reality, and at times it was really hard to discriminate between them, since the reality criterion was distorted in view of the absence of reliable signs.

On several occasions the treatment was in danger of being interrupted, whether because the grandmother decided they had to emigrate for her granddaughter's and her own safety, or because I felt in serious danger.

What was particularly "maddening" was the new category of those who had "disappeared": dead, alive, or dead without a grave; those who were no longer there, the N.N. corpses (the anonymous dead), the category to which Mariela's parents belonged. "When a complaint was lodged due to the absence of a loved person, we were faced with two types of situation: if he was alive in a concentration camp, we were led to consider him dead; and if he was dead and buried as an N.N. corpse, the answer was that he was surely abroad. This helped to create an atmosphere of confusion and ambiguity, and led to the loss of what the inclusion of the funeral rites implied for the access to the culture: if there is no grave, no corpse, then mourning becomes impossible, it remains suspended. The result is an open wound, open because of the hope, because of the no-name, because of the whole situation implicit in not knowing" (Cecchi et al., 1986).

We adults had no explanations to offer to this child. What had happened to her parents and why? Only uncertainty was left to us, and we had to live with that. How should we have referred to those parents, as living or as dead?

I will offer only one example of Mariela's attempt to work through this particular mourning and of her use of songs. I am referring to "Mambrú se fue a la guerra".[2] The contrast in this song between the content of a death and the cheerfulness of the music and the interjections was used by Mariela to express her perplexity in connection with what had happened to her parents and the ambivalence of her feelings. When the ambivalence decreased, the girl changed the music to adapt it to the lyrics. During a period of hope, Mariela cheerfully sang only the phrase: *They'll* come (using the plural) for Easter or for Christmas (she did not know about Trinity). As regards another song on the same record, "A lovely May morning", she repeated insistently: "I found my mummy watering the garden."

When the return of her parents became obviously unlikely, Mariela added to her Mambrú (always in the plural): they were killed in battle. It was only near the end of the treatment that she added the last part of this song, where the burial is mentioned, and at the same time, and obviously with intense grief, she dramatized her need to bury her parents, which was not possible. This attempt showed her guilt for regarding them as dead, for perhaps they might be alive, abroad, somewhere.

Final remarks

This child, normal until she was two years old, found herself suddenly confronted with a mother who was narcissistically withdrawn (because of her pregnancy but also for the reasons mentioned above), depressed and anxious, which in turn increased her withdrawal.

The child resorted to a schizoid defence mechanism and withdrew too. As we were able to confirm in the course of the analysis, her paranoid anxieties also increased. The outside, her mother, became dangerous on the one hand through the projection of her sadistic fantasies of attacking the mother's womb, and on the other hand because in fact the outside was dangerous and because her depressed mother, who was the victim of death fears, no longer provided the support that this child, in a fully fledged "rapprochement phase", required (Mahler, 1979).

The "catastrophic situation" which triggered her defensive autistic reaction was the abduction of her parents. Mahler describes the traumatic effect caused in the child by physical separation from the mother, and the pathological influence of that separation on personality development. The "separation-individuation" process presupposes the mother's physical presence; otherwise, the child experiences a catastrophic situation. Her aggressive fantasies against her parents were thus staged during the raid. On the one hand she was attacked and harmed; parts of her self were wounded, torn away from her together with her parents. She lost her parents and she lost parts of herself. On the other hand she identified herself with the torturers who fulfilled her fantasies. This little girl, overwhelmed by helplessness, broke down into autism. It is a break with an absolutely unbearable reality.

According to Freud (1926), the basic traumatic situation is that of helplessness, a state brought about by the experiences of loss (of the mother, the mother's love, the object's love, etc.), and all later traumatic situations refer back to it.

Mariela's psychic apparatus was suddenly flooded by an amount of external and internal stimuli that she could not metabolise. What happened then is what Meltzer (1975) called dementalisation: "the immediate and transient suspension of mental activity . . . an attempt at literally paralysing mental life . . . the mental apparatus breaks down in the double sense that it no longer works and it is broken to pieces".

In the course of the analysis, the material associated with the traumatic situation appeared constantly, like a leitmotif. At the beginning it did so with the prevalence of schizoid aspects, persecutory guilt and fear of retaliation. As these fantasies were gradually worked through—which diminished the patient's omnipotence—and fantasy and reality were gradually discriminated, strong feelings emerged in connection with the grief over her loss. The excellent relationship Mariela had had with her parents during the first two years of life was the "dowry" which made her recovery possible. Mariela's analysis was a long and painful task: to reconstruct her psychic apparatus, recover the good experiences and an internal object good enough to allow her to go on living and endow the external world with a higher degree of reliability.

Notes

1. This chapter was first published in the *International Journal of Psychoanalysis* 1990, 71.

2. "Mambrú has gone to the war / Chiribin, chiribin, chin, chin / Mambrú has gone to the war, who knows when he'll return / Ahahá Ahahá / He'll return for Easter or for Trinity / Trinity is over / Mambrú will not return / Mambrú was killed in battle / They take him to his grave / With four officers / And a chaplain / Over his grave / A little bird flies / Singing pío-pío and pío-pío pa." This song, together with "A lovely May morning", was included on one of the records found in her parents' house. There was a time when she listened to it practically all day.

94   VELLEDA CECCHI

References

94   VELLEDA CECCHI

References

Anzieu, D. (1979). The Sound Image of the Self. *Int. J. Psychoanal.* 6: 23–36.

Cecchi, V. *et al.* (1986). *Argentina: Psicoanálisis: Represión Política.* Buenos Aires: Ed. Kargieman.

Dolto, F. (1971). *Dominique. Analysis of an Adolescent.* New York: Condor Books, 1974.

Freud, S. (1895). *Project for a Scientific Psychology. SE 1.*

Freud, S. (1900). *The Interpretation of Dreams. SE 5.*

Freud, S. (1912). Recommendations to Physicians Practising Psycho-Analysis. *SE 12.*

Freud, S. (1913). The Disposition of Obsessional Neurosis. *SE 12.*

Freud, S. (1926). Inhibitions, Symptoms and Anxiety. *SE 20.*

Mahler, M. (1979). *Separation-Individuation. The Selected Papers of Margaret S. Mahler, Vol. 2.* New York: Jason Aronson.

Meltzer, D., Bremner, J., Hoxter, S., Weddell, D. & Wittenberg, I. (1975). *Explorations in Autism: A Psycho-Analytical Study.* Strathtay: Clunie Press.

Racker, E. (1952). Aportación al Psicoanálisis de la Música. *Rev. de Psicoanálisis* 9: 3–29.

Tustin, F. (1972). *Autism and Childhood Psychosis.* London: Hogarth.

Winniciott, D.W. (1958). *Collected Papers: Through Paediatrics to Psychoanalysis.* London: Tavistock.

CHAPTER FIVE

"Playful" therapy: working with autism and trauma[1]

Paul Barrows

Introduction

In much of the literature on autism, psychoanalytic psychotherapy enjoys a pretty bad press. It is not generally regarded as an appropriate form of treatment, and at times it is even felt to be potentially damaging. Howlin, for example, writes:

> In 1987, Howlin and Rutter noted: "one cannot conclude with certainty that it does not work, nevertheless, there is little evidence . . . to suggest that it does". Almost ten years later, Campbell *et al.* (1996) concluded that "psychoanalysis as a treatment for autism has a limited value" . . . Anecdotal evidence suggests that unless therapy is combined with direct practical advice on how to deal with problems, the outcome may be disastrous. Simply taking an individual back to his or her early childhood, or focusing (for example) on disturbed mother-infant interactions, is more likely to result in obsessional ruminations and laying the blame for all current problems on other people, rather than encouraging effective coping strategies. [1998, pp. 95–6]

This view seems, however, to be based on a misunderstanding of the way in which child psychotherapists now work with such

95

children. A recent paper (Alvarez, 1996) has sought to address these misconceptions and has described a model of therapy which is informed by both the most recent psychoanalytic models of early development and those provided by developmental psychologists such as Stern (1985) and Tronick and Weinberg (1997).

Rather than "taking an individual back to his or her early childhood", a key feature of this modified approach is the emphasis on making emotional contact with the child, by whatever means seem most likely to engage the child's attention. By working in this way, child psychotherapists probably come close to offering (at least in the early stages of the work) the kind of therapy that Baron-Cohen and Bolton see as being valuable, and which they refer to as "play therapy":

> If psychotherapy is considered for individuals with autism them-selves [rather than their parents], it should be borne in mind that it is unlikely to be of use to those with insufficient language skills. The alternative non-verbal technique for children with autism is *play therapy*. This practice is valuable in helping children with autism to control anxiety and play more creatively, but it can be counter-productive if the therapist makes interpretations of the child's play that simply confuse the child. [1993, p. 70]

The implied distinction between "psychotherapy" and "play therapy" would seem to be somewhat misleading. Child psychotherapists are familiar with using play as a means of communicating with non-verbal children, and indeed Klein (1955) originally developed her play technique as a "substitute" for the adult patient's (verbal) free associations. They are also concerned to make sure that their com-ments are pitched at the right level for the child's understanding. Where there may be a difference is in how the work develops if and when the child begins to emerge from their autistic state.

One difficulty, of course, for either kind of therapist is that *play*—in the sense of symbolic, imaginative play rather than repetitive actions—is precisely what autistic children are bad at. It is the absence of this capacity that forms one the classic triad of impair-ments described by Wing and Gould, namely "impairment of social interaction, repetitive activities in place of imaginative symbolic interests, and impairment of language development" (1979, p. 26). The three elements are closely interlinked, and in seeking to help the child develop their imagination and language, the psychoanalytic psychotherapist may use play as a route for engaging emotionally with the child, thereby addressing the underlying problem of social interaction. It is here that they may draw particularly on insights from developmental psychology about the processes of the ordinary infant's developing intersubjectivity.

In a recent comprehensive review of the literature on "primary intersubjectivity", Trevarthen and Aitken have underlined the therapeutic importance of this kind of emotional engagement, with particular reference to work with autism and language development:

> In the study of special education for autism, instruction in speech and language is naturally given great importance. However, speech therapy is not, by itself, generally effective . . . For more children with greater problems in communication, an approach that addresses the underlying interpersonal problem is more effective. Emotional engagement and joint attention appear to have a more fundamental role in furthering language development in autism than instrumental use of language (Rollins, 1999), and this approach may be applied for clinical intervention to enhance communication skills in autistic children more effectively than any training in thinking or belief (Astington & Jenkins, 1999; Rollins *et al.*, 1998). [2001, p. 32]

It is interesting to note that some forty years ago, Winnicott had already implicitly emphasised the importance of "emotional engagement and joint attention". I think this is what he was referring to when he wrote about the importance of "play". He spelt out that when play is not possible, the psychotherapist's primary task is to enable the patient to play:

> Psychotherapy has to do with two people playing together. The corollary of this is that where playing is not possible then work done by the therapist is directed towards bringing the patient from a state of not being able to play into a state of being able to play. [1971, p. 38]

A sub-group of autistic children

It is undoubtedly the case, however, that some autistic children who have been seen in psychotherapy have shown very little progress despite intensive input over many years, and have not recovered their capacity to play. When, as in the NHS, resources are severely limited (and this applies particularly to the availability of psycho-analytic psychotherapy), it would be hard to justify such a use of those scarce resources. The difficulty, of course, lies in identifying those children who may benefit from this particular approach.

The problems of assessment are many and complex, and I shall not be addressing them here (but see, for example, Reid [1999a] and Rhode [2000] for a detailed discussion). What I do wish to suggest, though, is that there may be a sub-group of autistic children for whom this form of psychotherapy is particularly appropriate. The group I have in mind is that originally identified by Reid. She described a sub-group of autistic children comprised of those who appear to have resorted to autistic defences in the face of overwhelming trauma. She calls this group *Autistic Post-Traumatic Developmental Disorder*, and she writes:

> I wish to draw attention to a remarkable similarity between the nature of the symptomatolgy in a small sub-group of children with autism and the symptomatolgy of Post-Traumatic Stress Disorder in children who are not autistic. I am hypothesising that an experience of trauma *in the first two years of life* may be a precipitating factor in the development of autism in this sub-group. Clinical experience seems to suggest that this factor may have combined with a biological or genetic predisposition in the infant which the traumatising event has then served to activate. [1999b, p. 93; my italics]

Reid also observes that these children may find psychoanalytic psychotherapy particularly helpful.

I shall describe my work with a young boy who I believe fits into this group. He initially presented with a query of autism and he certainly showed very marked autistic features, although there was a reluctance to make a formal diagnosis. When referred, he was not speaking at all, made little eye contact, and was obsessed with one particular video. He also had a number of stereotypies. He had been hospitalised at five months with a life-threatening condition, necessitating major invasive (and doubtless traumatising) medical interventions, and a link with this traumatic hospital admission was suspected. It is his remarkable development over the time I have been seeing him that forms the basis for this paper and for the suggestion that for some "autistic" children this kind of therapy may prove very beneficial.

Clinical material

Stephen was originally referred just after his third birthday. He is from an intact and caring family, with a sister who is three years older and a younger brother. In her referral letter, the Health Visitor described how he had spent a lot of time in and out of hospital, having been diagnosed at five months with a life-threatening illness. He had been rushed into casualty with difficulty in breathing, and had in fact suffered a respiratory arrest while in the casualty department. He had required several weeks of intensive treatment. At just over a year, he had had a relapse requiring further treatment.

However, she also noted that he had progressed well developmentally until he was about two, although his speech was slightly slow (though at the time of a visit he had a lot of jabber). At 2½, Stephen was still not speaking. He did not acknowledge the Health Visitor when she visited, and often seemed to be in a world of his own. He was not attempting to communicate either verbally or nonverbally. He made some noises but no conversational jabber, and there was no eye contact, gesturing or pointing. His mother reported to her that she had no idea when he fell asleep in his bed or woke up because she could just put him down and he would happily stay there, never calling out or crying. He did not go to his mother for comfort or cuddles. The Health Visitor noted that Stephen was being brought up in a lovely, well stimulated, caring environment.

It was clear that she felt Stephen showed many signs of being autistic, and she also mentioned that he showed hand-flapping and stereotyped movements. There had been some suggestion to the parents of him showing autistic features, but no actual diagnosis. The community paediatrician took the view that Stephen's difficulties could be understood as a response to the trauma of hospital admission, including some general delay occasioned by the time spent in hospital, but the Health Visitor did not agree: she felt his development had in fact continued satisfactorily subsequent to his discharge and had only become problematic later. She wondered if it might have been his measles-mumps-rubella injection that was responsible, as this came much closer in time to the onset of his difficulties.

In their own account of his early years, the parents noted: "We became increasingly concerned about Stephen's behaviour. He stopped talking and making eye contact, and lost all interest in his toys. He was only interested in 'Postman Pat' videos, climbing and rough-and-tumble play with his dad ... His levels of concentration were minimal and he was in his own world. He does not point to indicate his wants or choices. He also does not nod or shake his head ... If Stephen wants a drink, he will get a cup. If he wants you to go somewhere with him, he will take your hand and lead you."

During this time Stephen's paternal grandfather died and his maternal grandmother was very seriously ill. His mother meanwhile became pregnant. She noted that Stephen would shun physical contact with her and refuse to sit on her lap. She thought this was because many of the investigations that took place had involved him sitting on her lap (e.g. when doctors were trying to look in his ears) and so the two were closely associated in his mind. At age 2¼ his younger brother was born. Initially he had completely ignored the baby, acting as if he simply did not exist.

Initial assessment

Stephen and his family came for an initial assessment when he was 3¼. At this time his parents noted that there had been a marked improvement over the preceding six months in that he had become more affectionate and demonstrative towards them and was making more eye contact. However he still did not speak at all.

In the first session, with his parents, the eye contact was very apparent. However, it had an unusual quality in that it was very fixed and piercing. Similarly, he made a lot of direct approaches to me, coming up disconcertingly close and putting a pen in my mouth, and a couple of times looking as if he was coming to give me a kiss. Towards the end of this session, his mother commented on how fascinated he is now by his little brother. I also learnt that there was a long-standing problem with constipation dating from around five months of age—the time of his first hospital admission.

When I saw Stephen on his own, he did not speak at all, and he frequently made typically autistic stereotypical gestures. He became engaged in very repetitive play, and appeared to have no (or extremely limited) capacity for any kind of symbolic play. When he did any drawing it was very unformed.

I was puzzled by Stephen, and intrigued. I therefore decided to offer what was in effect a prolonged assessment, suggesting that I would begin seeing him weekly, and we would see how that went and if it seemed helpful. That was nearly three years ago, and I continue to see him once a week.

The therapy

I want now to give a brief overview of Stephen's therapy and to try and convey some of the ways in which he has changed over these three years. The changes have been quite dramatic. The Stephen I see today is extremely verbal, chats away to the receptionist in our clinic when he arrives, and readily engages in symbolic play in the consulting room. The stereotyped gestures have virtually disappeared. His language is at times still hard to understand, and there are features in his play that still give cause for concern, but he is nonetheless a transformed child. He is attractive, engaging and charming, and a delight to see. Indeed, he is almost too much of a delight, as he tends to use his charm to avoid confrontations and difficulties.

I will begin, however, by quoting from my notes of a session very early on to give some flavour of how Stephen was at this time:

> He took out some pens and drew one or two marks on the paper, but then left this and became very preoccupied with taking the pens out and putting them back in again. He removed the pens from their plastic wallet and then put them back in again, and repeated this many, many times. At one point he crunched up the plastic wallet and made it very clear that he wanted me to hold it, which I did. He did this two or three times, and then took it back and put the pens back into it without using them for drawing. He did not speak throughout any of this.
>
> At one point whilst he was doing this and moving the pens around on the table, I instituted a sort of game where I chased his fingers with my fingers. He laughed at this and seemed amused by it. This felt like a fleeting moment of contact in a session otherwise devoid of real contact. When I tried to repeat this game later using the pens rather than my fingers, there was absolutely no response from him.

Whilst the fleeting moment of contact here seemed hopeful, I was aware of similar hopeful moments in the early days of treatment of another non-verbal child patient which had not in fact led anywhere, and so did not feel overly encouraged by it. At this stage it seemed unclear how much it might be possible to make more sustained contact with him.

Throughout this first term I mostly felt ignored by Stephen, but he could occasionally become involved in a game I initiated, such as balancing the pens standing up so that he could knock them down. When I met his parents for a review soon after the Christmas break, he seemed to be showing continuing progress. At nursery, which he had recently begun, he was keen to go and ran in with no backward glance. But there was still no speech. His mother mentioned some of his recent play at home: for example, playing with Power Ranger figures and putting them inside his own shoes, which then served as a car or boat. She also described how he got very excited if he went in the front seat of the car. It seemed as if he was perhaps moving out of his autistic withdrawal, but into a state of identification with powerful and controlling figures. That Christmas, for the first time, he had shown a real interest in and awareness of what was going on.

Introducing aggression

During the second term of Stephen's therapy, I became increasingly aware of a certain stuck quality to the sessions and to his play. I felt a pressing need to make my presence felt, and play seemed the obvious medium for this. However, it was clearly going to need me to take an increasingly active role if I was to be able to engage with him in this way.

Here is an example from that term of the kind of game I would introduce in order to try to make some contact with him:

> He was poking a car and then a person through the gap/doorway in the middle of the dolls' house. I moved so as to have my fingers "hiding" behind a wall of the house. They would then jump out and push his car back at him. He squealed and giggled with delight when I first did this, and got very excited, so much so that he kept going off to fall on the floor . . . He was making a new and different kind

of noise today, but this soon became very repetitious, so that whilst at first it seemed to represent something new, it quite soon lost its interest.

There is, of course, already an element of aggression involved in this kind of play, introduced by me. In later sessions this became more explicit, although I would have to say this was not a consciously thought out strategy at the time. I think it felt rather as though it required some fairly robust response on my part if I was going to make genuine contact with Stephen, and that having initiated something, I would then to a large extent be guided by his response. His receptiveness would then lead to further elaboration. However, it will also be apparent from the above how quickly novelty could degenerate into something sterile and repetitive, and this was something to which I had constantly to be alert.

In the following session the theme of aggression became quite explicit:

> Today he was using quite a lot of proto-declarative pointing . . . gesturing at the window, although I was not quite sure what he was wanting me to look at. On several occasions he made it very clear what he wanted me to do (repeating a game we had played before— my fingers chasing him at the dolls' house), but he sought to do this by grabbing my hand and pulling it over to the house. Today I had a strong feeling that he was adamantly and stubbornly *refusing* to speak, and I was reminded of his constipation and the way he holds on to his faeces.
>
> I resisted repeating the game at the house for too long, and then introduced a new game using the shark puppet. I held the puppet and he came along offering me a felt tip pen; the shark grabbed the pen with its teeth with some force. I then extended the game, getting the shark to try to "bite" Stephen, his nose or his ear, in a playful way. He was quite delighted with this and giggled and squealed, then ran away. At times—as if it were a part of his excitement— he produced some of the stereotypic gestures he sometimes uses . . . However, when I gave *him* the shark to play with a little later, he seemed unable to get it to "bite" me.

This kind of "play fighting" then continued as an important element of Stephen's sessions for some time. It was also a lot of fun, and Stephen giggled as he was "attacked" and would then come back for more. It did not become repetitive, and it was also quite possible to introduce all sorts of variations into this play, as one might in horseplay with one's own children. Very gradually Stephen started to involve himself more in this play, and he would sometimes manage to take over the role of the shark and attack me—or rather the glove-puppet I was wearing—and the two puppets would have quite a tussle.

By playing in this way, at my instigation, Stephen seemed to be helped to start to "own" some of his more aggressive feelings. At the same time I think this material also illustrates a link that was becoming apparent with his language development: his non-speaking seemed more deliberate and in itself a sort of aggressive withholding. My taking the initiative in introducing the shark's aggression was in part, I believe, a response to this and a reaction against the passive role of allowing my hand to be led.

When we met to review progress at the end of the first year Stephen had acquired about 12 words that he would use, though not consistently, and was showing an increasing interest in pretend play. However, he still had problems with constipation—his parents felt that he was trying to stop his poos coming out. The Health Visitor thought there had been little change and that Stephen's mother was having to make huge efforts to get him to do anything. He had developed an interest in a video of crashing cars.

Aggression and sibling rivalry

During the course of the next term a characteristic pattern became established in Stephen's sessions. This involved all of the items in the room gradually being pushed off the table or other surface until everything ended up on the floor in an un-sorted jumble. The following session was typical:

> He came into the room carrying an Action Man doll with a hand grenade . . . He pulled the box of toys towards him . . . there was no eye contact as yet . . . He did some "drawings", making a mark on each sheet and then putting it to one side till he had used up all the paper. He had his back to me and there was still no eye contact.
>
> When he had finished, he rolled each pen in turn towards the edge of the table until it fell off the edge. Then he went back to the big table and moved all the fences to the edge of the table until they all

fell off. Then he tipped out the contents of the box onto the table and gradually pushed every item off the table onto the floor. He took the tea tray and tea set and moved this to the edge of the table till it too fell to the floor. Gradually everything in the room was pushed onto the floor and moved to be part of a large pile heaped up in the corner of the room . . .

When I began to clear up, he prepared himself to leave, picking up all his things and standing by the door. When I told him, as usual, that we had five minutes left, he stood nearer to the door, and I commented on him getting himself all ready to leave . . . Then he put the grenade between his legs and walked along. The second time he did this, the grenade fell to the floor. I commented on how it seemed as if this was like some bit of poo that drops out, and wondered to myself about the connection between this and all the mess on the floor and something very explosive happening.

At the time I was unsure how to understand some of this material, and therefore largely limited my comments to a description of what was taking place. The way in which the toys were allowed to simply fall to the floor had a rather passive quality to it, and I wondered if this perhaps represented everything simply falling out of his mind, the jumble on the floor being an image of his internal muddle. With the benefit of hindsight, however, I believe that what Stephen was doing was actually more like something that Houzel has described. He wrote about a child who behaved in a very similar way in his session, and how he came to understand that for this child all the objects in the room symbolised the other children the therapist saw when the child was away. He commented on how

> Every object is experienced as a rival baby . . . who has a right to everything of which the autistic child is deprived. The only way to soothe autistic distress would seem to be either *to ignore these rivals completely* by denying the existence of otherness and diving back down into the deepest of autistic states, or *to eliminate the rival babies by throwing them away* or otherwise destroying them—hence the fact that play is impossible for the autistic child. [2001, p. 135; my italics]

Stephen had originally ignored his baby brother's existence. Now he seemed to want to eliminate my other children. His attacks on them—even if not initially recognised as such by me—would seem to represent progress in that he does at least then acknowledge their existence and "otherness". Stephen seemed to be gradually finding it possible to own more of his aggression in this respect, and I would suggest that this was at least in part connected to his experience of "playing" at this with me.

By the end of his second year of treatment he had begun to use language most of the time, and once this process had started it seemed to take off dramatically. Stephen's growing awareness of my having other "children" in mind—and the concomitant recognition of *my* "otherness"—seem closely linked, therefore, both to the emergence of his capacity to acknowledge his aggressive feelings and to his growing wish to communicate through language.

The attacks on these rival children became increasingly explicit, and drawn into the treatment setting:

> He put the reindeer with the red head into one of the rooms of the dolls' house and then brought along a series of different animals which he also put in the room. The reindeer then picked up the intruding animal and threw it against one or two of the walls of the room and against the floor, and then threw it out of the house altogether. At first I could not quite catch what he was saying, but then it became quite clear that he was saying "out of my room" as each one was thrown away. This was repeated with a lot of different animals, including very big ones (like the elephant) which were huge compared to the reindeer.

Some months later he also whispered, as he was playing, that he did not want any more brothers or sisters.

I think we can see how, having started by exploring these feelings at one remove through my playing them out, Stephen was gradually able to move on to playing with them in his own right. This was well illustrated in the following, later sequence:

> He began playing with the puppets. First he picked up the shark, and I was given the white bear. He got me to bite the shark's tail and to bite his hand, and he played at being scared and hurt. Then he picked up another identical white bear and showed me that he wanted to put this on his other hand. I helped him with this. I commented on them being the same. He then had his puppet bite mine.

He then very explicitly said that he wanted to swap chairs with me and that he wanted to sit in my chair. I went along with this and sat in his chair, and then, on his instructions, we swapped puppets. Then his white bear bit my shark's tail and then started throwing my white bear against the wall—this seemed a very clear reference to the previous play in which the red-faced reindeer had thrown animals against the walls of the dolls' house. I talked about him feeling very cross and wanting to bite.

Here I think we can also see Stephen involved in a mental manoeuvre that Anna Freud referred to as "identification with the aggressor". She described it as follows:

> By impersonating the aggressor, assuming his attributes or imitating his aggression, the child transforms himself from the person threatened into the person who makes the threat. In [Freud's] *Beyond the Pleasure Principle* (1920) the significance of this change from the passive to the active role as a means of assimilating unpleasant or traumatic experiences in infancy is discussed in detail: "If the doctor looks down a child's throat or carries out some small operation, we may be quite sure that these frightening experiences will be the subject of the next game; but we must not in that connection overlook the fact that there is a yield of pleasure from another source. As the child passes over from the passivity of the experience to the activity of the game, he hands on the disagreeable experience to one of his playmates and in this way revenges himself on a substitute." [1936/1976, p. 113]

Whilst there is no specific reference to his earlier traumatic experiences in hospital, I found myself wondering how much this play was perhaps linked to that experience and the feeling of having to passively suffer what might have been felt to be an annihilating attack. Here he seems to have moved to a new position where he is now gradually more able to show his anger and wish to retaliate against his apparent attackers.

Benign doctors

The kind of playful working over of the theme of aggression that I have been describing continued to be a major feature of Stephen's sessions over the following two terms of work, bringing us up to the present. In the course of this time there have been two major developments.

One has been the growing tendency for Stephen to also identify with the playfulness of his object, such that he now sometimes takes the initiative in introducing novel elements into his play. This is not, of course, an entirely linear development, and it remains important to be alert to those times when his play slips into becoming something repetitive and sterile, when he needs a nudge to move on. But he is very responsive to such nudging, and it is sometimes at these moments that *he* then introduces a new element.

The second, very positive development has been the appearance in his play of a benign doctor figure or rescuer. This has emerged in the context of games where a horse is injured and then a rescuer appears who can tend to the horse's injuries. At times it has been specifically a doctor who has been named. The following example is typical of this:

> He went back to the previous game of playing at horse races. He moved all the horses (represented by felt tip pens) along except for one—the blue one—which was left behind. He then removed the top of this one, making noises as he did so, and it was clear that he was playing at being the blue horse *and being upset* at having lost his top. He then said something about the crocodile, looked through the puppets, and passed me the green one which had previously served as a crocodile. He gave it to me and made it very clear that the crocodile was to rescue—or at least help to rescue—the horse. He also told me that the crocodile had a house, and that there was a point on the floor near me which was the crocodile's house. When the blue horse/pen had been rescued, I held the bottom of the pen while he put the top back on. I, the crocodile, was then to put the horse in my house.

To my mind, this material illustrates an important shift. No longer am I just the aggressor he must identify with. We are now able to work together at helping to fix the damaged horse-pen, and my "house" has become a place where he can receive help.

Discussion

Stephen's material raises many issues. Here, however, I wish to focus in particular on the way in which traumatic early experiences may impact on normal developmental processes and precipitate a state of autistic withdrawal. I also wish to draw attention to the therapeutic implications of the ideas I shall be discussing.

The impact of trauma

Stephen would seem to fit very well Reid's description of the sub-group of autistic children affected by trauma. She notes that traumatic experiences might include severe medical conditions, a severe reaction to immunisation, and an extreme response to the birth of a sibling. She continues: "Our case histories frequently reveal the presence of more than one of these ordinary life situations coinciding at a particular point in time, and it is the coincidence of theses situations which seems to be more than some vulnerable or particularly sensitive infants can process" (1999b, p. 104). Stephen experienced all of these traumas in turn.

She also noted the particularly heightened impact of trauma when it occurs in early infancy, as the infant lacks the "backdrop of other life experiences" to call on:

> For very young children, however, fantasising a different outcome to traumatic events, or "rewriting" of personal history, is a developmental achievement which is unavailable to them. But the infant can withdraw to a world of auto-generated sensations where they can control the intensity, duration, frequency and type of sensation, thereby introducing some degree of self-will or potency. [ibid., p. 100]

This connection between trauma and autistic withdrawal (the extreme end of the dissociative response) has also been emphasised in recent work from the field of neuroscience. Perry's seminal paper on the neurobiological impact of trauma describes how, in the face of persisting threat,

> The child will move along the hyperarousal continuum or into the dissociative continuum . . . Dissociation is simply disengaging from stimuli in the external world and attending to an "internal" world. Daydreaming, fantasy, depersonalisation, derealisation, and fugue states are all examples of dissociation . . . Observers will report these children as numb, robotic, non-reactive, "daydreaming", "acting

like he was not there", or "staring off into space with a glazed look" . . .

Our clinical experience suggests that the younger an individual is, the more likely he or she is to use dissociative adaptations . . . The nature of the trauma seems to be important to the pattern of adaptation; *the more immobile, helpless, and powerless the individual feels, the more likely they are to utilise dissociative responses. When physical injury, pain, or torture . . . is involved in the traumatic experience, an individual will be more likely to use dissociative responses.* [Perry, Pollard, Blakely, Baker & Vigilante, 1995, pp. 281 and 282; my italics]

The factors Perry and colleagues identify as predisposing to a dissociative (or autistic) response—age of experiencing the trauma, immobilisation, pain, helplessness—were all especially relevant to Stephen's situation. They go on to note the potential long-term sequelae of this state of affairs, with obvious implications for the importance of early intervention: "If the child dissociates, and stays in a dissociative state for a long period of time (e.g. by re-exposure to evocative stimuli), the child will internalise a sensitized neuro-biology related to dissociation, predisposing to the development of dissociative disorders" (ibid., p. 283).

The link between trauma and autism is, of course, not new. As Maiello, writing about prenatal trauma, has summarised, "Tustin considered autism as '*a reaction that is specific to trauma*' (1994, p. 14). Trauma can have both external and internal origins, but in both cases it leads to what she described as these children's 'traumatic awareness of bodily separateness from the mother . . . before their psychic apparatus was ready to take the strain' (1986, p. 23)" (2001, p. 108).

I would draw attention to Maiello's comment about the origins of trauma being potentially either external or internal. In Stephen's case both seem to have been present: there was the external trauma of the necessary medical interventions he suffered and also the "internal" trauma of his response to the birth of a sibling. Perhaps also the "attack" on his own body from his illness could have been experienced as coming from within. It may be that it is precisely the coincidence of both sources of trauma that precipitates the extreme response of autistic withdrawal.

This argument extends Perry's view of dissociation as "simply disengaging from stimuli in the external world and attending to an 'internal' world", since the disengagement or retreat is actually from both. Schore has recently made a very similar point: "It is important to emphasize that in traumatic abuse the individual dissociates not only from the external world, from processing external stimuli associated with terror, but also from the internal world, that is painful stimuli originating within the body" (2001, p. 233). He also goes on to make clear the damaging impact this kind of dissociative response can have on neurobiological development. Whilst the response is an adaptive strategy at the time, the danger is that if prolonged, it can lead to permanent psychological damage rooted in changes to the very structure of the brain:

> It is now established that "dissociation at the time of exposure to extreme stress appears to signal the invocation of neural mechanisms that result in long-term alterations in brain functioning" (Chambers *et al.*, 1999, p. 274). In other words, infants who experience states of terror and dissociation and *little interactive repair*, especially those with a genetic-constitutional predisposition and an inborn neurophysiological vulnerability, are high risk for developing severe psychopatholgies at later stages of life. [*ibid.*, p. 213; my italics]

I will return later to the reference to "interactive repair", but would underline here Schore's further point, linking these changes in brain function to autism:

> In the previous article I proposed that the amygdala, anterior cingulate, and insula limbic structures play a role in pre-attachment experiences that onset early in the first year, and thus trauma during each of their critical periods would interfere with the experience-dependent maturation of these limbic structures.
>
> Indeed neurobiological studies indicate that damage to the amygdala in early infancy is accompanied by profound changes in the formation of social bonds and emotionality (Bachevalier, 1994) ... Abnormalities of the social functions of the amygdala are implicated in autism (Baron-Cohen, Ring, Bullmore, Wheelwright, Ashwin & Williams, 2000), and this would include autistic post-traumatic developmental disorder (Reid, 1999). [*ibid.*, pp. 221–222]

Trauma, aggression and language

I now want to consider what all this might mean at an emotional level. I am especially concerned with the link between the child's experience of trauma and the ordinary developmental processes involved in managing aggression. Klein has detailed how the infant normally comes to terms with his own innate aggression and how this process is vitally assisted by interaction with external reality: "From its inception analysis has always laid stress on the importance of the child's early experiences, but it seems to me that only since we know more about the nature and contents of its early anxieties, and the continuous interplay between its actual experiences and its phantasy life, can we fully understand why the external factor is so important" (1935, p. 285). What she has in mind is the way in which a benign external reality may modify the child's aggressive phantasies. However, when the child is exposed to trauma, external reality may, on the contrary, reinforce rather than modulate the child's fears about his own aggression.

It is my impression that for children in this group a very particular link comes into being between the experience of the trauma and the normal developmental task of coming to terms with aggressive feelings, such that the traumatising event or events are felt to be a violent, persecutory and retaliatory attack for having such feelings. These children then respond to this by getting rid of *all* their aggression, to the extent that this precludes any engagement with real life and leads to a state of lifeless autistic withdrawal.

This situation can then only be overcome by the active involvement of the therapist (or parent) in introducing the notion of aggression in a sufficiently modified and playful form to allow for its gradual integration. However, all too often in such situations the same experience that was traumatic for the child has been equally traumatising for the parents. In consequence, they have not been available to play this kind of modulating role. Gaensbauer, an American psychologist who has specialised in the area of trauma, has also noted "the disruptive impact of traumatically induced anger on young children's development and the importance of facilitating the appropriate expression of this anger in order that traumatic experience can be resolved fully" (2000, p. 374).

In the same paper he is also reporting on the case of a child "traumatised by a medical illness and its associated treatments prior to the onset of verbal fluency", and his patient, like Stephen, came from a "close and warm family" in which it seemed the direct expression of anger was problematic. He underlines the therapeutic implications of his understanding of the impact of trauma: "From the standpoint of therapeutic technique, the work highlights the crucial role of therapists and caretakers in actively facilitating the internal reworking of the young child's traumatic experience" (*ibid.*, p. 383). He writes of "the emergence of the capacity to express anger *as a critical turning point in relieving many of the child's symptoms* (Drell, Gaensbauer, Siegel & Sugar, 1995; Gaensbauer, 1994)" (*ibid.*, p. 384; my italics).

For Stephen too it seems to have been the emergence of his ability to express anger and aggression—through play with the puppets—that led to him having the strength to emerge from his autistic withdrawal. Aggression, as Klein noted, also has its positive aspects: "The aggressive component of feelings and of the personality is intimately bound up in the mind with power, potency, strength, knowledge and many other desired qualities" (1946, p. 8).

Interestingly, Gaensbauer also highlights an important link with the role of language, and suggests why it may be important to provide both non-verbal (play) *and* verbal input:

> Young children ... depend strongly on caregivers to provide psychological explanations and emotional labels for their experiences (Nelson, 1990). To be most effective, therapists and parents must *not only provide opportunities for young children to express their understanding, but must draw inferences from non-verbal behaviour and translate it into verbal terms.* [2000, p. 383; my italics]

My introduction of the aggressive puppet play into Stephen's sessions thus provided the opportunity both for him to express his aggressive feelings and, at the same time, for me to provide the necessary verbal commentary on them.

The role of sibling rivalry

When Stephen was referred, the dramatic and traumatic nature of his hospital admissions and subsequent treatments stood out, and it was difficult not to assume some link with his later autistic withdrawal. However, the Heath Visitor's reservations about this, and the fact that his development did appear to continue for a time after his hospital discharge, gave grounds for caution in assuming a straightforward cause and effect.

Moreover, the material from Stephen's sessions indicated that sibling rivalry actually played an important part in his psychological make-up. Both Reid (1999b) and Tustin (1990) have suggested that for certain particularly sensitive children, the birth of a sibling can be experienced as traumatic. I would suggest that in Stephen's case, it is quite possible that the birth of his brother, which in ordinary circumstances might have been quite manageable, was in fact also experienced by him as traumatic, the culmination of a whole series of traumas.

I would also emphasise, though space does not allow me to expand on this, that the role of the parents can be crucial in mitigating the impact of trauma on the child. This resource is generally unavailable, however, when the parents are also affected by the same trauma, as Stephen's parents were by his traumatic hospital admission. They additionally had to deal with the death and illness of their own parents.

Therapeutic implications

Finally, I want to consider the factors which have been operative in bringing about Stephen's improvement. I am very conscious both of the difficulty of ascribing cause and effect and of the major contribution also made by the care of his parents and the input from specialist teachers and speech and language therapists. In relation to his psychotherapy, however, I would suggest that the kind of more actively playful way of working that I have described does seem to be helpful—at least for children in this sub-group—in facilitating the development of their language and imaginative play. I would also suggest that it was particularly important that this more active role included taking the initiative in introducing aggressive themes into the play.

In doing this, I think what I found myself offering Stephen was not so much the chance of re-enacting the specific details of his traumas as the experience that aggression, aggressive feelings and anger could safely be introduced into our relationship, could be played with and played at, and hence could be explored in this way. This also meant that the exact attribution of those feelings—whose feelings they were—mattered less at this stage than the fact of their existence.

This way of conceptualising what was therapeutic in our work would be in line with the views of Fonagy in a recent Guest Editorial in the *International Journal of Psychoanalysis*. He argued against the importance of the explicit recovery of memories, and preferred to conceptualise the therapeutic action as consisting in the acquisition of a new way of being with the other, a change in the nature of procedural memory: "Intensive work within the transference has the non-explicit aim of modifying implicit memories, rather than of relatively superficial changes in autobiographical memory ... Psychoanalysis is more than the creation of a narrative; it is the active construction of a new way of experiencing self with other" (1999, p. 218). In my work with Stephen I believe I found myself "actively constructing" a new way of him experiencing himself with another.

A key feature of this approach is the reciprocal nature of the play thus instituted. This brings me back to the point alluded to by Schore about the importance of "interactive repair" (above). He also highlights the therapeutic implications of this point of view: "The interactive regulation embedded in the therapeutic relationship functions as a 'growth facilitating environment', specifically for the experience-dependent maturation of right orbitofrontal systems" (2001, p. 245).

With my active encouragement, Stephen in fact proved very responsive to the play fights we engaged in between puppets, and there was a genuine interaction. His responsiveness was no doubt due in large measure to the positive experiences he had enjoyed prior to his illness.

In short, I believe it was the mutuality and playfulness of our engagement with issues of aggression that was ultimately therapeutic. When Stephen and I were playing in this way we both had fun. I think we should not underestimate this fun element.

Acknowledgements

Preparation of this paper was made possible by a research grant from the Tavistock Institute of Medical Psychology, to whom I am very grateful. My thanks also to Margaret Rustin for ever thoughtful and thought-provoking discussions of Stephen's material.

Note

1. This paper was published in the *International Forum of Psycho-analysis*, 2004, 13. A more technical version has also appeared in the *Journal of Child Psychotherapy*, 2002, 28(1).

References

Alvarez, A. (1996). Addressing the Element of Deficit in Children with Autism: Psychotherapy which is both Psychoanalytically and Developmentally Informed. *Clinical Child Psychology and Psychiatry* 1: 525–537.

Astington, J.W. & Jenkins, J.M. (1999). A Longitudinal Study of the Relation Between Language and Theory-of-Mind Development. *Developmental Psychology 35*: 1311–1320.

Bachevalier, J. (1994). Medial Temporal Lobe Structures and Autism: A Review of Clinical and Experimental Findings. *Neuropsychologia 32*: 627–648.

Baron-Cohen, S. & Bolton, P. (1993). *Autism: the Facts.* Oxford: Oxford University Press.

Baron-Cohen, S., Ring, H.A., Bullmore, E.T., Wheelwright, S., Ashwin, C. & Williams, S.C.R. (2000). The Amygdala Theory of Autism. *Neuroscience and Biobehavioral Reviews 24*: 355–364.

Chambers, R.A., Bremner, J.D., Moghaddam, B., Southwick, S.M., Charney, D.S. & Krystal, J.H. (1999). Glutamate and Post-Traumatic Stress Disorder: Toward a Psychobiology of Dissociation. *Seminars in Clinical Neuropsychiatry 4*: 274–281.

Drell, M.J., Gaensbauer, T.J., Siegel, C.H. & Sugar, M. (1995). Clinical Round Table: A Case of Trauma to a 21-month-old Girl. *Infant Mental Health Journal 16*: 318–333.

Fonagy, P. (1999). Guest Editorial: Memory and Therapeutic Action. *International Journal of Psychoanalysis 80*: 215–223.

Freud, A. (1936). Identification with the Aggressor. In: *The Ego and the Mechanisms of Defence.* London: Hogarth.

Gaensbauer, T.J. (1994). Therapeutic Work with a Traumatised Toddler. *The Psychoanalytic Study of the Child 49*: 412–433.

Gaensbauer, T.J. (2000). Psychotherapeutic Treatment of Traumatized Infants and Toddlers: A Case Report. *Clinical Child Psychology and Psychiatry* 5: 373–385.

Houzel, D. (2001). The "Nest of Babies" Fantasy. *Journal of Child Psychotherapy* 27: 125–138.

Howlin, P. (1998). *Children with Autism and Asperger Syndrome.* Chichester: Wiley.

Klein, M. (1935). A Contribution to the Psychogenesis of Manic-Depressive States. In: *Love, Guilt and Reparation and Other Works.* London: Hogarth, 1975.

Klein, M. (1946). Notes on some Schizoid Mechanisms. In: *Envy and Gratitude and Other Works.* London: Hogarth. 1975.

Klein, M. (1955). The Psycho-Analytic Play Technique: its History and Significance. In: *Envy and Gratitude and Other Works.* London: Hogarth. 1975.

Maiello, S. (2001). Prenatal Trauma and Autism. *Journal of Child Psychotherapy* 27: 107–124.

Nelson, K. (1990). Remembering, Forgetting and Childhood Amnesia. In: R. Fivush & J.A. Hudson (Eds.), *Knowing and Remembering in Young Children.* Cambridge: Cambridge University Press.

Perry, B.D., Pollard, R., Blakely, T., Baker, W. & Vigilante, D. (1995). Childhood Trauma, the Neurobiology of Adaptation and "Use-Dependant" Development of the Brain: How "States" Become "Traits". *Infant Mental Health Journal* 16: 271–291.

Reid, S. (1999a). The Assessment of the Child with Autism: a Family Perspective. In: A. Alvarez & S. Reid (Eds.), *Autism and Personality.* London: Routledge.

Reid, S. (1999b). Autism and Trauma: Autistic Post-Traumatic Developmental Disorder. In: A. Alvarez & S. Reid (Eds.), *Autism and Personality.* London: Routledge.

Rhode, M. (2000). Assessing Children with Communication Disorders. In: M. Rustin, & E. Quagliata (Eds.), *Assessment in Child Psychotherapy.* London: Duckworth.

Rollins, P.R., Wambacq, I., Dowell, D., Mathews, L. & Reese, P.B. (1998). An Intervention Technique for Children with Autistic Spectrum Disorder: Joint Attentional Routines. *Journal of Communicative Disorder* 31: 181–192.

Rollins, P.R. (1999). Early Pragmatic Accomplishments and Vocabulary Development in Preschool Children with Autism. *American Journal of Speech-Language Pathology* 8: 181–190.

Schore, A. N. (2001). The Effects of Early Relational Trauma on Right Brain Development, Affect Regulation, and Infant Mental Health. *Infant Mental Health Journal* 22: 201–269.

Stern, D. (1985). *The Interpersonal World of the Infant: a View from Psychoanalysis and Developmental Psychology.* New York: Basic Books.

Trevarthen, C. & Aitken, K.J. (2001). Infant Intersubjectivity: Research, Theory and Clinical Applications. *Journal of Child Psychology and Psychiatry* 42: 3–48.

Tronick, E.Z. & Weinberg, M.K. (1997). Depressed Mothers and Infants: Failure to From Dyadic States of Consciousness. In: L. Murray & P.J. Cooper (Eds.), *Postpartum Depression and Child Development.* New York: Guilford Press.

Tustin, F. (1986). *Autistic Barriers in Neurotic Patients.* London: Karnac.

Tustin, F. (1990). *The Protective Shell in Children and Adults.* London: Karnac.

Tustin, F. (1994). The Perpetuation of an Error. *Journal of Child Psychotherapy* 20: 3–23.

Wing, L. & Gould, J. (1979). Severe Impairments of Social Interaction and Associated Abnormalities in Children: Epidemiology and Classification. *Journal of Autism and Developmental Disorders* 9: 11–29.

Winnicott, D.W. (1971). Playing. A Theoretical Statement. In: *Playing and Reality.* London: Tavistock.

CHAPTER SIX

The creation of psychic space, the "nest of babies" fantasy and the emergence of the Oedipus complex[1]

Didier Houzel
Translated by David Alcorn and Paul Barrows

In her introduction to *The Oedipus Complex Today* Hanna Segal (1989) emphasises Melanie Klein's view that it is necessary for the baby to have first established a good relationship to the breast if he or she is to be able to manage and work through the pains of the oedipal situation. She adopts the model proposed by Britton (1989, 1992, 1998) whereby a psychic space is delineated at the heart of the oedipal triangle within which the infant is able to maintain a differentiated relationship with each of his parents, a space that Britton conceives as being an extension of the relationship container-contained as described by Bion. In this space the infant also encounters a good relationship between his parents, a relationship which is one of container-contained but one from which he is excluded, in contrast with the original relationship between the baby and the maternal breast. This leads him to distinguish the nature of the parental relationship from the connection which he has with each of them separately, and involves him in the work of separation and individuation that characterises the depressive position. She adds to Britton's model that room for the new baby is implicit in the space thus delineated:

I would like to add a point to the idea as described by Dr Britton. An important part of the difference between the infant's relation to the parents and their relationship is not only that they exchange genital gratifications, but also—and, I think, importantly—the fact that the parental intercourse leads to the creation of a new baby. This is always so in phantasy, even if in reality there is no new sibling. When I think of Dr Britton's triangle as defining the space in which different links can be established between the child and the two parents, I think that space implicitly contains the room for a new baby. If a new baby appears inside the mother [. . .] before such a space can be established—and while the little infant is still heavily dependant on the phantasy of getting back inside mother—psychotic disturbances can easily ensue. [Segal, 1989, pp. 125–138]

Thus room for a new baby within the sibship should result from the creation of an oedipal space within which the relationships between the different protagonists can gradually become differentiated: an intimate relationship between the baby and the maternal container (Meltzer, 1971), identificatory relationships between the baby and each of his parents, a loving and sexual relationship between the parents in the fantasy of the primal scene. The brother or sister who bursts in upon the family constellation before this space has been created will be experienced by the elder child as an intruder, a persecutor, not to say a conqueror threatening to destroy the space in which he had begun to develop his psychic life. Perhaps psychotic or autistic states are always an echo of such a catastrophe.

However, even when the fantasies and affects relating to brothers and sisters, whether real or imagined, have been recognised as a constituent element of the family constellation which shapes the child's psyche, they have until recently (Mitchell, 2000; Coles 2003) received far less study by psychoanalysts than those concerning the parents. There are, of course, some notable exceptions to the historical lack of interest in the role played by siblings in psychic reality. In this chapter, I intend to focus on the contribution of Frances Tustin, who, through her description of the "nest of babies" fantasy, highlighted the importance, for autistic children, of imaginary brothers and sisters.

But before I do this, I would like to make a short detour via the history of psychoanalysis and its founder, for this may help to explain why so little is made of sibling relationships both in the

Freudian corpus *stricto sensu* and in psychoanalytic literature in general.

Freud and sibling rivalry

The topic of sibling rivalry is hardly ever discussed in Freud's writings. This may have something to do with the death of his younger brother Julius when he was only a few months old, and the impact this had on the infant Sigismund (as he then was). In his detailed biography of Freud, Jones gives the following account of this period:

> A more important occurrence [. . .] was his young brother's death when Freud was nineteen months old and the little Julius only eight months. Before the newcomer's birth the infant Freud had had sole access to his mother's love and milk, and he had to learn from the experience how strong the jealousy of a young child can be. In a letter of 1897 he admits the evil wishes he had against his rival and adds that their fulfilment in his death had aroused self-reproaches, a tendency which had remained ever since. [Jones, 1953]

The letter to which Jones refers was addressed to Fliess on 3 October 1897. In it Freud admits he felt jealous of his little brother Julius, who dethroned him from his privileged place in his mother's love. Freud, whose self-analysis was already under way (Anzieu, 1988), went on to discover the Oedipus complex, in which the little boy's jealousy is aimed at the father as the child's rival in accordance with the fantasy wish to possess the mother sexually. It is, however, instructive to consider Freud's somewhat confused account of the events that took place in his early childhood: he seems to telescope the death of his little brother and the sexual arousal he felt towards his mother, and the chronological errors he commits cannot be attributed simply to the fact that the events in question had occurred long before. It is as though Sigismund's oedipal feelings towards his mother served to mask his primitive and guilt-laden jealousy towards Julius. The studies by Anzieu (1988), Gay (1988) and Rodrigué (1996) will guide us in our attempt to unravel the tangled web of fact and fantasy we find in Freud's correspondence.

Let us begin by taking a closer look at the letter written on 3 October 1897. In it, delighted with the progress his self-analysis was making, Freud shares his most recent discoveries with his friend Fliess. These concern two topics which he develops one after the other: the erotic attraction he had felt as a young child towards his mother, and his ferocious jealousy towards his younger brother. The paragraph is well known:

> Later (between the ages of two and two-and-a-half) libido towards *matrem* was aroused; the occasion must have been the journey with her from Leipzig to Vienna, during which we spent a night together and I must have had the opportunity of seeing her *nudam* (you have long since drawn the conclusions from this for your own son, as a remark of yours revealed); and that I welcomed my one-year-younger brother (who died within a few months) with ill wishes and real infantile jealousy, and that his death left the germ of guilt in me. [1954, p. 219]

This extract is crucial in that it prefigures what was later to be expressed in Freud's theory as the Oedipus conflict. Indeed, he refers to it just twelve days later, in another letter to Fliess (15 October 1897). Yet it includes several chronological errors which cannot but make us think that some sort of defence mechanism has been at work. The journey from Leipzig to Vienna, during which Freud appears to have slept in his mother's bedroom and perhaps saw her naked, did not take place when he was two or two-and-a-half years of age, but when he was about four years old. The Freud family had left Freiberg (Moravia) when Sigismund was about three years of age. They had settled first in Leipzig for a period, the exact length of which is not known, but it must have lasted at least several months and perhaps even as much as a full year. In other words, the journey Freud mentions in that letter was the one in which they left Leipzig to settle permanently in Vienna. Further, Julius was not born just before Sigismund's first birthday; according to Peter Gay, Freud was 17 months old at the time: "Freud was born on May 6, 1856; and Julius, born in October 1857, died on April 15, 1858 (see the 'Chronology' in Krüll, Freud and His Father, p. 214). For these details, Krüll refers to Josef Sajner's research" (Gay, 1988).

For a complete picture, we would have to include the birth of Sigismund's sister Anna when he was two-and-a-half years old. As we know, he never liked her (Jones, op.cit.), and the feeling seems to have been reciprocated. Rodrigué (1996) says that Anna used to complain about the fact that in Vienna Freud had a room to himself whereas his sisters had all to share a single room. He mentions also the piano affair: Anna played the piano, and the noise distracted her older brother while he was studying, whereupon he simply persuaded his parents to sell the piano. Thus the age Freud mentions for the Leipzig–Vienna journey lies between his age when his brother Julius died (23 months) and that when his sister Anna was born (30 months). It is obvious that a process of condensation of two memories is at work here, with all that implies in terms of the toning down or even the masking of one event by another. My hypothesis would be that the memory of seeing *matrem nudam* (as he says so tactfully in Latin) at age 4 partly masks the impact on the infant Sigismund of his little brother's birth, followed by his death six months later, together with (though to a lesser extent) the trauma of his mother's subsequent pregnancy and the birth of his sister Anna.

He did, however, acknowledge some of the influence these births had on his fantasy life and subsequent relationships. In the letter to Fliess, he agrees that his jealousy towards Julius and, on the contrary, his alliance with his nephew John (the son of his half-brother Emmanuel), who was a few months older than Sigismund, were a deciding factor in all his subsequent relationships. He is even more explicit in the following extract from *The Interpretation of Dreams*:

> My emotional life has always insisted that I should have an intimate friend and a hated enemy. I have always been able to provide myself afresh with both, and it has not infrequently happened that the ideal situation of childhood has been so completely reproduced that friend and enemy have come together in a single individual—though not, of course, both at once or with constant oscillations, as may have been the case in my early childhood. [1900, p. 483]

Such an admission cannot fail to interest us when we think of the passionate friendships and quarrels that ran through all of Freud's life, and consequently affected the history of psychoanalysis. The splitting of sibling imagos that he describes in the above extract would thus appear to originate in the trauma he experienced at the time of Julius's birth and subsequent death. We may recall the analysis he made in *The Psychopathology of Everyday Life* (1901) of a screen memory combining the arrest of his nurse on charges of theft and the birth of his sister Anna; in this memory Freud's half-brother Philipp was suspected both of causing the nurse's disappearance and of responsibility for there being a rival baby in the maternal womb. Nevertheless, in Freud's thinking and in the theoretical models he left us, little importance is given to siblings, rivalry between brothers and sisters is toned down, and feelings of love between siblings and incest fantasies are obfuscated, all in the name of oedipal love and jealousy. A psychoanalytic reading of Freud's memories and of the mistakes he unwittingly makes in his account of them would lead us to believe that, far from being milder versions of oedipal fantasies and emotions, those involving brothers and sisters may be even more primitive and violent than those concerning the parental couple. The more certain phenomena have to be disguised and covered up, the greater their unconscious significance.

To summarise this period of young Sigismund Freud's life: his father already had grown-up children, and Sigismund was the first child of his father's third and his mother's first marriage; she was some twenty years younger than her husband. At 17 months of age, he was superseded in his mother's love by the birth of his younger brother whom, Freud later admitted, he hated for precisely that reason; the infant rival lived for only six months, dying when Sigismund was 23 months old. Julius's death prevented the infant Sigismund from processing and integrating what was, after all, normal sibling rivalry. His subsequent guilt-feelings probably facilitated the operation of splitting mechanisms with respect to the fraternal imago: on the one hand, an idealised one he sought after all through his life in his various friendships, and on the other, a persecutory one which constantly led to abrupt quarrelling in his passionate relationships. When he was two-and-a-half, his sister Anna was born; he was unequivocally hostile towards her all through his life, and that feeling appears to have been mutual. When he was about four years old, during the journey from Leipzig to Vienna, he shared a room with his mother and felt intense arousal at the sight of her naked body. That event was to operate like a screen memory, masking in part the earlier traumatic events, in particular those relating to Julius's birth and subsequent death, and giving rise to some chronological confusion which tended to telescope these events together. Consequently, the mother's body is absolved from the crime of carrying and giving birth to a rival baby and becomes instead an overwhelmingly attractive object, with the result that all rivalry is displaced onto the father as oedipal rival. Thanks to this displacement of the little boy's rivalry fantasies onto the paternal figure, and thanks also, as I have pointed out, to the splitting of the sibling imago into two parts, primitive sibling rivalry thereafter lies buried in the depths of the Unconscious.

As Freud's theory developed, brothers no longer appear as rivals but play the part of accomplices. This theme runs through the whole of *Totem and Taboo* (1912–13); Freud argues that the brothers, ganging up on the father, the tyrannical head of the primal horde, killed him and ate his body in order to acquire his power, then turned the symbolic representation of the father into a totem in order to prohibit all acts of this kind for future generations.

> For a long time afterwards, the social fraternal feelings, which were the basis of the whole transformation, continued to exercise a profound influence on the development of society. They found expression in the sanctification of the blood tie, in the emphasis upon the solidarity of all life within the same clan. In thus guaranteeing one another's lives, the brothers were declaring that no one of them must be treated by another as their father was treated by them all jointly. They were precluding the possibility of a repetition of their father's fate. To the religiously-based prohibition against killing the totem was now added the socially-based prohibition against fratricide [. . .] The patriarchal horde was replaced in the first instance by the fraternal clan, whose existence was assured by the blood tie. Society was now based on complicity in the common crime; religion was based on the sense of guilt and the remorse attaching to it; while morality was based partly on the exigencies of this society and partly on the penance demanded by the sense of guilt. [p. 146]

Such an emphasis on the sense of guilt and on the need for expiation which binds the brothers and, by extension, the members of the clan together might indeed lead one to think of the sense of guilt the young Sigismund may have experienced on the death of his rival brother, which he then had to expiate all his life through his passionate friendships followed by violent break-ups. Where, then, have fantasies of sibling rivalry and the underlying death wishes gone? They seem to have been subjected to quite massive repression. They do, however, reappear in Freud's writings, but with respect to femininity (Freud, 1933). He states that in her libidinal development, the little girl is originally attached to the mother, but gives up this attachment and changes her object, which will henceforth be the father, because of her initial disappointment at having lost the breast and her fantasy of having received too little milk from the mother. Freud goes on:

> The next accusation against the child's mother flares up when the next baby appears in the nursery. If possible the connection with oral frustration is preserved: the mother could not or would not give the child any more milk because she needed the nourishment for the new arrival. In cases in which the two children are so close in age that lactation is prejudiced by the second pregnancy, this reproach acquires a real basis, and it is a remarkable fact that a child, even with an age difference of only 11 months, is not too young to take notice of what is happening. But what the child grudges the unwanted intruder and rival is not only the suckling but all the other signs of maternal care. It feels that it has been dethroned, despoiled, prejudiced in its rights; it casts a jealous hatred upon the new baby and develops a grievance against the faithless mother which often finds expression in a disagreeable change in its behaviour. [p. 123]

According to some commentators, this is Freud "at his most Kleinian". He is very clear about the role played by rival babies in the primal cathexis of the maternal object. Yet it looks as though Freud projected onto women the fantasies he could not acknowledge and accept in his own psychic reality. Only little girls are said to bear a grudge against the mother because of the series of disappointments she inflicts on them, including that involving the conception of new babies. Freud continues to pretend that boys feel no ambivalence in their love for the mother, and vice-versa. It is possible, then, that he was thereby attempting to get rid of his own fantasies of primitive rivalry, though I would have to qualify what I have just said with a reference to his *Introductory Lectures on Psychoanalysis* (1916–17). There he states that the child's rivalry or even hatred as regards siblings is universal, though to my mind he did not draw all the metapsychological conclusions he might have:

In this connection it will be interesting to compare the child's attitude to his brothers and sisters with that towards his parents. A
small child does not necessarily love his brothers and sisters; often
he obviously does not. There is no doubt that he hates them as
his competitors, and it is a familiar fact that this attitude often
persists for long years, till maturity is reached or even later, without
interruption. Quite often, it is true, it is succeeded, or let us rather
say overlaid, by a more affectionate attitude; but the hostile one
seems very generally to be the earlier. This hostile attitude can be
observed most easily in children between two and a half and four
or five, when a new baby brother or sister appears. It usually meets
with a very unfriendly reception. Such remarks as "I don't like
him; the stork can take him away again!" are quite common. After
this, every opportunity is taken of disparaging the new arrival and
attempts to injure him and even murderous assaults are not
unknown. (p. 204)

I say that Freud did not draw all the metapsychological conclusions
he might have because in the remainder of the Lecture there is no
mention of this primitive rivalry; the only reference is to oedipal
rivalry and the child's ambivalent feelings towards the parents,
though Freud continued to maintain that there is no ambivalence in
the mother-son relationship: "This last [the relation between mother
and son] provides the purest examples of an unchangeable affection,
unimpaired by any egoistic considerations" [p. 206]. It would appear
that Freud felt he had to put aside any suspicion, however slight,
that a son might betray his mother; he did this by exonerating her
from what I call the crime of carrying and giving birth to a new baby.

After Freud

Until recently (Mitchell, 2000; Coles, 2003, for instance), few psychoanalysts after Freud explored the topic of sibling rivalry. Without
any pretence at being exhaustive, I will mention the contributions
of Jacques Lacan and Melanie Klein before going on to deal in more
detail with that of Frances Tustin.

In the article he wrote in 1938 for the *Encyclopédie Française*,
entitled "Family complexes", Lacan described what he called "the
complex of intrusion": "The complex of intrusion represents the
experience of the primitive Subject, when he or she sees that one or

usually several similar beings also participate in the domestic relationship: in other words, the realisation that he or she has brothers
or sisters" (pp. 35–36). In identifying this complex, Lacan refers to
mirror identification and primary masochism. Towards the end of
weaning, which in this paper Lacan puts at around six months, the
infant reaches the "mirror stage" of development, with recognition
of his or her reflection in the mirror; this unified image serves as a
matrix for unifying the child's mental experience and for combating
"fantasies of dismemberment and bodily dislocation" (*ibid.*, p. 44).

> Seen thus, the stage corresponds to the end of weaning, i.e. towards
> the end of the six months dominated mentally by feelings of unease,
> and the concomitant backwardness in physical growth, that express
> that pre-maturation of birth which is, as I have said, the particular
> basis on which weaning in human beings is founded. When the
> Subject recognises his or her reflection in the mirror, this phe-
> nomenon is doubly significant for the analysis of this phase: it
> appears after six months, and it then demonstrably reveals the
> tendencies which at that point constitute reality for the Subject. [*ibid.*,
> p. 42]

The brother or sister who resembles the Subject is initially cathected
as a mirror-reflection identificatory object which is both unifying and
alienating; as such, the sibling is experienced as an intruder, the target
of primitive aggressive impulses which Lacan likened to primary
masochism and the death instinct:

> As long as the likeness only fulfils its primary role, limited to expres-
> siveness, it generates in the Subject similar emotions and attitudes,
> at least insofar as the present structure of the apparatus allows for.
> But while subjected to such emotional or motor suggestion, the
> individual cannot distinguish between his or her reflection and the
> actual self. Indeed, with the characteristic discrepancies of this period,
> the image only adds the temporary intrusion of a foreign tendency.
> I shall call it narcissistic intrusion: the unity it introduces in the im-
> pulses will nonetheless contribute to ego organisation. But before the
> ego can assert its identity, it becomes confused with the image that
> both shapes it and fundamentally alienates it. [*ibid.*, p. 45]

It is greatly to Lacan's credit that in this article he highlighted
primitive rivalry and distinguished it clearly from oedipal rivalry,

which is much less violent and persecutory: "If, on the other hand, the intruder arrives after the Oedipus complex, it is more often than not adopted in terms of parental identification, denser in affect and richer in structure" (ibid., p. 47).

Lacan's reference to *Gestalttheorie*, which in the Fifties became a structuralist model, is an obvious problem insofar as it tends to evacuate the dynamic and affective aspects of object relations. His model is based on the image of the rival at the mother's breast much more than on the feeling of having been more or less evicted from mother's attentiveness and tenderness by the arrival of a new baby; this aspect becomes comprehensible only once we situate the sibling drama within the framework of the dynamic relationship between child and mother (or, in analysis, within the dynamic of the child's primitive transference to the analyst who is suspected of taking an interest in objects other than himself).

Melanie Klein considered primitive sibling rivalry and jealousy to be extremely important; for her, they were part of the early stages of the Oedipus complex which begins during the first year of life. The child, boy or girl, is frustrated by the breast and is pushed into attacking the contents of the mother's body, experienced as creating obstacles to the unlimited use of it that he or she desires. The contents targeted are the father's penis and the internal babies it is supposed to give the mother. The child's attacks are extremely sadistic and transform these contents into fearsome and dreaded persecutory rivals. Klein described this situation in her famous analysis of Richard: "He felt he had attacked and injured the imaginary babies inside his mother's body and they had become his enemies. A good deal of this anxiety was transferred onto children in the external world" (1945, p. 375).

Disappointed by the mother's breast, the child then turns towards the father's penis with the hope of being given babies; the simultaneous projection onto the paternal penis of the child's own oral, anal and uretheral sadism transforms it into a bad and sadistic penis which creates in the mother's body bad, sadistic and threatening babies:

[Richard's] hatred of children, as well as his fear of them, was partly derived from the attitude towards his father's penis. The destructive penis and the destructive and greedy child who would exhaust the mother and ultimately destroy her were closely linked up with each

other in his mind. For he unconsciously strongly maintained the
equation "penis = child". He felt, too, that the *bad* penis could only
produced *bad* children. [p. 393]

According to Klein, in the early stages of the Oedipus complex, the
initial oedipal triangulation involves the child and the child's
maternal and paternal part-objects (respectively, breast and penis);
this succeeds weaning, taken in the widest sense of the term, i.e.
including all the frustrations the baby experiences in the relationship
with the mother. This early oedipal situation is established at the
same time as the child realises that the satisfying breast, which had
been idealised, and the frustrating breast, experienced as persecutory,
are one and the same. Thus the part object oedipal constellation Klein
describes actually succeeds an even more primitive kind of triangulation, characteristic of the paranoid-schizoid position, in which
the two objects the baby has to deal with are the idealised good breast
and the persecutory bad one. The lessening of the splitting of these
two images of the breast leads ipso facto to the emergence of the
early Oedipus complex, with the displacement of some of the infant's
libido and aggression from the breast to the father's penis. Rival or
even persecutory babies are the product of a fertile relationship
between paternal penis and maternal body; the same relationship
also creates good internal babies which repair and restore the
mother's body, experienced as damaged by the infant's sadistic
attacks. In so far as the infant can acknowledge the reparative role
of the father's penis in giving the mother babies, feelings of concern
and guilt related to the fantasied sadistic attacks on the mother's body
may come to the fore, as is characteristic of the depressive position.
Klein (1955) emphasises that this acknowledgement is harder to
achieve for the only child or for the youngest child in a family, for
whom it is as if they had managed to prevent the birth of any more
babies. Speaking of "the child's anxiety about the mother who is
frustrated and neglected by the father, instead of being loved and
made pregnant by him", she goes on: "This anxiety is particularly
strong in youngest and only children because the reality that no other
child has been born seems to confirm the guilty feeling that they have
prevented the parents' sexual intercourse, the mother's pregnancy
and the arrival of other babies by hatred and jealousy and by attacks
on the mother's body" (p. 158).

These extracts make it obvious that Klein was particularly eager to call attention to primitive sibling rivalry, whatever the child's sex. She did, however, treat it as deriving from the early stages of the Oedipus complex, not as a distinct form of rivalry *per se*. It is the child's fantasy that it is the bad paternal penis (the penis onto which the child's own sadism has been projected) which has created bad babies in the mother's body that leads to feelings of hatred and persecution towards these rival brothers and sisters, be they real or fantasied (the unborn children).

The "nest of babies" fantasy

In her exploration of autism in children, Frances Tustin broke new ground in the psychoanalytic understanding of sibling rivalry. In her first book, *Autism and Childhood Psychosis* (1972), she described the two main stages in the treatment of autistic children: in the first the child has no sense of having an internal psychic life and it is the analyst's task to revive this; in the second they become aware of the fact that they do have a mind of their own, a mind which is quite distinct from any other person's. It is at the start of this stage that fantasies of rivalry begin to appear, and in particular what Tustin called the "nest of babies" fantasy:

> In this phase, when the child is beginning to be able to bear the awareness of a clear distinction between himself and other people, there invariably develops a fantasy which I have come to call the "nest of babies" fantasy. This is associated with the notion that there are "special babies" who are given "special food". [. . .] My "brain children", the children in my mind whom I am felt to feed when I am preoccupied and averted from him, are sometimes felt to be the recipients of this special food. There is the fantasy that he (the patient—the child who is receiving my therapeutic milk) is in competition with predatory rivals on the other side of the "breast" who want to snatch the nipple away from him—to take away his chance of life and sustenance. [pp. 177–8]

For Tustin, it is the awareness of otherness, corresponding to the individual's basic identity and discovery of his or her mind, which gives rise to initial feelings of rivalry, long before the establishment of even the early stages of the Oedipus complex and the construction of sexual identity. When the child begins to have his or her own mental life, there is an unbounded desire to possess everything; and when the infant realises that he cannot do so, he thinks: " 'But there are some who have it', to be followed by 'But it isn't me'. This leads to disappointment, rage, jealousy, envy and competition, all in terms of imaginary especially favoured entities" (ibid., p. 178).

The "nest of babies" fantasy develops when the child experiences rivalry too early in life. Tustin linked this to what was for her the pivotal experience of the autistic child: the premature awareness of bodily separateness from the object of instinctual gratification—in other words, "the world was not body stuff to be moulded in his own terms" (*ibid.*).

In the "nest of babies" fantasy, the child is faced with a vast number of greedy, threatening mouths, the principal source of paranoid anxiety. This anxiety lurks somewhere inside the autistic "black hole" that her first little autistic patient, John, described to her one day. One of the main issues in the analytic treatment of autistic children—as well as in dealing with autistic enclaves in many other pathological conditions—is how to identify this primitive anxiety, tolerate its expression (however violent this may prove to be), and try to understand its meaning with the patient, rather than attempting at all costs to reassure the child, which would merely fuel his omnipotent fantasies. Klein, referring to her patient Richard, wrote: "Because of his unconscious fear and guilt about his own oral-sadistic impulses, however, infants predominantly represented to him oral-sadistic beings" (1945, p. 393). Hitchcock's 1963 film *The Birds* seems to me to be a remarkable illustration of this fantasy: innumerable threatening beaks attack human beings in their most private of retreats.

Tustin (personal communication) went so far as to argue that in the development of autistic children treated by psychoanalysis, the initial forms of oedipal triangulation (i.e. taking into account the difference between the sexes) are in fact derived from the "nest of babies" fantasy: the father being experienced as the biggest of the babies, and therefore as a particularly dangerous rival.

In her final writings, Tustin made significant changes to her model of the psychopathology of autism. Firstly, she clearly renounced the hypothesis of a stage of normal primary autism (Tustin, 1994a), a hypothesis she had sustained in her earliest writings and which she had borrowed at the time from Margaret Mahler (1968), but which she latterly considered an error. Furthermore, she accepted that normally the infant experiences oscillations between states of fusion and separation from its mother, whereas the infant at risk of developing autism finds himself stuck in an illusion of continuity with his maternal object, whom he experiences as an inanimate object:

> As in all psychotic conditions, a normal reaction becomes exaggerated. In autism it has also become frozen. In *normal* infancy there are oscillations from "flowing-over-at-oneness" to becoming aware of separatedness from the mother and the outside world. In this "dual track", as Grotstein (1980) terms it, there are alternating flickers of awareness of space and of "no space" between infant and mother. In the infancy of autistic children, these normal oscillations have not taken place. Something that is normally fluid has become frozen. Such an infant has become traumatized and frozen in a state of panic-stricken clinging in an adhering way to a mother who is experienced as an inanimate object that can be clutched. [1994a, pp. 14–15]

In her last paper, "Autistic Children who are Assessed as Not Brain-Damaged", Tustin describes a pathological illusion of at-oneness between infant and mother the outcome of which can only be a traumatic rupture when the infant becomes aware of his separateness from the maternal object:

> Autism is a two-stage illness. First, there is the over-close association of mother and child, and then there is the sense of being traumatically wrenched apart. Autism develops to deal with the sense of broken-ness. It is like a plaster cast to support the brokenness. [1994b]

Thus it would seem that she postulates the existence of a third area from the very beginning of extra-uterine existence, as a precursor to the psychic space described by Britton and the "room for the new baby" referred to by Segal. It is this space which has never developed in the autistic child. The rival sibling can then only figure as a terrifying persecutor who comes along to destroy the illusion of at-oneness in which mother and child were living.

These last hypotheses of Tustin lead us to a completely new model of the development of object relations. This model no longer follows the path that leads from a state of fusion or symbiosis between mother and child towards a stage of separation and individuation (Mahler, 1968) followed by making room for the presence firstly of the paternal third, then of the siblings. Rather, it envisages the unfolding of that which was already present in the mother-child relationship: the space contained within the relationship between the parents (the primal scene), which itself implicitly contains room for the new baby. I have elsewhere developed the hypothesis of the importance of the bisexuality of the primary psychic container (Houzel, 2005), a bisexuality which is necessary for the psychic development of the infant but which is split in the case of autistic children, the masculine aspect of the container being experienced as menacing and destructive and projected onto the external world. I take the maternal container described by Bion as being bisexual to the extent that the mother, in exercising her containing function, needs the support of her internal objects, both maternal and paternal. The mother's internal objects, and their relationship to each other, would thus define an initial space, which the oedipal space belonging to the infant's own development would then further support. In those cases of psychogenic autism to which Tustin refers, it would seem that the mother has been unable to provide the infant with this initial space in which he could have established a non-adhesive relationship with her and begun the development of a capacity for symbolic thought. Instead, a purely sensual adhesive relationship develops which allows for no symbolisation. The illusion of at-oneness contained within this adhesive relationship leads to an experience of catastrophic ripping apart whenever a third object intrudes on the child's relationship to his mother. The "babies in the nest" described by Tustin, who enjoy the special food contained within the mother's breast, are then the persecutors who come to disrupt the charm and shatter the illusion on which this relationship was based.

A clinical illustration

To illustrate the "nest of babies" fantasy, and the difficulties faced in the creation of a psychic space, I shall describe an extract taken from the analysis of Cyril, an autistic child whose treatment I have discussed in greater detail elsewhere (Houzel, 1999). With the help of this material, I will try in particular to illustrate one aspect of the fantasy which, following Tustin, I would express thus: when the child acknowledges otherness and starts to become aware of his or her mental functioning, everything contained in the therapy room may be experienced as representing the rival babies who stay permanently inside the therapeutic setting. As such, they are supposed to take advantage of the young patient's absence and eat up all the "special food" of the analysis, as Tustin put it, of which the patient is deprived in the break between sessions.

For my part, I feel that this is one of the obstacles on the developmental road that should normally lead to pretend-play and the resulting expression of fantasy life which, as it becomes richer and richer, enables the child to tolerate frustration, waiting, separation and difference. The child is in a vicious circle, since the means which could be used for expressing the intolerable anxiety associated with the discovery of otherness remain out of reach because they are part of the very fantasies that fuel the anxiety.

Several analysts quite rightly make a distinction between autistic reactions and the autistic state or structure. I would suggest that in what I am about to describe we can see one of the criteria for differentiating between these two aspects. In the case of autistic reactions, as manifested at times of separation, emotional deprivation, infantile depression or simply in the "still-face" experiment (Tronick *et al.*, 1978), the child usually manages fairly quickly both to restore the relationship with other human beings and to use real objects as transitional ones—in other words, as objects which can be used as a vehicle for his projections and on which he can base the imaginary scenarios that help the mind to tolerate frustration and waiting without falling apart. In the autistic structure *stricto sensu*, however, this is not possible, since every object is experienced as a rival baby—a baby in the nest—who has a right to everything of which the autistic child is deprived. The only way to soothe autistic distress would seem to be either to ignore these rivals completely (by denying the existence of otherness and diving back down into the deepest of autistic states) or to eliminate the rival babies (by throwing them away or otherwise destroying them)—hence the fact that play is impossible for the autistic child.

Cyril's analysis began when he was three years old, and I saw him three times per week. He had been diagnosed as having autism. He is the elder of two boys: his brother is two years younger. Both parents are from a very cultured background. The father is in an intellectual profession; the mother had been in higher education but does not currently work. She has a deformity of the uterus which made her pregnancies difficult. She found herself pregnant with Cyril after three spontaneous miscarriages. She had to be on bed rest throughout her pregnancy with Cyril, which was a time of great anxiety. The baby moved very little *in utero*. The mother's impression was that by remaining very still, he was protecting himself from the uterine contractions that she experienced as being threatening to him, given the very little space that he had. So from the very first the mother found it extremely difficult to have a sense of herself as a good container for her baby; she even had the sense of being a threat to him from which he had to protect himself.

Cyril was a quiet baby. His sleep soon settled into a regular pattern. He was breastfed for six weeks, but this was very brusquely interrupted due to an infection of his mother's breast. Nothing was noticed at the time of this sudden weaning. Cyril's motor development was delayed: he only sat up at a year and did not walk until 22 months.

Mother's second pregnancy began when Cyril was 15 months old. During the final trimester there were complications which meant there was a danger that she would give birth prematurely, and this led to her having to remain in bed and then to being hospitalised for the last month.

Cyril's parents began to be concerned about him because of the delay in his motor development, but particularly because of his failure to develop language. In addition they noted behaviours they described as "strange". Cyril would bang his head against the floor or against the wall and he would rock backwards and forwards. At around 20 months his parents had the impression that he was withdrawing from the world, that he was "in his own bubble"; he showed very limited interests, for example in opening and closing doors and listening to music; he did not develop any symbolic play and very little pretend play; and he would take an adult's hand to obtain what he wanted and did not point.

After our first summer holiday break, Cyril inaugurated a new activity in the sessions: he emptied his box of toys, threw away the pens and paper I had prepared for him on a little table, climbed triumphantly onto this table and from there onto my lap, and exclaimed: "Big, big, big!" I interpreted this as his wish to grow into a big boy coming to see me and drawing support from me. I was initially more in tune with his wish to grow up than with the theme of rivalry with the objects he threw away, which represented, I think, the rival babies who (in his view) had stayed with me all through the long summer break (which had lasted a little over two months). In a subsequent session this aspect became clearer, as the following extract shows:

> Cyril threw the pens to the floor, then played with the water, attempting to flood the whole room in spite of my forbidding him to do so. Then he threw all the sheets of paper from the little table to the floor and climbed onto the table, saying in a triumphant tone of voice "Grown-up!" From there he climbed onto my lap (with my help), then back to the table. He picked up the pens, gave them to me to hold for him, then threw them back onto the floor. With one of the pens, he drew several long lines on some sheets of paper, saying they were "little cats". He then threw these sheets of paper to the floor and went through the whole sequence again: climbing onto the table, then onto my lap, then back to the table. He also made as if to bite me.
>
> I felt that the little cats he had drawn and then thrown to the floor in order to take their place on the table or on my lap represented rival babies whom Cyril wanted to chase away so as to be alone with me; I made an interpretation to that effect. He had tried to bite me, and that seemed to correspond to a fantasy of an oral attack against what I could contain inside myself. At the same time, he appeared to feel threatened by the little cats; he expressed this by trying to leave immediately after drawing them. I interpreted this to him as an expression of his fear that the little cats he wanted to attack and whose place he wanted for himself might attack *him* and chase *him* away.

In the following sessions, Cyril played out a repetitive scenario. He began by completely emptying his box and throwing all the pens and paper to the floor. Then, with a tumbler, he filled his box with water; he was often quite fascinated by the water flowing into the box. I interpreted this play as an expression of his wish to chase away the toys, the pens and the sheets of paper as representing rival children whom he thought of as hard and threatening; he wanted to replace them with mummy-water because he wanted me all to himself like a mummy full of good food that he could turn on like a tap, as and when he wanted (at times he would stand inside the water-filled box). He gradually started being able to put some toys or pens into the water and manipulate them there; he seemed to feel that they were less of a threat insofar as they were to a considerable extent imbued with this maternal element.

I have since had further confirmation of the way in which the "nest of babies" fantasy may emerge with respect to the objects in the therapy room. When he throws the pens and paper I set out for him on the little table onto the floor, I tend to try and preserve the cardboard folder in which I keep the few drawings he has produced (he is still at the scribbling stage) by, for example, picking it up and putting it on a chair. When I did just this in a recent session, Cyril opened the folder, took out his drawings one by one and threw them angrily as far away as possible; I interpreted this as an expression of the jealousy he felt when he saw me take such good care of these drawing-babies. On another occasion, he emptied his box of toys on his own head, saying they were hurting his head (they were indeed falling on it). I commented that the toys were perhaps the children he felt were always in the room with me, the children he wanted to attack and chase off, and of whose return attacks he was very much afraid.

By now Cyril had developed a language which enabled him to communicate his fantasies to me much more fully. He told me about his little brother Tristan, after whose birth he had retreated behind his autistic defences. For the most part he complained about Tristan: he was annoying, did stupid things, messed up everything in the house. Once, having spoken to me about Tristan, he said "break you" several times, which I understood at first in the sense of a similar French expression meaning "get lost" and interpreted in this way. However, he then brandished the scissors and made the gesture of cutting me in two down the middle. I then said to him that he had perhaps had the impression when Tristan was born that his mother had been cut in two, as he might have feared that I had been busy with another child during the Christmas holidays which had just finished, and that had cut me in two.

He now used the toys more, and in particular the plasticine. He frequently took lumps of plasticine to make people and used the point of a pencil to make two holes for the eyes, a hole for the nose and a slit for the mouth. Usually one of the characters was the father, another the mother and the third was the baby. The following extract from a session shows his efforts to construct a psychic space and to fill it with internal objects.

24 November 2005
He decided to play with the plasticine. He took it out of the box himself. For quite a time he played at letting it fall by tapping on the box and then putting it back in the box. Later he took the whole block, which was quite soft, and put it against his neck as if it were caressing him. Then he decided to make a father, a mother and a baby, which he did very crudely by cutting the block into three and marking out the eyes, the nose and the mouth with the point of the pencil. He made the father first, then the mother, and finally the baby. He gave the father a big caress and then immediately afterwards he squashed him.

He then proceeded to insult me, calling me a filthy beast, a shit, an idiot . . . I said that it seemed as if he wished to squash me with his insults, like the father whom he had caressed and then squashed. He looked at the figure which was the mother and gave a cry as if he were frightened, then he came and lay across my knees, and then turned himself over, calling for help and saying he was about to fall. I interpreted that when the father was squashed, the mother became dangerous, as if he were about to fall into her eyes as he seemed in danger of falling off my knees. He then talked to me more clearly than he had ever done before, telling me that they had left his house with some suitcases to go to granddad and granny. Then he told me about a big boy at his school who insulted him and told him he was an idiot, and he no longer wanted to play with him.

This extract illustrates how the containing function requires the necessary combination of paternal and maternal elements and Cyril's difficulty in achieving this. The maternal object becomes devouring and dangerous if stripped of all paternal aspects. But on the other hand Cyril wishes to eliminate the father, even if he does also experience some affectionate feelings towards him: he crushes him as if he were taking up too much room. The father is then confused, as Tustin describes, with the largest of the "babies in the nest". It is only gradually that he will become differentiated and that Cyril will discover his reparative function. The oedipal triangle is based on this distinction between the protective and reparative father and the rival babies, a distinction which has only recently emerged for Cyril. The obstacle he has to overcome to achieve this is specifically the confusion he generates between the imago of a reparative and protective father and that of his fraternal rivals, who occupy all of the maternal space available, which he must repossess by mercilessly crushing those rivals.

One aspect of the reparative function of the father has been highlighted by Simonetta Adamo and Jeanne Magagna in a paper given to the Second International Congress on Infant Observation (Tavistock Clinic, 1–4 September 1997). The father enables the infant to take over a new space, and thereby to free up the space occupied by the primal scene and the room for the new baby. The new space which is thus conquered is a product of the intimate relationship with the mother, but transformed, symbolised and internalised. By way of illustration, I would compare this conquest to the altitude restrictions imposed on aircraft which allow them to fly in the same corridor: if there were two aircraft flying in the same corridor and at the same height, then there would be a danger of collision. If, however, a sufficient altitude difference is imposed, a collision becomes impossible. The father needs to allow the eldest to elevate himself to the level of "big child" in order that the next born may occupy the lower level which is thereby made available. This is precisely what is lacking in the two-dimensional world of autism, which does not allow for any possibility of a change of level. The interpretation I made to Cyril, concerning the protective function of the father which is lost when Cyril crushes him, seemed to help him begin to make a differentiation between his image of his father and that of his rival siblings: he spoke clearly about going with his suitcase (his internal world) to "Papy" and "Mamy", somewhere he has always evoked as a place of security, which is at some distance from the family home, and where he has stayed on his own, away from his younger brother.

25 January 2006
At the beginning of the session Cyril said to me: "You are trying to understand! You are trying to save my life!" He talked about being very small and about difficult things, which led me to say that he was asking me to save the life of baby Cyril who had experienced some difficult things. He became absorbed in some repetitive water play,

filling a beaker, emptying it into another one or into the sink, etc. I asked him to stop this game. He didn't do so, but began to call me names, whilst excusing himself for using bad language.

I said that when I asked him to turn off the water he felt that I was like a mother who would not always give him good milk, and he was then very angry and called me names. He said that his mother had given him his tea before coming to see me. He talked of his mother being kind and how he loved her very much and wanted to be all on his own with her. Whilst carrying on with the water play he also continued talking to me: he told me that the girls were not kind to him, that Pierre (a school friend) was not kind to him and had given him a kick up the bum, and that he, Cyril, had told his parents. If Pierre did this again he would fight him and would kill him.

I asked him if he expected me to protect him from those who were unkind to him, as when he told his parents about Pierre giving him a kick up the bum. He began to describe situations with at least three protagonists in which some would ally against others and threaten them with death: sometimes it was he and Tristan who wanted to kill father and mother, or father, mother and me; sometimes it was father and mother or father, mother and me who wanted to kill him; then again sometimes he wanted to kill father, Tristan and me so that he could be on his own with his mother. At other times he said that there was a wolf which was going to eat us both, or that he was going to kill the wolf by throwing it onto the ring road (the road he uses to come to his sessions). The wolf would be crushed by a car. He finished by asking me to cry for the people who had died in these adventures, whilst announcing that he was happy. I pointed out to him that he wished to put all his sadness about the people he wished to kill when he was angry into me, in order to feel happy and rid of this sadness.

These three-person scenarios, in which alliances are made and unmade alternately, without any one object ever becoming fixed in the role of persecutor, are characteristic of the oedipal configuration. The infant needs to explore each of these alliances and their effects on the whole constellation of his internal objects in order to find the necessary equilibrium which will allow his sexual identity to be built, based upon an identification with the parent of the same sex. We can see in Cyril the shift towards depressive feelings and the struggle against guilt which accompanies his conquest of a space at the centre of the oedipal configuration: Cyril has an experience of sadness which he evacuates by projecting it into his analyst.

He still has a long way to go to complete his oedipal adventure. He needs to acknowledge his ambivalence towards each of his parental figures, to recognise fully the reparative role of the father, to accept the difference between the generations and, last but not least, to allow the other siblings, real or imaginary, their due place as the product of a procreative relationship between the parents, of a good primal scene. This presupposes an adequate integration of his own anality, which would enable him better to tolerate his negative feelings, to no longer project them externally, and to make use of his aggression in the service of individuation, that is to say to assume a certain distance from his maternal object, to claim his own space whilst respecting that of others.

Recently, Cyril has very movingly expressed this conflict: "Let me finish my sentence, then I will let you speak," he said, his whole body very tense. He talked to me about the night and about death. We were on the brink of a week's holiday, and I therefore linked this material to the interruptions of the sessions. I talked to him about the night between the sessions and about his anxiety about what would happen during that time. He replied: "You will be with someone else!" He took the plasticine to knead it a little, then held it out to me, saying: "Here's a present!" I thanked him and said that in this way we would not be entirely separated during the holidays. However, this positive and reparative aspect of his anality was quickly overwhelmed, and he was gripped by an uncontrollable urge to defecate. I had to allow him to go off to the toilet.

A particular aspect of the difficulty autistic children experience in approaching the oedipal triangle was highlighted for me by a scenario that Cyril enacted in various ways: he would grip the sink with both hands and then call me to help, asking me to give him a hand to help him detach himself—he would smear his hands with glue and then smear mine similarly, and then immediately want to rinse them vigorously to remove all traces of the glue, inviting me to do the same. I interpreted this material as representing his fear of finding himself stuck or glued to me like a mother who would not allow him to move away, and needing the Houzel-father-hand to help him detach himself (I also linked this to the frequent necessity I have to use my hand to set limits for him). My interpretation was confirmed in a discussion I had with his mother: she described to me an occasion when Cyril had cried, something quite exceptional for him. I commented that Cyril seemed to find sadness very difficult to manage. Surprised by my remark, she told me that when she is sad (it is quite likely that she had suffered from post-natal depression and she is of a depressive nature) Cyril will do all he can to make her laugh, as if to get her out of her sadness; she added that he glued himself to her at such times, which she found very difficult to tolerate as when she is not well, all she wants is to be left alone. She described a vicious circle to me: the more he glues himself to her, the more she becomes irritated and the more he then tries to glue himself to her. It seemed to me that what both were lacking in these circumstances was a paternal third party who would enable each of them to keep their distance and to preserve their own space, which links with Tustin's hypothesis of a deadly illusion of continuity.

Conclusion

The origins of sibling rivalry are related to the advent of "otherness", and hence predate any question of belonging to one sex or the other. As soon as the idea of the maternal other takes root, that of a third party claiming all or part of the mother's attention emerges. Psychoanalytic research on autism in children and on autistic enclaves, developed by Tustin and her followers, tends to confirm the hypothesis that the original image of the other is relatively undifferentiated and much closer to a kindred individual, a child-rival, than to the paternal object as third party. This may explain why there has hitherto been much less research into sibling rivalry than into the oedipal situation; oedipal rivalry seems to have more or less obfuscated this more primitive kind of rivalry involving siblings, which is often much more callous and severe than the oedipal version. Far from incarnating the paradigmatic version of primitive rivalry, the oedipal situation manifests a more tempered one. Sibling rivalry is often presented as a mere displacement of oedipal rivalry, which is regarded as the main issue for the growth of the mind and as constituting its pivotal conflict. However, seen in the light of the psychoanalytic studies I have mentioned, sibling rivalry is a more primitive and much more relentless version than its oedipal counterpart. By placing heterosexual and homosexual object relations into a libidinal context, oedipal rivalry and the ambivalence of affect it implies enable the individual to find a way out of this kind of conflict which would have been impossible in the pre-oedipal situation of primitive sibling rivalry.

I have put forward the hypothesis that in order for otherness to become possible and for the infant to be able to establish his psychic space, it is essential that from the very beginning of the relationship between him and his mother an early form of the oedipal constellation needs to be present involving the bisexuality of the containing function, based upon the internal parental objects of the mother and their protective and procreative relationship. I believe this to be a prerequisite for the development both of psychic space and, within that, of room for the new baby.

Note

1. This is a modified version of a paper originally published in the *Journal of Child Psychotherapy*, 2001, 27(2).

References

Anzieu, D. (1986). *Freud's Self-Analysis*. London: Hogarth.

Bion, W.R. (1962). *Learning from Experience*. London: Heinemann. Reprinted London: Karnac, 1984.

Britton, R. (1989). The Missing Link: Parental Sexuality in the Oedipus Complex. In: J. Steiner (Ed.), *The Oedipus Complex Today*. London: Karnac.

Britton, R. (1992). The Oedipus Situation and the Depressive Position. In: R. Anderson (Ed.), *Clinical lectures on Klein and Bion* (pp. 34–45). London: Tavistock/Routledge.

Britton, R. (1998). *Belief and Imagination: Explorations in Psychoanalysis*. London: Routledge.

Coles, P. (2003). *The Importance of Sibling Relationships in Psychoanalysis*. London: Karnac.

Freud, S. (1900). *The Interpretation of Dreams. SE 5*.

Freud, S. (1901). *The Psychopathology of Everyday Life. SE 6*.

Freud, S. (1912–13). *Totem and Taboo. SE 13*.

Freud, S. (1916–17). *Introductory Lectures on Psycho-Analysis. SE 15–16*.

Freud, S. (1933). *New Introductory Lectures on Psycho-Analysis. SE 22*.

Freud, S. (1954) *The Origins of Psycho-Analysis: Letters to Wilhelm Fliess, Drafts and Notes 1887–1902* (M. Bonaparte, A. Freud & E. Kris, Eds.). London: Imago.

Gay, P. (1988). *Freud: A Life for Our Time.* London: J.M. Dent & Sons.

Grotstein, J. (1980). Primitive Mental States. *Contemporary Psychoanalysis* 16: 479–546.

Houzel, D. (1999). Séduction et conflit esthétique. *Journal de la Psychanalyse de l'Enfant* 25: 122–127.

Houzel, D. (2005). Splitting of Bisexuality in Autistic Children. In: D. Houzel & M. Rhode (Eds.), *Invisible Boundaries* (pp. 75–95). London: Karnac.

Jones, E. (1953–57). *Sigmund Freud: Life and Work.* London: Hogarth.

Klein, M. (1945). The Oedipus Complex in the Light of Early Anxieties. In: *Love, Guilt and Reparation and Other Works.* London: Hogarth, 1975.

Klein, M. (1955). On Identification. In: *Envy and Gratitude and Other Works.* London: Hogarth, 1975.

Lacan, J. (1938). *Les Complexes Familiaux.* Paris: Navarin, 1984.

Mahler, M (1968). *On Human Symbiosis and the Vicissitudes of Individuation. Vol. I : Infantile Psychosis.* New York: International Universities Press.

Meltzer, D. (1971). Sincerity: a Study in the Atmosphere of Human Relations. In: A. Hahn (Ed.), *Sincerity and Other Works: Collected Papers of Donald Meltzer* (pp. 185–284). London: Karnac: 1994.

Mitchell, J. (2000). *Mad Men and Medusa: Reclaiming Hysteria and the Effect of Sibling Relations on the Human Condition.* London: Penguin.

Rodrigué, E. (1996). *Sigmund Freud: El Siglo del Psicoanálisis.* Buenos Aires: Editorial Sudamericana.

Segal, H. (1989). Introduction. In: J. Steiner (Ed.), *The Oedipus Complex Today: Clinical Implications* (pp. 1–10). London: Karnac.

Tronick, E., Als, H., Adamson, L., Wise, S. & Brazelton T.B. (1978). The Infant's Response to Entrapment between Contradictory Messages in Face-to-Face Interaction. *J. of Child Psychiatry* 17: 1–13.

Tustin, F. (1972). *Autism and Childhood Psychosis.* London: Hogarth.

Tustin, F. (1994a). The Perpetuation of an Error. *J. Child Psychotherapy* 20: 3–23.

Tustin, F. (1994b). Autistic Children who are Assessed as Not Brain Damaged. *J. Child Psychotherapy,* 20: 103–121.

CHAPTER SEVEN

Joining the human family[1]

Maria Rhode

P sychoanalytic work with children on the autistic spectrum sheds light on many issues of basic importance, but perhaps the most fundamental of these concerns the processes involved in being welcomed into the human family. Developmental and observational studies carried out over the last twenty-five years have immensely enriched our understanding of what tiny babies are capable of in the way of social relationships. In psychoanalysis, as always, the clinical study of what happens when there are problems—and particularly of what happens when these problems begin to be overcome—makes it possible to fill in some of the detail which the smooth, almost automatic quality of normal developmental processes can seem to obscure.

Psychoanalysts and developmental researchers agree that the personality develops in the context of relationships with other people, and psychoanalysts, like developmental researchers, write about how such experiences are internalised and contribute to the growing sense of self. In this chapter I wish to focus on the importance of a particular kind of imitation which presupposes (and in turn reinforces) the sense of being a human being like other human beings.

147

Some kinds of imitation are central to development and learning. Other kinds can serve to obscure the difference between self and other, so that the child may, for example, habitually speak in an adult's voice rather than his own. This is the kind of imitation that has mostly been explored by psychoanalysts: children tend to have recourse to it when their sense of self is fragile. However, in the longer term it perpetuates this fragility, since children who habitually blur the distinction between themselves and their surroundings will be less able to benefit from any opportunities for mutual relationships and for learning that their environment may provide.

The other kind of imitation—the kind that takes place within the context of a reciprocal relationship—may be observed in newborn babies, though its characteristics change over time. This kind of imitation has mostly been studied by developmental researchers: it is one of the channels by which communication takes place and feelings are shared. Clearly, it contributes to the development of the personality. Among psychoanalysts, Gaddini and Sandler have both suggested that this process has an important part to play in human relationships, and Sandler has likened it to Freud's concept of primary identification in one of its usages, that is, an identificatory process which is early and immediate.

This suggestion seems particularly valuable because it provides a psychoanalytic context for a phenomenon which is obviously central to development but has remained largely untheorised by psychoanalysts and psychotherapists. Psychotherapy with children on the autistic spectrum makes it possible to explore some of its emotional facets. Such children tend not to imitate others with the immediacy that is characteristic of other children; their avoidance of eye contact is well known. Many first-person accounts emphasise their experience of feeling different, of not belonging in the world of other people. Formative events can appear not to have fed into a stable sense of self, as though the capacity to take in experience were affected. Parents and teachers, as well as therapists, know that a child may be able to show capacities in one particular setting but not in others, and indeed that many different developmental levels may seem to co-exist in a baffling kind of patchwork.

In this chapter, I discuss clinical material from the treatment of two children on the autistic spectrum in terms of factors bearing on the emergence of their sense of self and of a shared humanity. Not surprisingly, the way in which they interpret eye contact is of prime importance. Winnicott (1967) argued that our deepest sense of who we are derives from the reflection of ourselves that we see in our mother's face, while Klein (1961) documented the way in which children can personify aspects of the mother's character and behaviour—a kind of fairy-tale world in which she can be experienced literally as a house with many mansions, each with its particular occupant that manifests itself in characteristic ways. Many factors, including neurological and sensory endowment, will enter into the way in which children with autism can relate to the world and to other people. However, I shall suggest that, like other children, they interpret their relation to the world in terms of phantasies about the nature of a supposed internal family which the mother is thought to contain and which is felt to manifest itself in her personality and behaviour. More particularly, I shall argue that the child must feel in balance with this family, neither overshadowing it nor being overshadowed by it, in order to feel like a human being amongst other human beings and to be able to grow by internalising relationships.

The study of very early imitation[2] was pioneered by Olga Maratos in 1973. We now know that alert babies in a secure situation will imitate tongue protrusion by a stranger as soon as forty five minutes after birth; that is, at a time which allows one to rule out any influence of learning (Kugiumutzakis, 1988). The quality of imitation evolves over the course of the first year of life, both with regard to the actions that elicit imitation and with regard to the deliberateness with which babies observe the adult who is modelling an action and purposefully persevere in the effort to reproduce it. In contrast, very early imitation has a quality which comes over as instinctive as well as being in the service of relationship. It is worth emphasising that the action modelled by the adult in this study—tongue protrusion— is within the behavioural repertoire of the newborn. Of course that would have to be the case if imitative behaviour is to be elicited, but it also implies that the adult is, as it were, offering himself as a conversational partner who speaks the baby's gestural language.

Developmental researchers (Trevarthen, 1979, 1998; Beebe, 2006) have made video recordings of mothers and young babies interacting face-to-face in which it is plain to see that mutual imitation can be used in the service of sharing feelings. Some of this is imitation in the strict sense: mother and baby reproduce each other's expressions, gestures and vocalisations. Sometimes it involves the reproduction in another sensory mode of each other's "vitality contours", to use Daniel Stern's phrase (1985). The baby may move his arms and legs in rhythm to the mother's speech, or the mother may use her voice to reflect the rhythm of the baby's movements or nod in time to his vocalisations. I will give two examples from infant observation reports which show these processes at work in a naturalistic setting. The first observation (by a colleague) concerns two-week-old Baby Jack, the youngest of four children, whose mother was noticeably at ease, relaxed and attentive.

> She held him on her lap, patting his back, and looked into his face, talking to him softly in the intervals of her conversation with the observer. The observer noticed that even at this early age, Jack seemed to have some control over his head, which did not flop about when his mother was not supporting it. When his nappy was changed, he fixed his eyes somewhat blankly on the ceiling, but found the observer's gaze almost by chance when he moved his head, and stared straight into her eyes. When his mother spoke, he moved his head in the direction of her voice until his eyes found hers. Later, his mother moved her fingers rhythmically around Jack's palm, and the observer noted that Jack moved his own fingers in just the same rhythm around his mother's thumb. Indeed, his hands were very expressive: he clutched his thumb with the fingers of the same hand while he was trying to bring them up to his mouth, as though enacting the desired constellation of a mouth-shape encircling a nipple-shape. At another moment, he curved his four fingers into his palm and moved his thumb back and forth along the row of the facing joints, as though his thumb were like his gaze moving over his mother's face or over the row of clouds whose movement he had watched intently through the window.

Jack is a baby who has a loving relationship with his mother, and whose bodily integration, capacity for eye contact and interest in his surroundings are all well developed. This observation of a two-week-old baby turning his head in the direction of his mother's voice illustrates the integration of different sensory channels.[3] Like other babies observed in a naturalistic setting (Bick, 1964; M. Haag, 2002), Jack seems to be using his hands to embody fundamental aspects of his relationship with his mother, as when his fingers encircle his thumb. Finally, we see him adopting, within the same tactile mode, the rhythm with which his mother moved her fingers around his palm. This does not feel like the kind of imitation aimed at taking over the other person's qualities: it seems an example of co-operative imitation in the service of communication and attunement.

The observation of Baby Daniel (Barker, 2002) illustrates how this process shades into something that feels like identification:

> When Baby Daniel was first observed at the age of three weeks, he was lying on his mother's lap at the end of a feed. His eyes were closed, and he held the nipple in his mouth without sucking. The observer noted a calm, harmonious atmosphere; classical music was playing in the background. Then the music, which had been serene and quiet, changed to a vigorous piano solo. Without opening his eyes, Daniel began to suck equally vigorously, with rhythmical head movements. Mother took him off the breast by inserting her finger in his mouth: he sucked it energetically, moved his arms and legs, and vocalised.

One might hypothesize that Daniel reacted to rhythmical vitality in the environment as though it were a feature of his mother, and that his own rhythmical sucking resembled Jack's adoption of his mother's tactile rhythms, though Daniel's response was in a different sensory mode. What I particularly wish to emphasise is that when he sucked his mother's finger, he produced his own rhythmical vocalisations as a musical accompaniment. In later observations, he continued to vocalise to accompany his sucking, whether of the breast or his own hand. In other words, we can witness how the developmental, co-operative kind of emotionally charged imitation—cross-modal in this particular case—leads into a process whereby Daniel continues to produce his own vocalisations to accompany his sucking even when no music is playing: a process which seems to me to be true, introjective identification—in which the self is enriched through the internalisation of experience—rather than superficial, transitory mimicry. Interestingly, Hobson and Lee (1999) have shown experimentally that children with autism were capable of the mechanical imitation of an action but not of identification with an adult's style.

As far as I am aware, the only attempts in the psychoanalytic literature to theorise this kind of developmental imitation are by

Eugenio Gaddini and Joseph Sandler. Gaddini (1969) had proposed that the imitation of early infancy evolved into identification. However, he did not spell out how this occurred, and his clinical examples in fact concerned patients who used imitation to blur the distinction between self and other rather than in the service of development.

Sandler (1973) linked the kind of reflex, sympathetic imitation that we retain as adults to the Freudian concept of primary identification. Historically, this concept has been used in two ways. On the one hand, it points to the kind of identification in which the boundary between self and other is blurred, and contemporary Freudians continue to use it in this sense.[4] However, Freud also used the term "primary identification" to mean "primary" in the sense of "early": "a direct and immediate identification" which "takes place earlier than any [psychological investment of another person]" (1923, p. 31; 1921, pp. 105ff). This seems to have the quality of a "given", of something genuinely primary or primal which does not require explaining, and to address precisely the area of unlearned neonatal imitation and of being welcomed into the human family with which I am concerned.

Sandler drew on his own experience for an example of instinctive, sympathetic imitation. While walking on the pavement, he noticed someone ahead of him stumble, and he instinctively righted himself as though he had stumbled too. He suggested that this kind of immediate response might play an important part in emotional communication; more specifically, in the way the analyst's unconscious tunes in to that of his patient. This seems to anticipate Schore's formulation according to which infant and mother resonate "right brain to right brain" (1994). It is also consistent with recent work on so-called mirror neurons which fire in the same way when someone performs an action themselves and when they see someone else doing so: this phenomenon has been invoked (see, for example, Mitrani, 2007; Trevarthen, 2005; Music, 2005) as a possible biological basis for empathy. The observation of two-week-old Baby Jack, which I discussed earlier, illustrates how these fundamental imitative resonances can enter into a co-operative reciprocity between the baby and a mother who is experienced as separate.

I shall now attempt to unpack some of the components of this developmental aspect of imitation in the light of clinical material.

Children with autism respond to being imitated: this forms an essential component of many diverse programmes of intervention for them, including psychoanalytic psychotherapy. However, they do not themselves imitate in the natural, immediate way that other children do. The difficulty of making a reliable diagnosis of autism before the age of eighteen months means that information about the very early capacities of children with autism is on the whole obtained retrospectively, and it is not clear how, if at all, a baby's individual pattern of imitating may relate to a subsequent diagnosis. Still, imitation is widely enough recognised as being impaired or unusual in children with autism to form part of a diagnostic scale (Adrien et al., 1992).

Something seems to be amiss with these children's capacity for primary identification in the developmental sense. I think most clinicians would agree that it is encouraging when a child with autism begins to imitate in a relational context rather than in the context of mimicry or impersonation. It is essential to be alert to this distinction, and to realise the developmental importance that imitation can have. For example, Donna Williams, whose books on the experience of having autism provide fresh insights as well as confirmation of many clinical findings, explains that she was actually trying to convey a message when she produced echolalic speech as a child: "Look! I can relate! I can make that noise too!" (Williams, 1992, p. 188). Obviously, echolalia—like other kinds of imitation— will often be a matter of mimicry; but not always. Equally obviously, Donna Williams was not relating to the meaning of what was being said to her; but she was trying to be recognised as a human being who did the kind of thing that other human beings did. Clinical work with children with autism can help to clarify the conditions that are necessary for this kind of imitation, which, in normal development, looks as though it were automatic.

Building up and sustaining a sense of self, whether bodily or emotional, depends on the capacity to take in and assimilate experience— the process we call introjection. This can be problematic for children with autism and for adults with autistic features however well developed their capacity for recall may be (see, for example, Barrows, 1999, p. 559). The difficulty is often linked to the concreteness with which children with autism apprehend experience: they can find it hard to distinguish between taking something in on a mental level and taking it over on a bodily level. The earliest example of this is Tustin's patient David, who built himself a suit of armour by plucking features from his father "as if he were a lifeless thing" (Tustin, 1972). A patient of my own, while drinking from a bottle of lemonade, passed the plastic ring back and forth between the neck of the bottle and his mouth. When it was on the bottle, he showed me that his mouth was open in the form of a hole; when it was in his mouth, he looked fearfully at the bottle, as though he were frightened of being attacked, and indeed, when the bottle was empty, he threw it in the bin and shrank away from it (Rhode, 1997). In other words, taking in nourishment was felt to despoil the source (bottle or caregiver), which might then become either damaged or vengeful. This child, like others I have seen (Rhode, 2004), appeared to be enacting a very primitive version of the Oedipus complex in that two objects (his mouth and the bottle) were competing for a third (the ring). Both mouth and bottle needed the ring, of which there was only one, in order to be complete. Such a model does not allow the child to feel that he is fundamentally like the other person—as he must be able to do if developmental imitation is to be possible. Equally, it means that he cannot take something in from another person without doing damage.

Indeed, I wish to suggest that in order for introjection to occur—for experience to be taken in, built up and assimilated—the baby's position in relation to the mother must be the position implied by the developmental kind of imitation. In this position, the baby is experienced and experiences himself as someone fundamentally *like* the mother—not identical to her—and therefore able to interact with her by matching (like Donna Williams echoing someone else's words). In contrast to the example of the lemonade bottle, the mother and baby who match each other's rhythms, gestures, vocalisations or actions are both complete: this means that their relationship is complementary and reciprocal rather than competitive.

Clinical illustrations

Anthony: towards developmental imitation

Anthony was a boy with moderate to severe autism whom I began to see when he was six years old. The material I will discuss illustrates some of the problems which may be encountered on the way to the position of developmental imitation.[5]

Anthony was capable of speaking emotionally, communicatively, even poetically, but this could be difficult to remember, since he mostly produced mutilated bits of words and sentences in an array of voices that were not his own. These included the voice of the cruel giant from *Jack and the Beanstalk*, who threatened to devour him; and that of a figure he called "cruel Mummy" and who (unlike his actual mother) seemed to be humouring him rather than taking him seriously. He repeated what seemed to be catastrophic birth sequences such as Winnicott (1949) and Tustin (1981b) have described, in which he fell off the desk, struggling to reach the safety of a chair. As he did so, his mouth twisted into a tortured, lopsided shape, and he clutched the drawstring of his trousers as though he thought it could support him. He looked tormented. The torments which he in turn inflicted on the toy animals by cutting off their muzzles, hooves, ears and tails suggested that he felt in danger of losing parts of his own body. Although the animals pleaded "Please don't do this to me", he habitually continued until I stopped him.

At such moments, Anthony's cruelty seemed to involve identification with two aggressors: a cruel giant father who actively inflicted these tortures and an impervious mother who took no notice. Indeed, he appeared to conceive of this parental couple as being mirror images of each other, with eyes for no-one else. For example, he tipped a toy cow forward so that it stood on its muzzle on the mirror, and, pointing to the reflection, he said, "Mummy and Daddy".[6]

The cusp between visually-based and skin-based identification

> At the age of ten, Anthony jumped at me suddenly in the waiting room, growling in the giant's menacing voice. In the therapy room, he quoted from a story about Thomas the Tank Engine, who disobeyed the Fat Controller and fell down a mine from which he had to be rescued. Anthony seemed to feel that taking over a father figure's powerful voice in order to break through a boundary (the interval between sessions) meant literally falling into an abyss inside me as a mother or inside the therapy room.

He then noticed three small indentations on the wall (not made by him). They happened to be arranged in a triangle, as though they were two eyes with a mouth below. He traced round them with his finger to make the outline of a face, saying, "Poor eye, poor eye" (which of course is a pun on "poor I"). He then made a sticking plaster for the eyes from a strip of J-cloth, and stuck it to the wall with glue to cover the indentations, as though he were mending them. One end of the strip curved away from the wall like a label. Anthony tugged at it, as though testing whether he could pull it off; he then tugged at the tongue of his shoe, and, with his teeth, at bits of loose skin on his fingers. When I removed the J-cloth "plaster" from the wall in preparation for the end of the session, Anthony rolled the remaining glue into little balls resembling nasal mucus, and ate them. He then picked bits of mucus out of his nose and ate these as well.

Anthony seemed to think that the openings in a face—the eyes and mouth—were signs of the damage which the child could cause by smashing into a "brick wall" person (the "cruel mummy") who he felt was taking no notice of him—perhaps like me between one session and the next. He appeared to equate these holes with the mine down which Thomas the Tank Engine had fallen when he disobeyed the Fat Controller. It was as though Anthony felt that the wait between sessions had been imposed through the prohibition of a controlling father element. In terms of the Face, this would be the J-cloth: it made the eyes blind to him, but it was also an essential part of the Face's tripartite, primitive oedipal structure comprising J-cloth, glue and holes. Anthony's sudden aggressive jump in my direction, presumably in defiance of this prohibition, served the purpose of making me take notice of him—in his terms, it made eyes in the Face. (Indeed, both at home and at school Anthony had got into the habit of getting himself noticed by being naughty.) However, being noticed seemed inseparable from damaging me as a mother-figure, so that he "fell down the mine" into me and needed rescuing. Psychotherapists who work with this kind of child are familiar with the impossibility of getting the distance right: the child seems to be forever oscillating between the twin dangers of falling off an edge into space, like Anthony falling off the desk, and of falling into the therapist ("down the mine") and being engulfed. This oscillation has been described in adults by Sydney Klein (1973), and also by Henri Rey (1979), who called it the "claustrophobic-agoraphobic dilemma".

In line with this dilemma, "mending" the damage in the wall by restoring its tripartite structure (using glue to stick the J-cloth skin over the hole-eyes) makes the eyes blind again: the child seems caught between an impervious object and a broken one. Eating—in this example, eating the mucus-like glue—is therefore not in the service of development. Instead, it means taking over the substance which should be binding together two essential parts of the Face and which is therefore essential to its structural integrity, as in the vignette of the lemonade bottle. One could imagine a nursing baby looking into its mother's face and blaming its own feeding for any sadness or withdrawal to be discerned there (Meltzer, 1975b). Later in treatment, Anthony did in fact manage a better solution: instead of sticking the J-cloth over the eye "holes", he turned them into seeing eyes that no longer looked broken by adding a coloured pupil with a felt-tipped pen. He had developed the concept of a helpful third party to an oedipal triangle, located in the realm of eye contact with the adult.

Developmental imitation and the "helpful third party"

Anthony's material, I believe, illustrates the delicate cusp that can exist between adhesive mechanisms on the one hand, and, on the other, the kind of primary identification I think is involved in imitation of the developmental sort. I shall consider the adhesive, skin-based mechanisms first. When the "eyes" were "mended" with the J-cloth, Anthony plucked at his cuticles and tugged at the tongue of his shoe in just the same way as he tugged at the protruding J-cloth "skin" of the Face. In other words, the integrity of his own skin seemed to depend on the integrity of the other person's skin. Similarly, he appeared to equate his own balls of nasal mucus with the balls of glue that he extracted from the Face after the J-cloth-plaster-skin had been peeled off—and, by implication, he was equating the holes of his nostrils with the holes in the damaged Face. Whether the eyes in the Face were damaged or shut, they could not see or recognise him in the way that is necessary for "primary" identification (developmental imitation). In contrast, an eye with a pupil is no longer unseeing: it contains a third object, but one which confers vitality and can be identified with, rather than one which blocks the child out. This is the kind of mirroring eye contact that makes developmental imitation possible.

In these reflections, I am drawing on two main strands of psycho-analytic theory. One is Winnicott's paper on the "Mirror role of mother and family in child development" (1967), in which he proposes that the baby derives its fundamental sense of existence and goodness from what it sees reflected in its mother's face: on that most basic of levels, we are what we see. If the mother's preoccupations intrude excessively for too much of the time, then these are what the baby will see in her face rather than himself.[7] Anthony's transformation of empty holes into seeing eyes through the addition of pupils suggests that Winnicott's line of thought could usefully be combined with an observation by Melanie Klein (1961, pp. 46–9), who proposed that small children tended to personify the mother's qualities. They do not think of these qualities as though they were abstract properties of her mind and character, but as though they were people who literally lived inside her body and manifested their presence through her behaviour. The mother may be felt to contain a benign internal family which receives the child with love, or a hostile internal family which makes her into someone angry, or may intrude into his relationship with her and undermine his sense of self. Preoccupation then would imply an impenetrable J-cloth eyelid, a mother who is completely filled up by an internal family which leaves no room for anyone else; an empty, damaged eye would imply a maternal inner world populated by ghosts (Barrows, 1999). Anthony's pun on "poor eye" and "poor I" indicates, I would suggest, this kind of fundamental, visually-based identification; though in this case, it is with another person who is felt to be damaged.

The difference between this visually-based identification with a damaged other and the visually-based reciprocal exchanges of developmental imitation seems to lie in the presence or absence of the third object: the pupil, which Anthony later added to make the eye into one that could see him. It is this internal occupant that lends the mother's eyes their essential quality of liveliness—provided, of course, that this does not become excessive in a way the child could experience as intrusive. For example, Anthony was fascinated by mirrors.[8] He generally seemed to look into them for confirmation of his own existence, though he might also enact the kind of communion with a mirror image that went on between the "Mummy and Daddy" constellation of the cow and its reflection, as I mentioned earlier. Usually he declined to catch my eye in the mirror, as though I were to remain excluded from the couple he made with his own reflection. When he ignored me, he seemed to be identified with this narcissistic parental unit; and indeed he would enact being his mother on the telephone—"Yes, all right, darling"—or a performer singing into a microphone that he held as though it were a mirror and he were receiving the adulation of an adoring public. However, on one occasion when he was feeling more robust, he did meet my eye in the mirror: he smiled, and spontaneously exclaimed, "Hullo, mirror!" The point I want to emphasise is that my reflection at that moment seems to have served the same function as the pupil he placed in the empty eye: that of enlivening the mirror, so that instead of being a mechanically reflecting object, it became a humanised reflective agent that could encompass both of us.

Lina: "I'm looking for myself"

I would now like to develop this theme with regard to Lina, a little girl with autistic spectrum disorder whom I began to see when she was six and a half, following the death of a close relative. As a small child, Lina had been echolalic and extremely withdrawn, but she had improved to a gratifying extent during treatment with a therapist in another country. Like Anthony, she was inhibited by her confusion between taking things in and damaging me as a mother figure; like him, she mistook my attributes for rivals who got in her way. Unlike him, however, she increasingly came to feel that these attributes and contents could be distinguished from me—that I was not completely occupied by them—and therefore that they could be accessed without my disintegrating. Instead of seeing nourishment as a kind of essential glue that bound together the components of a mother figure and must therefore not be taken in (like Antony's nasal mucus), she came to see it as liquid that could be drunk from a cup without damaging the cup's structure. This meant that she could begin to own and assimilate what she took in, and to grow within the context of a relationship. I shall attempt to link this with Lina's position relative to the internal family that she imagined the mother-figure contained.

Lina had always been clear that my qualities were a function of my internal occupants: she even brought along a plastic toy with a pregnant-looking stomach that she rotated in order to change the expression in the eyes from Happy to Sad to Angry to Surprised, as though the mother-figure's mood were indeed a reflection of her imagined internal babies. In addition, she was preoccupied with the difference between the reflecting side of the mirror and its opaque wooden back. She linked the wood to the door of the therapy room, which felt shut to her between appointments, and also to the wall, which she tried to run through with predictably painful results. In contrast, seeing herself reflected in the mirror seemed to feel like finding the doorway into my eyes and mind. She became capable of much more enduring eye contact, though she could still feel in danger of being engulfed, and habitually made rafts for the toy animals to save them from drowning in the sink and being eaten by the crocodile on the bottom.

I would read this as a vivid illustration of Lina's desperate, precariously-balanced clinging to surfaces, and of her fear of dangerous depths in other people and in herself. However, she did manage to differentiate this version of a malign internal family from a helpful one which could provide support. This was represented by the solid trunk of a pot plant on the draining board, on which the farm animals sought refuge so as not to sink into the depths. Lina tended to attack this plant, as though she felt it to be a rival who was always in my room; but gradually she began to want to look after it. It was as though she had come to value the enduring presence of an object she had not been able to get rid of, and the solidity of which saved her from being engulfed, just as the presence of the father serves to regulate the distance between mother and child. Unlike Anthony, she began to feel that it was possible to get through emotionally without destroying the paternal function and ending up "down the mine".

In parallel with these developments, Lina took courage to be "naughty" and rebellious, whereas previously she had had the fairy-like, somewhat unreal quality that is characteristic of some children on the autistic spectrum. She seemed initially to experience this unintegrated naughty side of herself as though it were a double or alter ego, like Bion's imaginary twin (1950). The presence, in a glass-fronted cupboard, of some toys used by the colleague with whom I shared the room had long been a matter of annoyance. She had similar toys of her own, but the fact that the ones in the cupboard were, as she put it, "not playable" understandably felt tantalising and provocative, so that they became connected in her mind with my own supposed internal occupants.

One day she took a mouthful of water after some play at the sink, and held it in her mouth without swallowing while she stood gazing into the cupboard. She swallowed, then became acutely distressed. She wailed, "My sister Flo—I'm looking for my sister Flo", and had to run to the lavatory. As I waited for her, it struck me that her panic had been triggered by the act of swallowing, as though she feared that it might have destructive consequences. She was still quite distraught when she emerged from the lavatory, and in the room went back to stand in front of the cupboard, talking about her sister Flo whom she could not see. I said to her that perhaps, when she felt annoyed about things in the cupboard or in me that seemed to get in her way, she might feel muddled about different ways of taking things in. One way involved the kind of swallowing that she needed to do in order to grow; but perhaps she confused this with the destructive effect of what she had previously called her angry "monster mouth", which bit anything and anybody that obstructed her. That might make her feel guilty about swallowing and retaining the water inside her, and instead she let everything "flo(w)" out of her. She calmed down, and went to look at herself in the mirror as though to reassure herself that she was still there. In the next session, she again swallowed a mouthful of water while standing in front of the cupboard, and I asked whether she was looking for her sister Flo. "No", she answered in an assured tone of voice, "I'm looking for myself". Addressing her hostile impulses towards the supposed rivals inside my cupboard (or me) allowed her to look for her own reflection without feeling that this wiped them out, and to retain for herself the water she had swallowed, instead of equating herself with me as someone that water "Flo'ed" out of.

Some weeks later, in a pivotal session, Lina developed the theme of her position relative to the mother's internal occupant:

Lina drew many little circles in different colours on the surface of the mirror. (Previously, this had been in the context of wondering how babies were made: she had said that the circles were created by

Mr Green, Sir Blue, and so on). Now she said, a bit defensively, "I'm only trying to make stained glass". I said that perhaps she thought stained glass looked beautiful—all those colours with the light coming through—and that she was curious about how it was made, and would like to make some. In terms of her and me, this would be like feeling that it was she who elicited the expression—the colour—in my eyes when I looked at her: it was important to feel that she could make something nice like that happen, instead of imagining that a baby inside me determined my expression. She wiped the coloured circles off the mirror, and said, "It looks grey now", moving her hand furtively past her bottom as she threw the tissue in the bin. Wiping off the coloured circles, which in fact did get in the way of her own reflection, made her feel that my mirror-gaze was empty—grey, messed up, depressed, like Anthony's "poor eye".

Now she drew a bull on the mirror, with angry-looking eyes, coloured in red as though it were bleeding. She turned the mirror over, and seemed to be trying to see herself in the wooden back. I commented that one couldn't see oneself in that side, but that perhaps she was also wondering whether that was where the picture of the bull came from. She held up the mirror at an angle to the window, and said, "Now the light is shining through". In fact, of course, it wasn't; but I said she was looking for a situation where the light could shine through without being blocked by the picture: where there was space for life to go on behind my eyes in a way that encompassed her, and did not get in the way of room for her feelings.

Lina responded, "You can do something else, too". She took the mirror to the sink and, balancing it carefully, filled it up to the rim of the frame with water, so that the picture of the bull was now beneath the surface. She bent over it, as though, again, she were looking for herself; this time, however, she said, "I can see myself". I agreed that the water was different from the mirror, because it had actual depth, so that the picture of the bull did not get in the way of her seeing herself reflected.

I would suggest that these two related issues—firstly, of the way the child is positioned in relation to the mother's supposed internal occupant; and secondly, of depth within the mother which this occupant does not fill—are centrally important in allowing primary identification or imitation of the developmental sort.

In such a situation, the child's way in is not blocked; space is available for emotional containment; the light "shining through" makes the child feel that he can elicit a response; and, at the same time, the presence of the internal object means that the child is not in danger of being engulfed or of feeling responsible for an empty mother-figure. In other words, mother and child are both complete: they can evolve reciprocal interactions, like Baby Jack and his mother, which the child can internalise, like Baby Daniel. I believe this is the constellation underlying that particular kind of eye contact which allows children with autism to begin to imitate the therapist.

After this pivotal session, Lina took some major steps forwards. Her constructions at the sink evolved to include the vertical axis (a surfboard with a sail) as well as the horizontal one (the raft for the animals). Equally, her conception of space developed: she began to cut shapes out of paper to make patterns, while previously she might have been worried by the holes. It seemed she was moving away from the model of adding to herself by cutting or biting bits off another. Her ninth birthday soon afterwards encouraged her to feel that she was growing up and that she could have children one day, in identification with me as a woman whose internal husband and children left room enough for her own separate individuality to be reflected upon.

Discussion

The balance between the child and the mother's internal occupant

It seems that the position of the child relative to the mother's internal object is an expression of the oedipal constellation in relation to eye contact. This is on a very primitive level which concerns the child's experience of existing. These oedipal conditions must be in place for developmental imitation and introjection to go ahead.[9]

Children who do not have autism, even if they suffer from considerable disturbance, move readily from the experience of being recognised to taking an interest in the experience of the person who recognised them (Schacht, 1981). In terms of cognitive theories of autism, they develop a theory of mind. Indeed, in their therapy this may happen so quickly as to suggest the unfolding of a natural process which has been unblocked. For children with autism, on the other hand, this move, if it does happen, involves much time and labour. Tustin (1990) proposed that their failure to develop empathy might be traced to an insufficiently robust sense of self: putting themselves in someone else's shoes might feel like losing any sense of their own identity. Such a state of affairs implies an imbalance between the position of the child and the position of the mother's internal object.

In order for the child to feel supported rather than intruded into, the parent's internal family must be felt to be located at the optimal "depth". Early in treatment, for example, Lina meticulously arranged two calves face to face, one on a plate, one outside it, in such a way that they were equidistant from the rim. Where this balance is felt to be right, the baby can bring his own qualities to engage with the mother's, as in developmental imitation. Where the child cannot elicit a response or be recognised, he may (mis)interpret this as meaning that the parent's internal family lies too deep, as in the case of Anthony's "poor eye/I". Where the mother is preoccupied, so that the child does not experience being reflected (Winnicott, 1967) or find sufficient space for containment, he may feel that his way in is blocked by an internal family *that he (mis)interprets as lying too far forward*. (If the mother's preoccupation concerns transgenerational issues, as with Fraiberg's ghosts in the nursery [1975], the child may feel that his own "niche" is concretely filled by someone from the past.) In terms of introjection, the mother's capacity to distinguish between her own internal occupant and her actual external baby in turn supports the baby's capacity to distinguish between the mother herself and the mother's internal occupant, and therefore not to confuse taking in from her with taking away from her and damaging her structure.

Very schematically, one could speculate that when the balance is right, the child can identify with the parental figure, as Lina did when she began to think of herself as containing unborn children like me. When the balance is not right, the child may identify instead with the parent's internal occupant, like Kate Barrows' adult patient (1999 and this volume) who identified with her parents' dead or damaged siblings. For instance, a boy with Asperger's syndrome changed from being very withdrawn, when he was identified with ghostly inhabitants of a parental figure, to being highly excitable, with much bizarre phantasy, when instead he was identified with a vengeful persecutory sibling figure who he thought was coming out of the television in order to attack him.

It is important to emphasise that I am not implying a causal link between mother-infant interactions and autistic spectrum disorder: there are far fewer children with autism than there are depressed mothers or "ghosts in the nursery". My point is rather that phantasies about the mother's internal occupants can get mapped onto the way the child experiences his or her life circumstances. These circumstances may include aspects of the parents' capacity to pay attention. They may equally include neurologically-based feelings of being invaded by loud noises, which are then personified as intrusive father or sibling figures (Rhode, 1997). These phantasies, I believe, are central to the sense of identity, and psychotherapy with autistic children allows us to explore some of their ramifications.

Eye contact which feels emotionally significant to both parties implies the right balance between the child and the mother's internal occupant, and therefore allows primal (or primary) identification— imitation of the developmental sort—to take place. This can be observed clinically with regard to both immediate and deferred imitation. For example, following a rare moment of profound eye contact, a mute four-year-old boy with autism painstakingly imitated the round shape of my lips as I made the sound "o". Sometimes children who are not yet sure of the difference between introjection and despoiling the other person need to re-establish eye contact, with the proper balance between themselves and the other person's internal occupant, in order to be able to own and show what they have taken in. For instance, a three-year-old boy with autism treated by Christine Robson gazed deeply into her eyes, and then spontaneously hummed a song she had sung during the previous session. This could be seen as an example of the process that developmental researchers call deferred imitation. The fact that this instance of deferred imitation occurred after an emotionally charged moment of eye contact suggests to me that this child needed to re-establish the "position" for primary identification, in which he could feel at the right distance from his therapist's internal occupant, in order to be sure that he had not concretely damaged her by possessing the memory of her song. Once he had done this, he could show what he remembered.[10] The implication would be that this properly balanced position for primary identification provides the conditions in which introjection and assimilation can take place, and also, therefore, in which the child can grow within the framework of a relationship.

Children on the autistic spectrum can feel alien in the world of other people; and they can feel like "strangers in a strange land". The titles of first person accounts often bear witness to this sense of alienation—*Nobody Nowhere* (Williams, 1992), *Pretending to be Normal* (Willey, 1999), and *A Real Person: Life on the Outside* (Gerland, 1996), to mention only three. Factors which have been invoked to explain this include sensory impairments and biologically-based deficits in the capacity to mind-read, among others. My aim has been to illustrate some of the feelings and phantasy constellations which can accompany such experiences, whatever may have caused them. The work which had to be done so that Lina could establish a balanced position vis-à-vis the therapist's internal family and find her own reflection in the mirror illuminates some of the conditions that must be in place for developmental imitation and introjection to go ahead. Within the context of any specific limitations, the child can then begin to grow into his or her potential as part of the human family.

Notes

1. This is a revised version of a paper published in the *Journal of Child Psychotherapy* (2005); some of the material is discussed elsewhere in different theoretical contexts and is reprinted by permission.

2. See Nadel & Butterworth, 1999.

3. This is a process which a number of psychoanalysts (Bion, 1950; Meltzer, 1975; S. Klein, this volume, Chapter Eight; G. Haag, 2000) consider to be fundamental to the sense of self, a view supported by the good results that "sensory integration training" often achieves for children with autism.

4. For example, Kut Rosenfeld and Sprince (1965) describe the struggle of borderline children to maintain their precarious sense of a separate individuality: when under stress, they resort to "primary identification" to relinquish their hold on their own identity and take on the characteristics of significant adults.

5. This material was previously discussed in a different theoretical context (Rhode, 2003).

6. It is important to stress that Anthony's actual parents were very different from these hostile internal figures.

7. See Fonagy *et al* (2003) for a discussion of later work on the failure of mirroring.

8. An extensive experimental literature exists concerning mirror-recognition and its implications in children both with and without autism, consideration of which is beyond the scope of this paper (see, for example, Zazzo, 1995, Athanassiou-Popesco 2006).

9. They must also be in place, I believe, to allow for the much more sophisticated shifts in identification and point of view which are implied by Britton's work on the third position (Britton, 1989; 1998) and by Hobson's Relatedness Triangle, which addresses the relationship between the infant's attitude towards the world, the other, and the other's attitude towards the world (Hobson, 2002, p. 107).

10. This may partly explain why some children with autism can find it hard to access in other settings the capacities they show during sessions.

References

Adrien, J.L., Barthelemy, C., Perrot, A., Roux, S., Lenoir, P., Haumery, L. & Sauvage, D. (1992). Validity and Reliability of the Infant Behavioural Summarized Evaluation (IBSE): a Rating Scale for the Assessment of Young Children with Autism and Developmental Disorders. *Journal of Autism and Developmental Disorders 22*: 375–94.

Athanassiou-Popesco, C. (Ed.) (2006). Représentation et Miroir. Paris.

Barker, G. (2002). "How can the Start and the End of Vomiting in the First Six Months of Life of a Baby be Understood? A Reflection on a Good-Enough Relationship Between a Baby and his Mother." Unpublished MA Dissertation in Psychoanalytic Observational Studies, Tavistock Clinic/University of East London.

Barrows, K. (1999). Ghosts in the Swamp: Some Aspects of Splitting and their Relationship to Parental Losses. *Int. J. Psychoanal. 80*: 549–62.

Beebe, B. (2006). Co-Constructing Mother-Infant Distress in Face-to-Face Interactions: Contributions of Microanalysis. *International Journal of Infant Observation 9*: 151–64.

Bick, E. (1964). Notes on Infant Observation in Psychoanalytic Training. *Int. J. Psychoanal. 45*: 184–8. Reprinted in A. Briggs (Ed.), *Surviving Space: Papers on Infant Observation*. London: Karnac, 2002.

Bick, E. (1968). The Experience of the Skin in Early Object Relations. *Int. J. Psychoanal. 49*: 484–6. Reprinted in A. Briggs (Ed.), *Surviving Space: Papers on Infant Observation*. London: Karnac, 2002.

Bion, W.R. (1950). The Imaginary Twin. In: *Second Thoughts*. London: Karnac, 1984.

Bion, W.R. (1959). On Arrogance. In: *Second Thoughts*. London: Karnac, 1984.

Britton, R. (1989). The Missing Link: Parental Sexuality in the Oedipus Complex. In: J. Steiner (Ed.), *The Oedipus Complex Today*. London: Karnac.

Britton, R. (1998). Subjectivity, Objectivity and Triangular Space. In *Belief and Imagination*. London: Routledge.

Fonagy, P., Target, M., Gergely, G., Allen, J.G. & Bateman, A.W. (2003). The Developmental Roots of Borderline Personality Disorder in Early Attachment Relationships: a Theory and Some Evidence. *Psychoanalytic Inquiry 23*: 412–59.

Fraiberg, S., Adelson, E. & Shapiro, V. (1975). Ghosts in the Nursery: a Psychoanalytic Approach to the Problems of Impaired Infant-Mother Relationships. In: *Clinical Studies in Infant Mental Health*. London: Tavistock, 1980.

Freud, S. (1921). Group Psychology and the Analysis of the Ego. *SE 18*.

Freud, S. (1923). The Ego and the Id. *SE 19*.

Gaddini, E. (1969). On Imitation. *Int. J. Psychoanal. 50*: 475–84.

Gerland, G. (1996). *A Real Person: Life on the Outside* (trans. J. Tate). London: Souvenir Press, 1997.

Haag, G. (2000). In the Footsteps of Frances Tustin: Further Reflections on the Construction of the Body-Ego. *Infant Observation 3*: 7–22.

Haag, M. (2002). *À Propos et à Partir de l'Oeuvre et de la Personne d'Esther Bick. Volume I: La Méthode d'Esther Bick pour l'Observation Régulière et Prolongée du Tout-Petit au Sein de sa Famille*. Paris: Privately printed.

Hobson, R.P. & Lee, A. (1999). Imitation and Identification in Autism. *Journal of Child Psychology and Psychiatry 40*: 649–659.

Hobson, R.P. (2002). *The Cradle of Thought*. Basingstoke: Macmillan.

Klein, H.S. (1973). Emotion, Time and Space. *Bulletin of the British Psycho-Analytical Society 68*.

Klein, M. (1961). *Narrative of a Child Analysis*. In: *The Writings of Melanie Klein, vol. 4*. London: Hogarth, 1975.

Kugiumutzakis, G. (1988). Neonatal Imitation in the Intersubjective Companion Space. In: S. Braten, (Ed.), *Intersubjective Communication and Emotion in Early Ontogeny*. Cambridge: Cambridge University Press.

Kut Rosenfeld, S. & Sprince, M. (1965). Some Thoughts on the Technical Handling of Borderline Children. *Psychoanalytic Study of the Child 18*: 603–35.

Maratos, O. (1973), "The Origin and Development of Imitation in the First Six Months of Life." Paper presented at the British Psychological Society Annual Meeting, Liverpool.

Meltzer, D. (1975). The Psychology of Autistic States and of Post-Autistic Mentality. In D. Meltzer *et al*, *Explorations in Autism, a Psycho-Analytical Study*. Strathtay: Clunie Press.

Mitrani, J. (2007). "The Problem of Empathy: Bridging the Gap Between the 'Mirror Neuron' Concept and Frances Tustin's Understanding of the Psychogenesis of Autism." Paper presented at a conference of the Australian Psychoanalytic Society, Melbourne.

Music, G. (2005). Surfacing the Depths: Thoughts on Imitation, Resonance and Growth. *Journal of Child Psychotherapy 31*: 72–90.

Nadel, J. & Butterworth, G. (1999). *Imitation in Infancy*. Cambridge: Cambridge University Press.

Rey, J.H. (1979). Schizoid Phenomena in the Borderline. In J. Le Boit & A. Capponi (Eds.), *Advances in the Psychotherapy of the Borderline Patient*. New York: Jason Aronson. Also in: E.B. Spillius (Ed.), *Melanie Klein Today, Volume 1: Mainly Theory*. London: Tavistock/Routledge.

Rhode, M. (1997). Going to Pieces: Autistic and Schizoid Solutions. In: M. Rustin, M. Rhode, A. Dubinsky & H. Dubinsky (Eds.), *Psychotic States in Children*. London: Tavistock/Duckworth.

Rhode, M. (2003). Aspects of the Body Image and Sense of Identity in a Boy with Autism: Implications for Eating Disorders. In: G. Williams, P. Williams, J. Desmarais & K. Ravenscroft (Eds.), *The Generosity of Acceptance. Volume I: Feeding Difficulties in Childhood*. London: Karnac.

Rhode, M. (2004). Different Responses to Trauma in Two Children with Autistic Spectrum Disorder: the Mouth as Crossroads for the Sense of Self. *Journal of Child Psychotherapy 30*: 3–20.

Sandler, J. (1973). On Communication From Patient to Analyst: Not Everything is Projective Identification. *Int. J. Psychoanal. 74*: 1097–1107.

Schacht, L. (1981). The Mirroring Function of the Child Analyst. *Journal of Child Psychotherapy 7*: 79–88.

Schore, A. (1994). *Affect Regulation and the Origin of the Self: The Neurobiology of Emotional Development*. Hillsdale, NJ: Lawrence Erlbaum.

Stern, D. (1985). *The Interpersonal World of the Infant: a View from Psychoanalysis and Developmental Psychology*. New York: Basic Books.

Trevarthen, C. (1979). Communication and Co-operation in Early Infancy: a Description of Primary Intersubjectivity. In: M. Bullowa, (Ed.), *Before Speech*. Cambridge: Cambridge University Press.

Trevarthen, C. (1998). The Concept and Foundations of Infant Intersubjectivity. In: S. Bråten (Ed.), *Intersubjective Communication and Emotion in Early Ontogeny*. Cambridge: Cambridge University Press.

Trevarthen, C. (2005). First Things First: Infants Make Good Use of the Sympathetic Rhythm of Imitation, Without Reason or Language. *Journal of Child Psychotherapy 31*: 91–113.

Tustin, F. (1972). *Autism and Childhood Psychosis*. London: Hogarth.

Tustin, F. (1981). Psychological Birth and Psychological Catastrophe. In: *Autistic States in Children*. London: Routledge & Kegan Paul.

Tustin, F. (1990). *The Protective Shell in Children and Adults*. London: Karnac.

Willey, L.H. (1999). *Pretending to be Normal: Living with Asperger's Syndrome*. London: Jessica Kingsley.

Williams, D. (1992). *Nobody Nowhere*. London: Transworld Publishers.

Winnicott, D.W. (1949). Birth Memories, Birth Trauma, and Anxiety. In: *Through Paediatrics to Psycho-Analysis*. London: Hogarth, 1958.

Winnicott, D.W. (1967). The Mirror Role of Mother and Family in Child Development. In: *Playing and Reality*. London: Tavistock, 1971.

Zazzo, R. (1995). *Reflets de Miroir et Autres Doubles*. Paris: PUF.

PART II

AUTISTIC FEATURES
IN ADULTS

CHAPTER EIGHT

Autistic phenomena in neurotic patients[1]

H. Sydney Klein

In recent years there has been an increasing awareness amongst analysts that behind the neurotic aspects of the patient's personality there lies hidden a psychotic problem which needs to be dealt with to ensure real stability. This was particularly highlighted by Bion in his seminal paper on the differentiation of the psychotic from the non-psychotic part of the personality (1957). However, I do not feel that this is still fully recognised. In the course of a periodic review of the progress of my analytic practice, and particularly of my patients' habitual modes of communication, I became aware that certain among them whom I thought of initially as being only mildly neurotic, some of whom were also analytic candidates, revealed during the course of treatment phenomena familiar in the treatment of autistic children. These patients were highly intelligent, hard-working, successful and even prominent professionally and socially, usually pleasant and likeable, who came to analysis either ostensibly for professional reasons or because of a failure to maintain a satisfactory relationship with a husband or wife. It gradually became clear that in spite of the analysis apparently moving, the regular production of dreams, and reports of progress, there was a part of the patient's personality with which I was not in touch. I had the impression that no real fundamental changes were taking place. There is an obvious parallel with what Winnicott has called the false self (1960), and which Rosenfeld has termed "psychotic islands" in the personality (1978), but I do not think these terms quite do justice to what may be described as an almost impenetrable cystic encapsulation of part of the self which cuts the patients off both from the rest of their personality and the analyst. This encapsulation manifests itself by a thinness or flatness of feeling accompanied by a rather desperate and tenacious clinging to the analyst as the sole source of life, with an underlying pervasive feeling of mistrust, and a preoccupation with the analyst's tone of voice or facial expression irrespective of the content of the interpretation. There is a constant expectation of hostility and a tendency to become quickly persecuted at the slightest hint of the analyst's irritation or disapproval. Consciously the analyst is idealised as an extremely powerful and omniscient figure who also occurs in this guise in the patient's dream. As a concomitant, the patient denies his persecutory feelings in spite of the evidence subsequently given by dreams and other analytic material. For example, one patient offered to raise her fees as she felt so well, and I accepted her offer. The next night she dreamed of a large white vampire bat and of a baby wriggling to escape from a tube being put into its foot for a blood transfusion. It was obvious that although she had offered to raise the fees herself she experienced me as a vampire-like breast which was sucking her dry instead of filling her with life. Nevertheless her fear of me led to a firm denial of her persecutory feelings.

Another feature of the analysis is the tendency to bring up some topic which the patient seizes upon with obsessional rigidity but which is never worked through because of the inability to take in interpretations and deal with the problem. There is a striking similarity with the behaviour of autistic children who play with a ball or toy in a compulsive repetitive way and who scream and resist any attempt to interfere with or change the pattern of play.

Sooner or later, however, the patient's personality structure is made clearer by references in a projected form. For example, one patient said: "I can never get through to my mother. She seems to have an encapsulated relationship inside herself." Another described an autistic child she had seen in exactly the same terms. Yet another patient described herself as drifting away from me, even though she was interested in what I was saying, in exactly the way autistic babies are described as drifting away from their mothers. As soon as I was able to draw the patients' attention to these phenomena in themselves, they began to dream about being in walled towns or fortresses, stone buildings, etc. In addition, crustaceous creatures began to appear in their dreams, such as cockroaches, armadillos, lobsters, and so on (cf. Tustin, 1972). Previously these encysted parts of the self had been dealt with by projection into the body, producing various types of psychosomatic symptoms, or into other people.

I would like to describe one patient in some detail to illustrate my point. This female patient had politely but consistently denied all feelings about weekend or holiday separations even though the material pointed quite clearly to feelings of exclusion from the parental couple. Just prior to the second holiday break she suddenly developed acute abdominal pain and was rushed to hospital for removal of what turned out to be an inflamed ovarian cyst. Prior to the next analytic break she developed an acute swelling in her breast which was operated on and diagnosed as acute cystic inflammation. However, despite the operation she continued to complain of pain and swelling in both breasts. Subsequent sessions indicated that the swellings were equated with omnipotent appropriation by projective and introjective identification of her mother's genital and breast creativity. This was shown by a dream in which she had two swellings on either side of her body, to which she associated sitting between two pregnant women at a dinner party. This was followed by phantasies of attacks on "the goose that laid the golden eggs". Moreover when she spoke of her feelings of insecurity and inability to maintain her confidence, which she equated with a structure of bricks collapsing, it became apparent that this was due to her attacking the cement which bound her together, namely my interpretations. Her own association of cement with semen showed her hostility to the creativity of both parents, who were not allowed to come together in her mind. Nevertheless, there was no overt expression of hostile feelings towards me, which remained completely split off. Indeed, there was little feeling of immediacy of emotional contact in the transference. Even when she agreed with what I said, I did not feel we got any deeper. The model was of a baby with the nipple in its mouth but not taking in the milk.

However, after I had consistently drawn her attention to the lack of real emotional contact, in a Monday session a short time later she told me two dreams. In the first dream she was driving up a hill in a red car. Her association was that when she is without me at the weekend, she stops going forward and feels like a child. She then told me the second dream, in which she was lying in a hospital bed in a room with her mother. There were cockroaches in the room, and her mother was very angry with the nurse while my patient was quite calm. Her associations were that in her late teens she had had an operation for the removal of a dermoid cyst. Her mother came to visit her and was very angry with the nurse because she was very impatient and could not tolerate anything dirty in the room.

I interpreted that she was afraid that I was like her mother and could not tolerate anything dirty in her like a cockroach, but this was also because she was putting into me her own impatience and intolerance of anything which was not ideal. She agreed and said rather ruefully that she supposed she expected a land of milk and honey. She then added that she hated cockroaches. She remembered being with a girl friend and killing a big fat cockroach which her girl friend had been very frightened of. She laughed and said it was an act of friendship.

Now in the previous session there had been veiled and scattered, but increasingly hostile references to this girl friend, who had recently started analysis herself and had told my patient she was doing well. It seemed to me that under the guise of friendship she was denying her jealousy of her girl friend, who in her phantasy was a new baby coming to me, and I interpreted that she turned me into a dirty cockroach and killed me off because of the hatred and jealousy that she experienced towards me at the weekend as a pregnant mother containing her baby sister and father's penis instead of being the ideal mother and breast who was there just for her. She said: "You have said this before but I don't see it. I must be blind. It is like looking at letters and not being able to put them together to make words out of them. It is the same with my husband. He gets furious with me and says that I don't take things in." There was a reflective pause and she said: "I must be a difficult nut to crack." There was another pause, and she added "but it's only like this when you talk about separation." I said that she kept herself in a shell in order to avoid the painful feelings I had just described.

To summarise, the dream of going up the hill in the car which then changed into a pedal car showed how the patient functioned by identification with me and my analytic potency. However, the fact that this defence failed at the weekend and she regressed to being the helpless child indicates that this identification was predominantly a contact one or what Bick has called "adhesive identification". In the infantile position, her anger with me as the mother containing father's penis and babies leads her to attack me and turn me into the black cockroach which then has to be killed off. The whole process has been previously encapsulated, i.e. in the dermoid cyst, which had then been dealt with by being cut out.

This patient had previously described how her mind drifted away in meetings because she felt afraid of her male colleagues, and how she had always felt her father's words like bullets. In the next session she now returned to this theme and said that she was like a hedgehog: if she was feeling attacked either her quills shot out or she collapsed inside herself. When I interpreted that she was putting her own hostility into myself as father she said she did feel hostile. What was so painful was her feeling that he had no time for her. Every time she telephoned him he just said "Hello", and passed her over to her mother. As a child and adolescent she always felt he was battering her with lectures and had no interest in her feelings or in common everyday events. She then recounted with intense feelings how she used to take her boyfriends home and how they had completely ignored her but sat adoring her father, who also ignored her. It was the most painful experience of her life, she said bitterly. "He robbed me of my femininity." When I tried to relate this to her feelings about myself and other patients, she denied it. She was quite sure this wasn't so; I was kind, attentive, etc. However, she sounded quite hurt, and I then pointed out how she did feel hurt by me because when I interpreted her negative feelings she felt I ignored her positive, loving feelings. In fact a constant feature of the analysis at this time was that any interpretation of her negative feelings immediately made her feel extremely persecuted. During this period I had to proceed extremely cautiously, but little by little she was able to voice feelings and produce dreams in which I was experienced successively as a hard-shelled beaked lobster, a cruel and treacherous Stalin who pretended to be genial but was really murderous, and then as more human but cold, hard and formal.

After this period she told me two dreams which shed some light on her difficulty in taking in understanding. In the first dream her husband was talking on the telephone to a young girl who was staying with them, and she cut the wire. When I interpreted that not only was she cutting the links between her husband and the girl because of her jealousy of the relationship, but she was also jealous of the link between myself and my analytic babies, she said "I don't understand". I then added that she didn't understand because she was also cutting the links between us as a result of the envy of the good link between us, and especially the link with the dependent part of herself. She then said: "I do understand that. It's like being in a boat and cutting the ropes pulling me ashore so that no one can help me. I am too proud. I take small things but not big ones." She then told me a second dream.

She was in the hairdresser's, and was kept waiting until the shop was empty. She then got so angry that she smashed two pairs of plates, each pair consisting of one large and one small. Her association was that she had been to the hairdresser and changed her hairstyle, but her husband had not noticed. The plates symbolised her capacity to receive and understand the analytic food for thought, which she smashed up when she could not bear the frustration experienced when she felt she was overlooked, especially if she felt that I, like her husband, did not notice her attempts to change for the better. Her reaction to this interpretation was to say: "My father looked at me but did not see me and never listened either." After a pause she said she now realised that her sexual phantasies towards her father and her wish for babies from him and other men, which we had previously seen, meant that she was prostituting herself to get concrete proof that she was cared for. I told her that if she did not get all the food and care she wanted, she destroyed what she did get: it was all or nothing.

At a later stage in the analysis, towards the end of the second year, what also emerged was her realisation that she was using me as a processing plant in which I had to act as her eyes and her judgement, and function as someone refining and enriching her like a uranium factory, or giving her a blood transfusion. She revealed that the reason why she projected her senses and her capacity to think into me was that if she stopped to think and make a decision as to what course of action to take, she was afraid that she would become so paralysed by doubts about other possible courses of action that she would never move. Instead she got rid of her capacity to think, and consequently behaved in a completely blind and confused way. This was described very vividly by her as pseudo-bravery, in which she acted very fast and destroyed what she called the monsters of doubt, which made her behave in what she called "constant hysterical action". It also became apparent that her paralysis by doubt was due to her fear that if she went ahead and committed herself to the analysis, this would result in her throwing herself completely into me, body and soul. This was partly due to her need to prove her commitment as a result of the projection of her expectations from others, particularly her father and myself. She admitted that she had always felt she needed her father's whole physical involvement because she had had so little of it as a child.

At the same time her fear of throwing herself inside me was due to the impulse to occupy and possess me as a mother full of imagined riches. This was felt as being carried out in such a violent way that she feared that she would get stuck inside me and would be unable to extricate herself. Even worse, she feared that in the process she would destroy my inside containing herself, expressed in phantasies of being buried alive in a mining shaft whose walls collapsed, a volcano erupting with tons of lava, and a steam roller which could flatten everything.

However, as another holiday drew nearer at the end of the second year, it became clear that behind the possessiveness and jealousy of her more adult self there was a desperate need to keep herself inside me because of the intense anxiety aroused in the infantile part of her by the approaching break. This time the impending separation brought into consciousness terrible feelings of me dying or abandoning her, and of consequently dying or falling to pieces herself. She said she felt as if she were in a black space screaming for help. "I feel worse than an unborn baby, more like a mindless dog which can only be happy when its master returns." These primitive feelings of needing the analyst/mother in order to hold the infant together and protect it from death and disintegration are basically what underlie the autistic defences I have previously described. The patient herself referred to her behaviour being like that of a child playing with a ball, which could not stop (just as I described the behaviour of the autistic child) because any suggestion of the idea of it not going on for ever was like a small dose of death.

The interpretation of these intense anxieties brought a measure of relief to the patient but then led to phantasies that she could only get stronger by eating her way out of me, and guilt at taking in life at my expense. As this was due to the feeling of being inside me again we could then see that apart from the primary infantile anxiety of separation she also got rid of the adult part of herself in order to make herself small enough to get inside me, like Alice in Wonderland, this time because of a stubborn anger and spite at the separation. For the first time she was able to admit to murderous feelings about being left, both towards myself and towards the other babies felt to be taking her place inside, and in particular, anger at being made so much better that she could no longer regress to being the helpless infant.

This patient and others like her had a preoccupation with and a fascination for words. On one occasion when her husband had been away and not replied to a letter she had written him, she dreamed of a letter being wrapped in wool. The meaning of this dream was that no-words were experienced as cold and hostile. Similarly, in order to disguise her own hostile reactions she had to wrap up her own words to make them warm. This sensitivity to the analyst's tone of voice, which is partly due to the need to hang on to something for life and support, and partly due to the expectation of hostility, requires him to be alert to his own reactions. While there is no doubt that the visual deprivation caused by lying on the couch plays a part in the importance of the analyst's voice, it also has its roots in early infancy.

My patient's earlier difficulty in expressing her feelings seemed to be due partly to identifying me with a fragile mother who could not stand anxiety without breaking down, and partly due to identifying me with an omnipotent father who would crush any aggression or defiance or reject her love. It was this lack of a good stable container which I think led her to use her body as a container instead, with the consequent production of psychosomatic symptoms. In fact all my patients in this group experienced their mothers as anxious, insecure, controlling, over-protective and hypochondriac, while their fathers were described as being either physically absent in their child-hood or emotionally absent in the sense of being remote intellectuals heavily invested in academic or professional interests outside the family. However, the patient's material about being battered by words, and her excess of concrete thinking seemed to be related at a deeper part-object level to attacks by an object which contained by production the split off hostility aroused by a frustrating nipple and the need to preserve it from this hostility, and the additional aggression towards this object for taking the infant's place. In this connection I should like to mention that my patient had made various references to guilt and anxiety about incest. A dream in which her body was split in half was understood in terms of splitting off her sexual feelings from her oral ones. In the context of the session this led me to suppose that this incest taboo was originally based on the guilt and anxiety caused by primitive sexual feelings and desires directed towards the nipple, which was felt at the same time to be in danger of being destroyed. In this connection it is striking that for many years there seemed to be a taboo on the word nipple in the analytic literature. Although Freud used the word as early as 1905 in his paper on "A case of hysteria", even Melanie Klein hardly ever used it in spite of her voluminous writings on orality, and there have only been scattered references to it since, as Bradley described in his well-documented paper (1973). A systematic differentiation of the nipple as a structure separate from, but part of the breast, the confusion of nipple and penis, etc. was first described by Meltzer in 1963, i.e. nearly 60 years later.

Confirmatory material was furnished by another patient, who described how his 4-week-old baby girl started to cry when he stopped talking to his wife when she was feeding the baby. As soon as he started to talk again, the baby settled down. A few weeks later the reverse occurred. When he began to speak to his wife during feeding, the baby began to cry. In the context of the session it appeared that there is a change from an early experience of a good third object felt to be supporting the nipple to one in which it becomes hostile and intrusive. In others words, the absent third object, later called "father", is experienced as what might be called an aggressive masculine nipple. This was shown in a dream in which the patient was being run down by a Jaguar car with a small rubber protrusion at the front, to which he associated a teat on a bottle.

Now, as Bion (1957) has pointed out, the fragmentation and projection of the sensory apparatus by the psychotic part of the personality leads to a penetration and encystment of the object, which then swells up with rage. As a consequence words are not experienced as words but as hostile missiles, as my patient described. Seen in this light, the acute cystic swellings of the patient I have described in detail can also be understood as being due to phantasies of projection of aggressive feelings and parts of herself into her internal objects, namely mother's nipple, breast and reproductive organs, which then swelled up and became persecutors. Bion also describes how in an earlier phase of development, i.e. pre-auditory, the infant has difficulty in using ideographs to form words. My patient's reference to not being able to put letters together to make words is relevant here, and was due to her both attacking the links between objects and losing the capacity to restore them. In connection with the projection of the sensory apparatus, it is interesting that another patient, who was much more disturbed, had a dream in which an old-fashioned gramophone horn was listening to him. In this case the capacity to hear had been projected so that the gramophone was then felt to be listening instead of playing. At a later stage he also dreamed of looking at a breast which had an eye in the centre looking at him, so that here the capacity to see had been projected.

To summarise, the autistic defence is primarily due to the avoidance of the pain caused by the intensity of the fear of death and disintegration caused by the absence of the containing nipple or breast. This surfaces as analysis progresses, not only at weekend and holiday separations but every time the patient makes a step forward and becomes more separate. In the patients I have described, these anxieties had previously been avoided, whether by projective identification with me and phantasies of being unborn and living inside me, by introjective identification with me as a hard-shelled object, or by adhesive identification leading to clinging to me as a placenta-like object which both feeds and detoxicates at the same time. The impact of these terrifying feelings on the analyst may be considerable, as they may have been previously modified by the reassurance gained from the fact that he usually retains professional contact with his own analyst or institute, or indeed from using the institute itself as a container.

Technically, it is obvious that the patient's sensitivity to the tone of the analyst's voice must be matched by the analyst's equally sensitive but non-paranoid alertness to the underlying tone of voice and mood of the patient. In a previous paper on mania I described how the manic patient talked incessantly as a defence against feelings of inner emptiness. The type of patient I have described here does not, of course, have the same degree of disturbance, but it was noticeable that they were all extremely verbally fluent, and two were informed by their parents that they could talk before they could walk. It seems that the premature development and hypertrophy of speech may be partly a defence against underlying feelings of emptiness and non-existence, and partly to overcome the infant's anxiety that these primitive feelings are not understood and contained. This precarious situation becomes confounded when the hypochondriac mother uses the infant as a container for her own anxieties. In any event, speech was certainly used by these patients at certain periods either to maintain a link with the analyst or to avoid the link, rather than as a means of communication.

In other words, we have to recognise that although the patient appears to communicate at one level, there is also a non-communication corresponding to the mute phase of the autistic child, and what is not communicated are not only the aggressive but also the loving feelings which accompany the growth of the sense of separateness and the associated sense of responsibility for the self and objects. Limentani (1977) also stressed the importance of learning to understand the moods and feelings of the silent patient and his difficulty in conveying his experience to students and colleagues. Is not this paralleled by the difficulty the pre-verbal infant has in conveying his sensations and feelings to his mother, especially the experience of being alone in a silent world?

It is my impression that recognition of the existence of the encapsulated part of the personality reduces the length of the analysis considerably, and moreover may prevent further breakdowns in later life. This was borne in on me when I treated several patients who had been analysed at earlier periods in their lives and who became very disturbed in the course of the process of ageing. There is one other important feature which repays observation in these patients, and indeed in all patients, namely the process of oscillation, which repeatedly occurs, for example, between states of omnipotence and helplessness, activity and passivity, adulthood and infancy, psychosis and neurosis, primitiveness and sophistication of thought, and paranoid and schizoid depressive. Analysis of the oscillation leads hopefully to a more balanced state of mind and personality,

in which the knife-edge of opposites is broadened to become a more
solid basis of reflective thought.

Summary

I have described a group of patients who are seemingly successful
in their professional and social lives, and who seek analysis ostensibly
for professional reasons or for minor difficulties in their relationships. However, sooner or later they reveal phenomena which are
strikingly similar to those observed in so-called autistic children.
These autistic phenomena are characterised by an almost impenetrable encapsulation of part of the personality, mute and implacable
resistance to change, and a lack of real emotional contact with either
themselves or the analyst. Progress of the analysis reveals an underlying intense fear of pain and of death, disintegration or breakdown.
These anxieties occur as a reaction to real or feared separation,
especially when commitment to analysis deepens. In the case I have
described in detail, the patient used various projective processes
to deflect painful emotions either into other people, including
the analyst, or into their own bodies. As a consequence, the various
objects or organs of the body swell up and became suffused with
rage as a result of having to contain the unwanted feelings. This
process leads in turn to intense persecutory fears and a heightened
sensitivity to the analyst's tone of voice and facial expression. It
would seem that the initial hypersensitivity of part of the personality
is such as to lead it to anticipate danger to such an extent that it expels
feelings even before they reach awareness. The sooner the analyst
realises the existence of this hidden part of the patient, the less the
danger of the analysis becoming an endless and meaningless
intellectual dialogue, and the greater the possibilities of the patient
achieving a relatively stable equilibrium. Although the analyst has
to live through a great deal of anxiety with the patient, I feel that
ultimately the results make it worthwhile.

Note

1. Published in the *International Journal of Psychoanalysis*, 1980.

References

Bion, W.R. (1957). Differentiation of the Psychotic from the Non-Psychotic Personalities. In: *Second Thoughts*. London: Karnac, 1984.

Bradley, N. (1973). Notes on Theory Making, on Scotoma of the Nipples, and on the Bee as Nipple. *Int. J. Psychoanal. 54*: 301–314.

Freud, S. (1905). Fragment of an Analysis of a Case of Hysteria. *SE 7*.

Limentani, A. (1977). Affects and the Psychoanalytic Situation. *Int. J. Psychoanal. 58*: 171–182.

Meltzer, D. (1963). A Contribution to the Metapsychology of Cyclothymic States. *Int. J. Psychoanal. 44*: 83–96.

Rosenfeld, H. (1978). The Relationship between Psychosomatic Symptoms and Latent Psychotic States. Unpublished paper.

Tustin, F. (1972). *Autism and Childhood Psychosis*. London: Hogarth.

Winnicott, D.W. (1960). Ego Distortion in Terms of True and False Self. In: *The Maturational Processes and the Facilitating Environment*. London: Hogarth, 1965.

CHAPTER NINE

The rhythm of safety[1]

Frances Tustin

And came on that which is, and caught
The deep pulsations of the world,

Aeonian music measuring out
The steps of Time—the shocks of Chance—
The blows of Death. At length my trance
Was cancell'd, stricken thro' with doubt.
                Tennyson, *In Memoriam*, XCIV

This chapter was originally presented as a paper to a conference in Paris organised by the Continuing Education Seminars of Los Angeles. The neurotic adult patient discussed in it was one of those seemingly perennial patients whose functioning is based on the avoidance of endings. Insights derived from my work with autistic children have released this patient from the fetters of her autistic practices, so that she has become able to generate fundamental understandings which have made termination a reasonably safe possibility for her.

Clinical work which is influenced by psychopathology as elemental as childhood autism is bound to seem strange to those psychoanalysts who work in terms of ego psychology. It may also seem somewhat different, at least in the early stages, from clinical work which has been influenced by Melanie Klein. The influence of Bion and Winnicott on the chapter will be apparent. With this introduction let me present to you the patient who is the subject of this chapter, Ariadne.

The patient

Ariadne was first referred to me at ten years of age for learning difficulties. As a result of this childhood treatment her capacity to learn in a formal way improved, but I never felt that I was in touch with her very fundamentally. At thirteen she went to boarding school. At age twenty-five, on her own initiative, she returned to me for more psychoanalytic help because she had had a very frightening panic attack in which she had gone cold and frozen like a corpse. She had spent the whole night begging the woman friend who was with her to take her to mental hospital. We arranged that she should have two sessions a week.

A dream which started off the train of thoughts to be developed in this chapter occurred after Ariadne had been back in treatment for three years. Although both she and I were concerned that she should be able to finish treatment, we never seemed to reach the point where it seemed safe to do so. The dream and the understandings it stimulated in both of us have now made termination a real possibility.

The dream

The dream occurred in a session following a five-week interval during which, for various reasons, we had been unable to meet. In the dream, Ariadne was going happily towards an interesting, characterful house in which she knew that both her grandparents and great-grandparents had lived, and where her parents lived now. However, before she could reach the house, she found herself in the chasm of a huge black wave which was arching over her. The arch of the wave had glistening black ribs of water, in which there struggled drowning people rather like the people in a Hieronymus Bosch painting. The wave was so high that Ariadne could barely see the white crest on the top. She was terrified that it was going to engulf her.

This dream brought to my mind the remark Ariadne had made when we had both realised that because my lecturing trips abroad would be followed by events in her own professional life, there would be an interval of five weeks before we could meet again. She had asked anxiously, "Won't that break the continuity?"

As an infant Ariadne had had an overly caring mother who had been grief-stricken as the result of the death of an earlier boy child. This caused the mother and the infant Ariadne to have an unduly close association with each other from which the father had been virtually excluded. Ariadne had remained over-dependent on this mother, who had been used as her constant prop, support and stay. This over-dependence had been transferred to me.

In this session I reminded Ariadne of her anxieties about the breakdown in continuity caused by the five weeks' interruption of our meetings. I said I thought that the undue closeness to her mother, as an infant and small child, had engendered false hopes that her body was continuous with that of an external, ever-present mother and so could never come to an end. When she could no longer avoid awareness of their bodily separateness from each other, she had felt catastrophically let down. She had realised that she was mortal and that her body could come to an end. Since then, she had spent her whole life trying to reinstate the delusion of bodily continuity with this everlasting mother. The difficulty was that she was forever hoping that I was this immortal being, and she tried to manipulate the analytic situation to give credence to this belief. She did this because her whole sense of existence and of identity seemed dependent upon bodily continuity with an immortal being who went on forever.

The recent five weeks' interruption to the continuity of coming to see me had re-evoked the catastrophic infantile experience of finding that her body was in fact separate from that of the mother. It was possible that her going to boarding school, which had interrupted the flow of her first analysis, had been a similar re-evocation of what she felt to be an irremediable wound. (As I hope to show later, this feeling of irremediableness came from her lack of belief in the creative inner forces of healing.) In the session I went on to say that the five weeks' interruption had made her feel that I had left her in the lurch of a huge black wave of tempestuous feelings which had threatened to overwhelm her.

After this session I realised that in going towards the house in which her forebears had lived, Ariadne was beginning to see herself as part of a continuous process of generation succeeding generation. This would have been a compensation for giving up the unrealistic notion that her individual body could go on forever without ever coming to an end. However, this movement towards seeing herself in perspective as part of biological, evolutionary and genealogical continuity had been abruptly broken by the upsurge of over-whelming terrors about her personal survival. In the elemental depths, Ariadne did not "think" about death; she experienced it in a sensation-dominated way.

This was not the threat of death as we know it as an objective fact about what happens to people. It was a horrifying sense of bodily discontinuity which brings rage, grief and terror of endings. The body seems to come to an end in a fulminating way. The child feels forever at risk. To get some sense of safety, there is a reaction to re-establish the delusion of bodily continuity with an everlasting "being" who is for them alone. This "being" is not shared with a father or other children. It is difficult to find words for this elemental phenomenon; it is sometimes called "the environmental mother", and sometimes "the earth mother". It is a "being" who is felt to guarantee the child's own sense of being. These are "all or nothing" states. Everything is total and forever. Ariadne was freeing herself from these constricting autistic delusions. Let me describe this more realistic forward movement, which she called a "rhythm of safety".

The rhythm of safety

In my reflective preparations for Ariadne's next session, I read James Grotstein's paper about primitive mental states in borderline patients (1980), and was struck by the phrase "the infant must develop a sense of safety from its primary background object of primary identifica-tion". "Yes," I thought, "what Ariadne has lacked is a primary back-ground object of safety." (Since then, I have also come upon Joseph Sandler's paper on the background of safety [1960].)

However, Ariadne had also been reflecting on this matter of safety for, as soon as she was on the couch, she said thoughtfully: "You know, over the past week I think I've developed a rhythm of safety." I was surprised and delighted, both by this insight and by the phrase she had used to describe it. I asked her to tell me more about it. Ariadne went on to tell me a dream she had had following the session about the black wave. She had been in a very constricted space and had thought to herself: "I must get out of here." She had looked for a way out and had seen a chute down which she slid. But this sliding did not bring her to safety.

Metaphorically speaking, she went out of the frying pan into the fire, for she found herself in a large amphitheatre which was full of extremely evil people. She thought to herself: "I can't possibly walk through this place." However, although she was very frightened, "taking her courage in both hands"—significant phrase—she had walked through the evil amphitheatre to the other side; whereupon she had said thankfully: "I've got a rhythm of safety." The way in which she said this made it sound like a paean of thanksgiving. I suggested to her that having the courage to *face* her fear, instead of her usual practice of sliding away from it, had enabled her to become aware of resources within herself which had helped her to cope with it.

Let us think about the possible origins of this "rhythm of safety". Ariadne's use of the word "rhythm" brought to my mind a tape recording, made by a former student of mine, of a baby feeding at the breast in the first two months of life. At first the baby could not co-ordinate the rhythm of its own sucking and breathing, so that it synchronised with the pulsing rhythms of the milk from the nipple of the breast. However, as the baby's muscular co-ordination improved, and as the mother got to know her baby, mother and child adapted to each other. From the baby's rhythms and from the mother's rhythms a *new* rhythm developed. It was a "creation" they had made together. The student commentator records as follows: "The baby's mouth formed a safe hermetical seal around the nipple of the breast so that mouth, tongue, nipple and breast worked together and a synchronised rhythm came into being."

In Ariadne's terms, the infant developed a "rhythm of safety". Brazelton speaks of mother and baby interacting with each other to create what he calls "a reciprocity envelope". Fortunately, due to the flexibility of human nature, this infantile interactive situation can be created in later life. This is especially the case in an analytic situation in which the use of the "infantile transference" is understood. The primitive mind works in terms of correspondences, clang similarities and analogies. In certain states, the analytic experience is so deeply felt that it feels analogous to the baby feeding at the breast.

For the "rhythm of safety" to occur, Ariadne had had to develop an interactive reciprocal relationship with me which had deep infantile roots and in which the upright father element came into focus. This father element is hinted at in the 23rd Psalm, which is dealing with these elemental levels. You will remember it says: "Yea, though I walk through the valley of the shadow / Of death, I will fear no evil . . . thy *rod* and thy *staff* they comfort me" (my italics).

Ariadne's behaviour, in which she used the phrase "rhythm of safety", indicated that a deep, reciprocal relationship with me was developing. It was unusual for her to plunge straight away into a deep discussion as she did on this occasion. The previous pattern of most of her sessions had been that she would tell me in minute detail all that had happened to her since we had last met. This helped her to feel that we had not been separated and that our bodily continuity was re-established.

It had other satisfactions also. She was a charming and amusing raconteuse, and by thus capturing my interest she hoped to ensure that my physical presence would always be with her. However, on the day when she reported the development of a "rhythm of safety", a reflective interaction developed between us in which she recognised more fully than ever before that I was separate and different from her. For one thing, she recognised in a deep way, and not merely verbally, that the five weeks' gap had arisen from our mutual adaptation of each other's activities. Between us, we evolved the phrase "adaptive reciprocity" for this way of responding. Ariadne realised that this was very different from the "me"-centred, mechanical routines which she had valued so highly. These had consisted of expecting the sessions to occur with clockwork regularity, of coming precisely on time, and of going through the same procedures each time she came.

I had often pointed out to her that such expectations arose from the notion that I was part of her body like the beating of her heart. As a child and adolescent, Ariadne had been addicted to romantic women's magazines, and she reacted to me as if I were her "heart-throb" for evermore. This sentimental, individualistic and body-centred notion was now being replaced by a rhythm which was the creation of both of us. It was a shared experience. This was a much better protection against the evil of which she now became aware than the slippery evasive reactions which had previously dominated her functioning. The dream was a kind of parable about dealing with evil.

Verena Crick has drawn my attention to the similarity of Ariadne's dream to the theme of Mozart's opera *The Magic Flute*, in which, by the playing of a magic flute, the hero and heroine go safely through the dangers which beset them. Indeed, the coming into being of the intangible "rhythm of safety" from tangible, sensuous, physical interactions between mother and baby is a kind of magic. Such a transformation is beyond our rational understanding. It is an everyday miracle.

As Ariadne emerged from the constricted enclosure of her autism, she became aware of her vulnerability and her fears of being assailed by evil. Let us now study the possible origins of Ariadne's sense of evil, which she became able to face when she got in touch with her "rhythm of safety".

Ariadne's sense of evil

Work with autistic children has alerted me to the fact that one of the earliest differentiations is between "clean" and "dirty". This differentiation would seem to come from the inbuilt hygienic dispositions which human beings share with the other animals. Instead of the normal differentiations, autistic children and obsessional patients such as Ariadne have developed rigid splits between "clean" and "dirty"—as also between other sensuous conditions such as "full" and "empty", "wet" and "dry", "hard" and "soft", "light" and "dark", "strong" and "weak", etc. They are afraid that if they experience one contrary state alongside the opposite state, one will destroy the other in a total way. For example, "dryness" will totally dry up "wetness"; "hardness" will totally destroy "softness"; "darkness" will totally extinguish "light"; "weakness" will totally weaken "strength"; and so on.

A dictionary definition of the word "rhythm" goes as follows: "movement or pattern with regulated succession of strong and weak elements, opposite or different conditions". It would seem that a regulated rhythm—that is, a shared rhythm which is outside the bounds of exclusively "me"-centred restrictive practices—provides the possibility for contraries to be experienced safely together, for they can modify and transform each other. A creative intercourse is born. Having developed this rhythm of safety, Ariadne could now become aware of what she felt to be "evil", because she no longer feared that it would totally destroy what she felt to be superlatively "good". Prior to this, her autistic practices had enabled her to feel "good" by covering up what she felt to be the evil part of herself. Such patients often feel that they are whited sepulchres; in an attempt to get away from feeling a sham, they react by naïve, ill-judged, obsessional attempts at "total honesty", which leads them into trouble with the people around them.

Let us now study the origins of what is felt to be so superlatively good. In terms of inbuilt hygienic dispositions cleanliness is felt to be "good", and this notion is embodied in the homely maxim "Cleanliness is next to godliness". However, for patients such as Ariadne, "dirtiness" became associated with unmitigated evil, and "cleanliness" became associated with absolute purity. Although Ariadne had a great deal of charm, she was also a goody-goody and a prig. Her holier-than-thou attitude caused her friends to call her Miss Perfect. This notion of herself as being pure and perfect had been achieved by dissociating herself from the dirty, smelly, unacceptable parts of herself which became "not-me". Thus the amphitheatre of the outside world into which Ariadne felt that she was "born" (both physically and psychologically) from the constriction of her autistic, "me"-centred existence was a "not-me" situation which had become imbued with the "evil" which was "not-me". She had felt that she had been born into a world that was hostile to her "going-on-being". This had been made even more "evil" by her own "not-me" projections.

Also, anything which comes from inside the body is felt to be contaminating, contaminated and dirty. So being born from inside a mother made her dirty. Such patients make a rigid split between the inside and the outside of the body. They feel that their inside is turgid with the stink and filth of their unaccepted and unacceptable erotic excitements, rages, panics and griefs, all of which are experienced in a sensation-dominated way as irritating, dangerous body stuff which will be there forever. This is partly because what is inside cannot be seen and is therefore uncontrollable and dangerous. Thus they live an artificial sort of life. They are an empty fake, a hollow sham. They live solely in terms of outside appearances and body surfaces in order to avoid the inner, unknowable darkness about which they are in despair.

I talked with Ariadne about this in relation to the explosive shit of her tantrums, which were provoked by the frustration and terror of bodily discontinuity from the elemental being with whom she had struggled to feel eternally continuous. This shit was felt to be evil and obnoxious, and offended her prudery about bodily processes. I suggested that her reaction was to see the dirty evil of the panic and rage of her tantrums in other people. Following this interpretation, Ariadne had a flash of inspiration about the delusional jealousy which had plagued her for many years, and about which I had not been able to give her fundamental insight. She said: "I've just thought that perhaps I do the same with my ecstasy. I can't bear it so I see other people enjoying it and then I'm jealous of them." (This piece of insight was typical of the reflective interplay which characterised the session.) But why had Ariadne been driven to such desperate extremes of splitting between the "me" and the "not-me"?

Splitting between the "me" and the "not-me"

Autistic children have shown me that at elemental levels the rage, panic and grief of their infantile tantrums about frustrations, and their infantile ecstasy about satisfactions, were associated with bodily discharges. Such discharges are not acceptable to a depressed or obsessional mother who feels them to be obnoxious and unclean. Thus they are not acceptable to the developing sense of "me-ness" of the baby, for whom parental approval is important. This means that they are experienced as "not-me". The passive baby often becomes the "unusually good baby" described by so many mothers of autistic children. As several writers have found, those autistic children who have an early history of tantrums (or fits without organic cause) usually have a more favourable prognosis than those with the "unusually good baby" type of early history.

This splitting also operates in another sphere of such patients' functioning. Purity (cleanliness) becomes associated with the intellect and, because primitive emotions are associated with bodily discharges, the emotions become associated with dirtiness and are experienced as "evil". The scrupulously "clean" intellect becomes overvalued at the expense of the "dirty" emotions. As Dr Sydney Klein has said: "The sooner the analyst realises the existence of the hidden part of the patient [by which he means the autistic part], the less the danger of the analysis becoming an endless intellectual dialogue" (this volume, Chapter Eight). Becoming aware of the hidden autistic part of such patients enables us to understand their deeply rooted fear of emotion, and also helps us to avoid becoming trapped by their arid intellectualism. Let us now study their fear of emotion and other intangibles.

The autistic fear of intangibles

For autistic children, feeling safe is dependent upon the delusion of feeling in absolute control of a mother's body, which is felt to be a part of their body. The manipulation of autistic objects supports this delusion. These are not symbols of the mother's body; they are felt to be actual tangible bits of the mother's body experienced as part of their body which can be controlled at will. In Hanna Segal's terms they are "symbolic equations" (1957). The intellect can be used in a formal way in the service of this control and manipulation. It can narrow things down to what the child feels they should be, rather that helping him to see what they are. But emotions are a very different kettle of fish. They cannot be controlled and manipulated as tangible physical objects. To autistic children, however, only what can be controlled and manipulated in a tangible way seems real and safe. Thus emotional states either feel unreal or are felt to be bodily substances which are exceedingly evil and dangerous. If we talk to these children about emotions, they either do not know what we are talking about, or they turn away because it feels dangerous and unsafe. They may even feel that we are pelting them with dangerous bodily substances. The reassuring, enriching, intangible, safe-making aspects of emotions are not available to them.

It is the same with the reassuring, intangible processes of growth and healing. These cannot be seen, touched and manipulated, and so they cannot believe in them. Such children feel that they can make themselves grow by sticking extra bits onto their bodies. This is imitation of a quite concrete kind. Since they also feel that these bits are plucked from other bodies who will want to retrieve them, these reactions bring terror in their wake. Because they are so afraid of letting things happen to them over which they have no control, the reassurance that growth takes place naturally, without their having to do anything about it, is not available to them.

Similarly, autistic children have no reassuring awareness that they have inherent healing processes which will collaborate with therapeutic interventions. The whole of their efforts are directed towards "covering" or "blanketing" (to use Daisy's terms) the many holes and wounds which seem to afflict them. Thus such children live almost wholly in terms of manipulative, body-centred evasions and artificial fabrications associated with sensuous experiences on body surfaces. They derive no sense of safety from the natural, spontaneous processes which go unseen and uncontrolled by them.

As well as being cut off from the reassuring processes of growth and healing, these children are also cut off from the reassuring intangibles of fantasies, imaginations, memories, and reflective thought. Such children's potentialities for these activities are relatively untapped and unused. Thus in working with autistic children we come upon unrealised potentialities.

As Ariadne's autistic constriction became relieved, she became aware of another reassuring natural potentiality. This was her biological reproductive capacity. Realising this assuaged her distress about not being eternal and immortal. She helped me to be aware of this in the following way. She had been to see one of the productions of a fringe theatre group. The production, which was called *Vulture Culture*, made a great impression upon her. It was about the turtles which come up from the water onto the seashore to lay their eggs, which are immediately vandalised by humans. She realised that in walking through the evil amphitheatre she had been protecting her "eggs" which were threatened with being vandalised.

As well as her biological potentiality to have offspring which would carry her seed from generation to generation, and so help her to achieve a kind of immortality, Ariadne realised that these "eggs" were also her creative capacities which had been "vandalised" by her autistic predations. Until we had worked this over, she could not leave me. But we could not work this over until her autism had been modified, and she had developed more authentic means of feeling safe by realising that she was part of a creative process which would go on after her mother's body and her own body were no more. To extend Marion Milner's saying (1969), not only is the analyst "the servant of a process", but so is the patient. Ariadne was becoming able to be lived by her life, and so she developed a "rhythm of safety", the capacity for which she had previously been unaware that she had. It was beyond her manual and intellectual control. Like growth and healing, this potentiality was a "given". It occurred without her arranging that it should happen. It gave her a much greater sense of safety than her own puny manoeuvres. The possibility for her awareness of this creative capacity was the result of a significant breakthrough in our work together, which came about in the following way.

The significant breakthrough

About six months before Ariadne had the dreams which stimulated her important forward movements, and when she was in a state of despair about ever being ready to finish coming to see me, I began to wonder whether she was using parts of her body as autistic objects, as autistic children did. So I asked her quite directly whether she sucked or bit the inside of her cheeks, or sucked and bit her tongue, or wriggled her bottom to feel the faeces in her anus. She willingly told me that from being a little girl up to the present day, she had bitten and sucked the insides of her cheeks. Such autistic manoeuvres are hidden and secret. I had never seen Ariadne using them, and she would never have thought to tell me about them unless I had asked her directly.

I dealt with them in a similarly direct way by saying that it was important that she should try to stop doing these things. I explained to her that I thought she did them in order to delude herself that she had a fleshly bit of an everlasting mother always with her, so that she could feel that her body was continuous with that of an eternal fleshly being who completely ensured both her safety and her existence. This was an important turning point in Ariadne's treatment and cleared the way for the dreams which stimulated her awareness of the "rhythm of safety". This, at depth, arose from an acceptance of the rhythm of life with its joys and with its sorrows. (I remember an autistic child for whom this was exemplified by the inevitability of the changes of the seasons as he came through the country lanes to the converted pony-shed which I used as a therapy room.) Ariadne has since told me that my disciplining firmness in telling her to stop sucking and biting her cheeks made her feel that I really cared about whether she grew up in the right way. She will now sometimes tell me that in moments of stress she has found herself sucking her cheeks, and has immediately stopped doing it. Benign authority was becoming part of her experience of me.

After discovering Ariadne's use of part of her body as an autistic object, I concentrated on showing her how these "techniques" (as she came to call them) had prevented her from coming to terms with the inevitable facts of bodily separateness. She began to realise that her manipulative techniques had led her to delude herself that absences and partings could always be avoided. Thus mental activities which bridge the gap of separateness—such as fantasies, imaginations, thoughts, memories and metaphors—were very underdeveloped. No wonder that as a child she had been referred to me for "learning difficulties". Sadly, at that time I did not understand her autistic handicaps and so could not help her as fundamentally as I have been able to do in the second phase of her analysis.

I have come to realise that the autistic part of the personality is the part which avoids coming into the analysis. It is the intractable part of infantile experience which could not be "digested" and has been hidden away. As well as being locked away in autistic objects and autistic shapes, it can also be locked away in idiosyncratic movements and tics. I am reminded of James Robertson's film of Laura, the two-year-old, very controlled little girl who was separated from her mother by being hospitalised. She shut away this "unthinkable" experience by the tic of brushing her hand across her face, as if wiping away the tears she could not shed. On a more sophisticated level this hidden autistic part can be seen in some children's excessive preoccupation with tongue-twisters, conundrums and riddles. This was also characteristic of the ancient Celts described by Daphne Nash (in Tustin, 1986). It is the twisted part of the patient which feels unknown and unknowing because bodily separation from the mother has been experienced as an obliterating catastrophe.

Autism is anti-life, but "anti-life" is not synonymous with death. Dying is an inevitable part of the life process. Autistic techniques are reactions to avoid becoming conscious of the "black hole" of separation, of partings, of endings, and ultimately of death. In so doing, they cut the individual off from life. It is only as we become aware of the fact of death that we fully value life. In the second phase of treatment Ariadne began to realise that for her, endings and partings were not merely experienced as rejections (as they would be by more normal neurotic patients), they were experienced as a violent tearing apart of her body from that of a being with whom she had felt continuous, and who had unrealistically seemed to guarantee the continuity of her bodily existence. The wounds from this violent ripping apart needed to be healed before she could bear to end her bodily contact with me. As De Astis and Giannotti (1980) have shown, the caesura of birth is healed for both mother and baby, in normal development, by their mutual interactions with each other.

The autism had been a kind of plaster cast which had immobilised this wounded part of her. As she gave up her autistic practices, Ariadne became aware of her own intrinsic forces of healing, and also of the firm but tender care by which she was surrounded. In short, she became aware of "love", not of the sentimental "heart-throb" kind but as an adaptive adjustment to her needs which arose from reflective thought, which also became possible for her. She began to be able to experience the agony and the ecstasy of being a fallible, finite human being who could die. Instead of evading them, she began to face the conflicts, difficulties and pains of ordinary living. She found that there were joys as well as sorrows, and that as she experienced uprightness in herself and in me, she became able to bear both. Her fear of madness associated with dirt and disorder, against which the autism had been a protection, was also alleviated. She no longer feared that the discharge of uncouth feelings would pollute the *absolute* purity of her body and cloud the *absolute* clarity of her mind. These extreme splits were modified as she became aware of a shared integrative rhythm of adaptive human reciprocity which embraced both the acceptable "me" and the rejected "not-me".

For this development to become possible, Ariadne had needed to be sternly encouraged to give up her massive evasions of reality. Quite concretely, she had put her own narrow construction upon the outside world. Her autistic contrivances had made her stilted, narrow-minded and rigidly conforming, to the point of passivity and timidity. But underneath this shying away, she had felt very special.

All this had protected her from the inevitable pains of being a human being, but had also shut her away from being aware of, and of becoming capable of, love in its functions of empathy, interest, attention, consideration, compassion, care and understanding. The uncouth, brutal aspects of her nature had remained unmodified and had shocked her when she had encountered them.

Conclusion

Those fortunate individuals who, early in infancy, have been able to enjoy and internalise emotional experiences of a rhythmical, adaptive interaction of the mouth differentiated from the breast are receptive to later experiences such as human sexual love, and aesthetic and religious experiences. For such people, these are not used in shallow and stereotyped ways as autistic evasions of the inevitable realities of human existence. They are deeply felt experiences which build upon, enrich and revitalise that intrapsychic creation which Ariadne so aptly called "the rhythm of safety". This intangible creation is primitive but complex. It is what the autistic child should have achieved but has not.

Experiences at the breast—or bottle experienced in terms of an inbuilt expectation of the breast—provide a foretaste of the inevitable life situations to come. In relatively normal development these are met in the protected situation of the reverie of maternal preoccupation (Bion, 1962a; Winnicott, 1958). If this is disturbed, the infant is left in the grip of atavistic, savage terrors which played a part in human evolution but which are now vestigial. In normal development this savagery is humanised and civilised by that transforming empathic communion between mother and baby which is the earliest form of communication.

Early, basic, bedrock processes set the pattern for later experiences. If, for any reason, evasion becomes the predominating reaction, evasion becomes the way in which all later difficulties are dealt with. It is a long and arduous task for both therapist and patient to bring about changes in these basic structures. But the effort is worthwhile, for these patients give us new ways of catching the meaning of those wordless intangibles which are of such deep significance in human living. They also free us from the jargon and clichés of words that have been worn smooth by use. They stimulate us to evolve more feelingful ways of expressing things. As a result, the mental and spiritual life of both analyst and patient is strengthened. The reflective interactions which developed between Ariadne and myself have meant that for both of us, immortality has come to be seen in less crude terms than mere bodily survival. Thus this chapter has been written as a tribute to Ariadne, as also those recovered autistic children who, like her, have had the courage to face those mortal terrors which these patients experience with such hypersensitised intensity.

Note

1. This chapter was originally published in *Autistic Barriers in Neurotic Patients* (see below).

References

De Astis, G. & Giannotti, A. (1980). Birth and Autism: Some Considerations about the Early Mother-Child Relationship. Unpublished in English.

Mahler, M. (1961). On Sadness and Grief in Infancy and Childhood: Loss and Restoration of the Symbiotic Love Object. *Psychoanalytic Study of the Child 16*: 332–51.

Milner, M. (1969). *The Hands of the Living God*. London: Hogarth.

Sandler, J. (1960). The Background of Safety. *Int. J. Psychoanal. 41*: 191–198.

Segal, H. (1957). Notes on Symbol Formation. *Int. J. Psychoanal. 38*:391–7.

Tustin, F. (1986). *Autistic Barriers in Neurotic Patients*. London: Karnac.

Winniciott, D.W. (1958). *Collected Papers: Through Paediatrics to Psychoanalysis*. London: Tavistock.

CHAPTER TEN

The autistic object: its relationship with narcissism in the transference and countertransference of neurotic and borderline patients[1]

Mario J. Gomberoff, Carmen C. Noemi and Liliana Pualuan de Gomberoff

Introduction

Our concern with neurotic and borderline adult patients and children who present similar and specific difficulties in the development of psychoanalytic processes led us to study the autistic object described by Frances Tustin in several publications (1972, 1981, 1986). This autistic object was originally observed in children presenting infantile autistic psychosis. However, some authors, such as H.S. Klein (Chapter Eight), Oelsner (1986, 1987a, 1987b) and Tustin herself (1972, 1981, 1986) apply this concept to other clinical phenomena and syndromes.

We are particularly interested in transference and counter-transference, because we think that the relation established with the autistic object is expressed in the analytical situation as a phenomenon likely to be clearly defined through a transferential relationship with the analyst, who acts countertransferentially without being able to realise that the analytical process is arrested. The analyst is trapped in a transference-countertransference relation which constitutes an autistic amalgam, a fusion which operates as an element, not only shared but established as a prolongation of his own self and the patient's. Such fusion distorts the analytical function, precluding observation. A barrier is formed which is difficult to eliminate through interpretation. We will finish this paper by discussing a clinical case in an attempt to illustrate what has been described.

Preliminary considerations

In a previous paper (1987) we attempted to make some developments on a model of the mind previously referred to by many psycho-analysts. In this model, prior to the emergence of the mental representation itself which is allowed by symbolisation (and thus before the consolidation of the representation of object relations with separateness between self and object), the forerunners of these phenomena become imprinted in the organism, forming mosaics. These imprints are subsequently followed by those of the mental representations of object relationships in the classical dynamics— symbiotic, transitional, partial, total, etc. Prior to these last imprints, there are some phenomena which also become imprinted, forming very primitive mosaics, which have been conceptualised as autistic, of primitive or primary identification (Freud, 1923), of fusion of the self with the object (Kernberg, 1976), of the agglutinate nucleus (Bleger, 1967), and so on. Tustin (1981) designates the period when these primitive phenomena occur the auto-sensuous state. In this period she distinguishes normal auto-sensuous objects and autistic pathological objects. The conceptualisations of Mahler (1975) and Kernberg (1976) explain, in our opinion, the fused object relationship of the autistic stage. Each primitive or complex object relation constitutes a subsystem of the mosaic which in turn is part of new, broader configurations that form supra-systems.

In contrast with what takes place in a real kaleidoscope, in the mental one the mosaic images persist, though only the last created are consciously perceived. The surface or depth of the mental kaleidoscope can be focused from different referential schemes. The vision resulting from these approaches will be either macroscopic or microscopic—with always limited and more or less encompassing visual fields.

The fusion of the autistic object with the self implies that separation produces laceration, a kind of mutilation. The autistic object may be something material, hard, a gesture or a stereotyped behaviour, or a particular ordering of elements. It is rigid, inflexible and inanimate; it precludes growth, fantasy and thought. Separateness which would allow suspense, delay, illusion and idea only causes anger and panic: the "nameless dreads" (Bion, 1962). Mother and autistic child or patient and analyst may therefore remain in a "static cocoon of ecstasy", constituting a prolonged autistic relationship.

We postulate that the relations with auto-sensuous and autistic objects remain in the configuration of the most primitive mosaics. Nevertheless, in neurotic or borderline patients, under certain circumstances (mourning, the onset of analysis, etc.) some pieces of these mosaics which had taken shape in the past may become reactivated and emerge in the present mosaics. In these cases, segments of the personality, current object relations, may remain static, as if the kaleidoscope movement had become stuck in certain sections of the mosaics.

Relations of the autistic object with the concepts of narcissism

We would like to discuss certain relations between the concepts of narcissism and those of auto-sensuousness and autism proposed by Frances Tustin. Several authors, including H.S. Klein (Chapter Eight), Oelsner (1986, 1987a, 1987b), Innes-Smith (1987) and Rosenfeld (1987) among others, have been concerned with the clinical applications of the concepts developed by Tustin (1981).

According to Tustin, sensations predominate in the auto-sensuous state. Only subsequently, during narcissism, upon the separate development of the self, could certain mental products which require a higher degree of organisation, like emotions, begin to predominate. In Tustin's opinion, in the earlier stages of development, the child begins to react to the external world in connection with his own body, according to innate dispositions and inherited behavioural guidelines. At that time the child believes that the mother is a part of his own body, constituting "sensations", hence we could call her a "sensation object". At this stage the postulate of a mental structure with representations is not yet required. The infant's processes are almost exclusively neurophysiological. Rosenfeld (1987) and Bion (1980) call these phenomena projective identifications, although they state that they correspond to a more primitive process than the traditional one. Rosenfeld points out that they could be considered as forerunners of the projective identification itself. Steiner (1982) and Felton (1985) also describe phenomena with similar characteristics. We think that projective identification requires on the part of the child at least the presence of a certain awareness of this physical separation from the mother. Some of these previous processes, fore-runners of projective identification, had already been described by Hermann in 1929; they were recalled by Tustin (1972, 1981) as "flowing-over-at-oneness" to recover the sense of "primal unity". This concept is related to the scattering of Oelsner (1987b), the imitation of Gaddini (1969), and the adhesive identification of Bick (1968) and Meltzer (1975). What would lead to this "overflow" would be the urgency to reconstruct the primary unity with the mother, the fusion which would have been broken, threatening survival.

The actual separation from the mother in these early stages is endured through the utilisation of an auto-sensuous object, which permits the recreation of the primitive illusion of self-satisfaction and self-sufficiency. If that auto-sensuous object should not exist, the actual separation from the mother would be felt as a laceration of the body. The auto-sensuous object and "good mothering" (Winnicott, 1971) will favour the development of inner representations, the consciousness of the self and of the object. The constitutional incapacity of the child to use the auto-sensuous object makes him liable to develop autistic pathological processes.

The different approaches of Freud (1910, 1913, 1914, 1923) to the subject of narcissism permitted other authors later to develop diverging conceptualisations or to use them with other meanings. Mahler (1975) agrees with Freud (1923) about primary narcissism in a non-object stage of his theory of development. She starts from non-differentiated states between self and object until the mental representations of self and object are consolidated separately. How-ever, Mahler (1960) proposes to extend the concept of object relation to anything which in a field of interaction—physiologically or otherwise—may affect the organism in intrauterine or extrauterine life, without discussing whether or not mental representations exist in such processes.

Tustin (1981) agrees with Freud's conceptualisation (1914) that the appearance of narcissism would be preceded by auto-erotism. When Mahler (1975) speaks about primary narcissism in this stage, we must assume that she is referring to the libido in the id and not in the ego, inasmuch as the latter has not yet developed sufficiently. Tustin (1981) agrees with Mahler in regarding the existence of this autistic phase as part of normal development, in which bodily sensations would predominate. Tustin does not consider this a non-object phase. She states that object relations operate from the beginning of life, though permeated by primary auto-sensuousness, so that there is a non-differentiation between the baby and the objects which are felt as a sensorial continuity of his own body.

Jacobson (1964a) reserves the term "primary narcissism" exclusively for the period prior to the development of self and object images. In her view (1964b), the libido cathexis of the fused representation of self and object marks, at the same time, the origin of self-love (or narcissism) and of object-love, so that both develop simultaneously.

According to Kernberg (1976), narcissism and object cathexis are simultaneous, which implies that the concept of primary narcissism becomes less important. Melanie Klein (1952a, 1952b) and her followers assume the existence of an ego and of part objects from birth. Fusing of the self and the object, according to Klein and her first disciples, would be only partially possible, in projective and introjective identifications. For Klein, the possibility of primary narcissism does not exist inasmuch as object relations—as we said before—are established from birth.

We think (1987) that even before the possibility of mental representation, there exist relations of physiological response to external objects which will be the forerunners of the object relation, which will become fused in its first representation. The stage we are referring to could be named "unobjectal", in the sense that there are no object representations, provided that this does not mean disregarding the intensive dynamics of exchange between subject and objects, with the acute need of the former for the latter. We could accept that this stage is one of intensive narcissism which may be called primary as long as we accept that primary narcissism does not presuppose the existence of ego, and that the libido, in a phase previous to the consolidation of mental representation, operates from the id, producing exchanges with the environment. In this context, let us recall that Freud, in "Inhibitions, Symptoms and Anxiety" (1926), refers to the narcissism of germ cells.

We could postulate a first phase dealing predominantly with environment relations, essentially with neurophysiological and biological characteristics and without mental representations; and a second phase where there will be undifferentiated, fused mental representations of self and object. Later on, self and object representations would become differentiated and separated. The first two phases could be assimilated to a phase of auto-sensuousness. When we wonder whether the above-mentioned phases are unobjectal or whether primary narcissism predominates in them, the answers will depend on the theoretical scheme we use. If in the auto-sensuousness phase we accept narcissism and the existence of objects as neurophysiological stimuli subsequently fused with the self, we could propose that Tustin's autistic object is a crystallised aspect of pathological narcissism in this stage, whereas the auto-sensuous object is a crystallised aspect of normal narcissism in the same stage.

Given that Melanie Klein is among the authors more distant from this concept of autism, her recent followers are possibly those who have referred most to this early period of the psyche. Tustin makes constant use of the Kleinian conceptualisation. Bleger (1967) refers to the "glischrocaric" stage as one previous to the paranoid-schizoid position, a stage where the notion of object as conceived by Klein would not exist. Bick (1968) and Meltzer *et al.* (1975) described defensive mechanisms which are more primitive than the projective identification that supposes a relation with a differentiated object. Such mechanisms correspond to very primitive identifications of an imitative type. Bick described adult patients who "stuck themselves" or "adhered" because they had difficulties in experimenting with the necessary space for introjection using projective identification. Meltzer described subjects expressing behaviours which were substitutive formations close to imitation, but hiding intensive disintegration states. The later authors describe very precocious processes and dynamics having normal or pathological sources and common denominators. The differences we find among them depend on the various referential schemes they use.

The autistic object in transference and countertransference

Different types of patients with characteristics similar to ours have been described recently: the "anti-analysing" and "disaffected patients" of Joyce McDougall (1978, 1984), the "scattered" patients of Oelsner (1987), and those of S. Klein who present "cystic" phenomena, among others.

Liberman (1958), while not referring to the autistic object itself, appears to describe clinical phenomena very similar to those described by Tustin. He designates the type of relation established by the patient in the analytical situation as transferential autism. The effect of such transference can be expressed by a halt in the projection-introjection interplay, in the transferential relation, where the analyst gets involved. The clinical elements described seem quite similar to those pointed out by us in the autistic phenomena.

Rodrigué (1966) describes two types of autistic transference. One of them is very much like that described by Liberman, which corresponds to Bleuler's concept of autism. It is not easy to detect, because the patient would appear to be connected to the analyst: he receives the interpretation and responds to it with interesting and confirmative material; yet this is a "pseudo-response". Rodrigué describes this as a refractory outward attitude, where nothing penetrates inside the patient, who becomes a mirror in which the analyst is reflected. The analyst would act as Narcissus, becoming fascinated by the reflection of his interventions, looking repeatedly at himself and not at the patient proper. The other type of transferential autism would be that described by Kanner, where the "analyst object" does not exist for the patient, yet the patient's inner world is perfectly clear and visible to the analyst, but completely inaccessible, as if there were a glass in between.

Kanner points out that interpretation in such a situation should have the characteristics of active incision, of perforation of the mirror of the glass. The words used by Liberman, Rodrigué and Tustin are quite consistent in their description of the phenomena: "inaccessible", "refractory", "hard", "mirror", "glass", "perforation", "incision".

However, Liberman and Rodrigué refer to a more global type of relation, of a narcissist character, and they do not use the concept of autistic object. We believe that clinically it is possible to distinguish when these phenomena obey a more global and extended situation of narcissism and when they are due to the emergence of an autistic object. The latter, however, could appear as a consolidation of the more extended phenomena described as narcissistic. It is precisely in such cases that we suggest that perhaps the autistic object is what consolidates and crystallises the narcissistic processes, self-carrying and hiding the narcissistic structures of both participants.

Boschan (1987) emphasises the importance of countertransferential aspects in order to detect autistic and narcissistic phenomena, differentiating autistic defences from narcissistic defences in countertransference. The autistic-type modality evokes a countertransferential state of disconnection and incapacity to think; the narcissistic modality evokes frustration due to lack of response; moreover, the patient's indifference causes inattention, annoyance and forgetfulness of material in the analyst.

The repercussion in the countertransference of transferential autism was described in 1979 by Pualuan, who pointed out that the patient's withdrawal and avoidance of contact with the analyst and with himself can produce phenomena which may be designated by the generic term of countertransferential autism. The characteristics of this are similar to those described by Boschan in the countertransferential record of patients with autistic transferential modality. In our opinion, the analyst may not only get in touch with his own objects when these are evoked or awakened by the analysed patient, but he may also impose his own objects on the patient. This situation involves the risk of transforming the analysis into a process where the analyst imposes his image and/or his objects on the patient, endangering the development of the analytical process. The analyst could "fascinate" the patient with his own autistic objects and share the "autistic cocoon" created by both of them. The patient may respond with fascination to the theory, consolidated rigidly and without movement on the part of the analyst. As a consequence, both enter into the "cocoon" of theory, and moreover, the analyst registers clinical confirmation of it. If the patient does not confirm the analyst's theory and is neither fascinated by it nor accepts interpretations derived from it, it is possible that in his conceptualisations and actions the analyst may consider this patient's reactions as a negative therapeutic reaction, as an "impasse" such as jealousy, aggressive constitutional impulses, etc. These new secondary theories could be used to cover the emptiness and the gap felt by the analyst in face of the lack of confirmation and consistency from the patient with respect to his own "autistic object theory". If the patient does not respond to the theories, the analyst is liable to become disorganised and unstructured. In this case, he may seek support from other people: colleagues or supervisors. He will defend himself against the feeling of disintegration caused by the lack of response from the patient who did not agree to place himself in the proposed counter-transferential "cocoon". The supervisor's contributions are likely to be used as a new proposition by the analyst to the patient for entering the "cocoon".

As Schumacher Finnell says (1985), "not always can the narcissism in the analyst be a reaction to the narcissism of the patient; it may even be detached from the pathology of the patient". Chasseguet-Smirgel and Grunberger (1979) say, along the same lines, that as analysts we must not impose our narcissism on the patient and that we must be aware of such a possibility. The analyst may impose his own narcissism on that of the patient instead of giving him back the one which legitimately belongs to him. Gaddini (1969) states also that if as analysts we put our image into the analysand instead of discovering who he or she is, the outcome will be an imitative analysand, or a double, in the image and likeness of the analyst. Sydney Klein (Chapter Eight), though not speaking specifically of the autistic object, refers to autistic phenomena in neurotic patients which could go unnoticed by the analyst, and, if not detected, might transform analysis into a fruitless and arrested situation.

The later authors emphasise the importance of countertransference for the detection and solution of these autistic and narcissistic transferential phenomena. Autistic transference is detected only through the emotional response of the analyst who resounds in very similar aspects to those of the patient. The partial fusion of analyst and patient consolidates and establishes the autistic object. The patient may establish the autistic object by taking aspects from the setting or from the analyst, the latter not being aware of what is going on. In other cases, the patient acts, urging the analyst to respond, and this becomes a repeating situation. The patient's action has a conventional meaning which is familiar to the analyst; yet for the patient it is not the same: to him this action becomes an autistic object. The transferential and countertransferential phenomena described by the rest of the later authors possibly do not have the rigidity, stability, hardness and borderline quality presented by those of the autistic object. They are also more accessible to interpretation.

Clinical case

This case is that of a 40-year-old patient. A successful artist, he has had diverse psychotherapeutic experiences which became good friendships. After breaking up a couple relationship one month before coming to the therapist, the patient suffered from violent crises of anxiety, involving his physical and psychic condition. He had a sensation which he described as disintegration and laceration. He felt paralysed and was unable to cope with his work.

The onset of treatment developed in a very special atmosphere. The patient spoke about the different stages of his life and certain painful episodes, using a rich language full of beautiful metaphors. Analyst and patient together made important and fascinating discoveries in relation to what happened to him during his mother's pregnancy and the birth, generating fantasies which emerged in the analytical relation and which were verified when the patient investigated after the sessions. For instance, during one of the sessions the patient suffered from distressing fantasies: he felt he was drifting in a viscous fluid which led him to a fatal abyss: all this was stimulated by the feeling of being rejected by the analyst. He asked his mother and found out that when she was expecting him she had symptoms of abortion and haemorrhage throughout the nine months of her pregnancy. The distress that usually accompanies this kind of experience was alleviated or virtually disappeared, concealed under the enthusiasm and pleasure experienced by the analytical couple upon uncovering such interesting and dramatic events. The intense symptoms that led the patient to see the therapist readily disappeared. It seemed as if the analysis had replaced the lost object, whose lack had triggered the symptoms.

After some months of this treatment, the analyst had the feeling of contemplating the development of an analytical process virtually in the control of the patient himself. Furthermore, the interpretations of the analyst were taken as material which the patient eventually used for his artistic creations outside the sessions, so that he seemingly formed with the analyst a couple which gave rise to artistic production.

The analytical process went deeper without causing suffering. Sometimes the analyst had to make an effort to remember that he was working. All this began to induce a growing discomfort which turned into a feeling of loss of the analytical function; but at the same time this was covered by a sensation of enchantment. During a session in the third year of analysis, as the analyst had been absent for the two previous days, the patient began to refer to this fact, at the same time relating diverse interesting fantasies about it. However, the analyst was overcome with a feeling of emotional emptiness and felt as if the patient were just "making noise" and not communicating. He interrupted him and showed him how he was referring only to his thoughts: "You are telling me that you think this or that, and you don't say what you feel!" Then he asked directly: "What do you feel?" The patient was silent for a while and answered that he had been very anxious those two days, with problems of tachycardia, extrasystole and "body noises", as he called them. He believed that there had been no reason to justify such a state, except that he had drunk too much coffee one day and that had undoubtedly caused his troubles. He stated that he did not connect them with the absence of his analyst because his was a "violent, distressing physical state with acute pain"; "maybe angina pectoris?" he wondered. He added that tranquillisers readily soothed his pain.

The analyst then showed him the connection between the kinds of sensations he described, associated with deadly anxieties connected to situations in which he felt lonely and abandoned. The patient agreed enthusiastically and said that curiously enough, abandonment and proximity evoke almost the same thing: both of them are speaking from two opposite poles, but at the same time they are so closely linked. He said that he should be all right, that everything was quiet, he was able to live alone and at peace, and had everything very well organised. He had a maid who was in charge of the shopping, the meals, the bills. He had solved his work problem, which allowed him to continue his analysis without risking interruptions. He had established non-stable, transient relations with three women, two during the week and one at the weekend. Despite all this, he would undergo this state, somewhat organic, when he suffered from a feeling of loneliness. He recalled other situations in which he had undergone what he called "body noise". He spoke, and the analyst felt that the patient was theorising and that he was referring to other factors, listing them and connecting them to explain what happened to him. He made a synthesis of what he said, recalled situations of his childhood. He spoke about a friend, a psychologist who once told him that he had an anaclitic depression, and said that he did not know what that was, despite having looked up the term and read its meaning. The analyst heard just a blabber. The patient said happily: "It's like I'm making science". The analyst interrupted him sharply: "You are not making science, you are just making noise; you are trying to cool off everything that is going on!" The analyst caught himself talking angrily, pointedly and more loudly than usual. He lowered his voice at once and continued his interpretation in the usual manner, saying that the patient "spoke and exhibited himself as an adult, but he actually felt very small, terrified and afraid of dying because he was left alone, and instead of complaining or getting angry produced this word-noise". The patient changed his attitude, became anxious, and began to talk in a different pitch, modulating less and omitting syllables. Most unusually, he appeared as a disorganised patient, at loss without the support of the language and of his intelligence which allowed him to use attractive conceptual images. The analyst was concerned and thought he might have been too energetic and abrupt, feeling responsible for the patient's defencelessness.

The patient said: "Should I get angry? I don't know how to do it. Something happened that I'm not like this and I get cooled down and get paralysed without being able to do 'anitin' . . . I have a knot . . . like a knot down here, that's stopping me, I don't want to be like this . . . 'latht' week . . . I felt very much like making the effort, how do I do it? Tell me, even only as a behaviourist, there must be some way to learn to react: I don't feel nothing with 'ye' . . . not resentment, or anger, 'notin' . . . " The analyst interpreted this by telling him that apparently he would not be resentful or angry, but he felt very lonely and scared because the analyst had failed him and he thought about behaviourism, or whatever might replace him. He stayed quiet, hesitated, and said that he did not mean what he had said. He didn't speak for a while; however, he quickly recovered and made a beautiful image of a river with two kinds of noises: the upper and the lower noise. The upper noise was at the surface; it was very beautiful and was seen and heard by everyone. The lower one was that of the deep regions, of slippery rocks, dark rocks, not seen or heard, and having nothing to do with the analyst but with his own mother, and so on. Again, the analyst began to hear blabber. Once more he interrupted him abruptly, and interpreted that he was using the language and his intelligence to create in the analysis a superficial and aesthetic relationship that he could control, in order to prevent the analyst from getting into the depths, not letting him sink in the turbid waters of the river bed, which was full of slippery stones. The patient, who at first was scared, began to smile as he listened to the last sentences, and the analyst then realised that he had colluded in the same expressive, superficial and aesthetic use of the language that the patient utilised. At that moment the analyst interrupted himself and said firmly: "I am also using a language that is sheer noise, but you smile, you are soothed because my noise allows you to move away from something which pains you very much and which is hard for you to understand and to communicate."

The patient was again distressed and said confusedly that on arriving he had a feeling of deep mistrust, that he did not want to tell him about it because he thought: "What I feel has 'notin' to do with 'ye' . . . it's with my mummy . . . I thought that but I felt 'notin' to do with ma . . . it's with 'ye' . . . I saw you exactly like my mummy, I distrusted you absolutely . . . But what happens if I distrust 'ye' . . . there . . . 'whaaat' . . . if I can't trust 'ye' . . . I don't care about anything else, I'd rather let it pass . . . this is a . . . crazy 'ting' of mine . . . I'm going crazy, it's that I'm mad because of the deception, I know 'notin' . . . "

The analyst told him that this sensation of madness, of despair because of the absence was terrible and dark, a feeling of drifting with nothing to hold on to. The patient said that he himself did not realise at first what was happening to him, he thought that the analyst had been absent because of a cold, but all of a sudden he began to doubt everything. He said: "From inside I felt a crazy thing . . . what do I do with another person? I felt that you were somebody else. I don't accept impostors; an aunt took care of me, another woman gave me milk, I did not accept impostors for my mamma [he moaned, his voice was broken], I wanted her. I am terribly insecure, I understand everything from my brain and justify it . . . I imagine that you lie and I am scared, unsure, resentful, distant, 'evryting' together [he hesitated and spoke in a tearful tone] . . . and I think that I like 'ye' but I have to be 'caarful'; in the depth of the river the rocks are darker, uglier, 'slipary', even 'noisiless' . . . "

The analyst told him that what he felt when he thought the analyst had abandoned him was so painful, ugly, dangerous and slippery that he would rather not speak about it or feel it, but preferred to get away and produce noises, words, in order not to feel the pain. He remained silent, and sighed deeply. The analyst asked him what he was feeling. He answered, very touched, that he did not know for certain, he could not describe it; he felt like weeping, like grief; he was struggling against this, because he was going to burst into tears and "go through a black hole inside". He said that from a very early age he had become an acrobat who had learned to clutch at anything in order to survive.

Comments on the clinical case

From the very beginning of the analysis the patient made use of and proposed to the analyst autistic objects which were often difficult to detect. The material we submit shows the utilisation of some aspects of the verbal language as one of these objects.

On describing the case, we commented that in the first stages of the treatment the analyst was struck by the verbal language of the patient: rich, poetical, full of metaphors, used with intelligence and great aestheticism. The analyst did not realise at first that this tool was being used not for useful communication but rather for pseudo-insight, pseudo-communication and pseudo-analysis. The interpretations of the first stages of the analysis were taken by the patient to form autistic objects. The patient clung to the words of the analyst, inserted them into his speech, and made them fit into a compact whole. He made every effort to ensure that his discourse should not disagree with that of the analyst. In this way there was no "me" and "not-me", there was no gap, there was only one. Patient and analyst fused into a single discourse, constructed by the patient. The difficulty of the analyst in detecting the autistic object the patient offered him allowed the existence of a kind of cocoon within which both were mutually fascinated by the game of words. This greatly hindered the opportunities for detecting the autistic object.

With time, the patient has managed to use verbal language for more useful communication. He speaks less than in the first stages of his treatment; sometimes he has difficulties in expressing himself. However, upon an abrupt and unexpected absence of the analyst, the patient once again underwent the sensation of brutal and premature disappointment that he had experienced in the first days of his life, when he felt his mother had abandoned him. The patient attempted to reduce the intolerable pain and catastrophic anxieties that tormented him by reverting to an artefact, the verbal language, again used as an autistic object which allowed him to alleviate these sensations.

The analyst is liable to reinforce the autistic quality of some aspects of the patient's language when his interpretation follows too closely the patient's turn of speech and style and he leaves aside his own expressive mode.

The material we have presented shows the difficulties of the analyst in removing the autistic object. When he has seemingly achieved it, the patient re-arms himself and again has recourse to his artefact. The analyst feels that the only way to penetrate the hard autistic carapace of the language is through very violent interpretative manoeuvres which are not in keeping with his usual methods. Through his autistic object the patient attempts to avoid "slipping", "being aborted", and "drifting through a black hole", and this is why, like "an acrobat", he clings to it.

The clinical case and the kaleidoscope

Using the kaleidoscopic model, the mosaic formed by the patient in the analysis and the way his analyst envisions him is agreeable, aesthetically beautiful, but motionless. The countertransferential reactions allow and force the analyst to alter his usual style of working in the analysis. Through an action that we could describe as abrupt—even aggressive—movement is re-established, as if the analyst had shaken the kaleidoscope to loosen the immobility of the mosaic. This movement discloses very primitive aspects, much earlier mosaics of the patient's mental kaleidoscope. The relationship which the patient then establishes with the analyst is characterised by regression and the appearance of extremely childish elements. The language deteriorates and pre-verbal aspects arise in the patient, together with bodily sensations felt in the earliest stages of development. It would seem that the jolt undergone by the mental kaleidoscope of the patient had obliterated the more integrated levels which allowed better organised mosaics: as if something had been broken, and wants, absences and gaps emerged. The movement is restored in very primitive areas associated to sensations of awe and anxiety both in the patient and in the analyst. In our current experience with these patients the previous functioning levels are eventually re-established. This is because the patient quickly seeks to restore the same autistic object or tries to find a new one. Only step by step, and after going through periods of great anxiety and pain, is the patient able to resort to a separate live object, instead of seeking the autistic object.

There is a deficit in the patient's structure which is felt like an emptiness, a hole. This becomes a threat for the integrity of the patient. To plug these holes, the patient has had recourse, from the earlier stages of his development, to what we term autistic objects. Such objects become part of the scaffolding that supports him.

In this case, the patient comes to the analysis bearing in his structure words which are used as an autistic object. He displays them to the analyst, who in turn becomes entangled in them, not realising that this link precludes the use of verbal language for true communication within the analytic process. A transferential-countertransferential relationship has been created through a mutual autistic object.

We believe that the only way to analyse patients' structural autistic objects is to undergo—within the framework of the analytical relationship—the experience of sharing the autistic object with them. Nonetheless, this implies the risk of arresting the process, at least in part, if the analyst does not realise its existence.

Note

1. This chapter was originally published in the *International Journal of Psychoanalysis*, 1990, p. 71.

References

Bick, E. (1968). The Experience of the Skin in Early Object Relations. *Int. J. Psychoanal. 49*: 484–6.

Bion, W.R. (1962). *Learning from Experience.* London: Heinemann. Reprinted London: Karnac, 1984.

Bion, W.R. (1980). *Bion in New York and São Paulo.* Strathtay: Clunie Press.

Bleger, J. (1967). La Simbiosis en el Reposo del Guerrero. In: *Simbiosis y Ambigüedad* (pp. 39–75). Buenos Aires: Paidos, 1975.

Boschan, P. (1987). Dependencia y Resistencias Narcisísticas en el Proceso Psicoanalítico. *Rev. Psicoanál (AP de BA) 8*:183–199.

Chasseguet-Smirgel, J. & Grunberger, B. (1979). El Narcisismo del Analista: una Introducción. *Rev. Psicoanál (AP de BA) 1*:135–150.

Felton, J. (1985). Personal communication cited by H. Rosenfeld in *Impasse and Interpretation* (pp. 185–186). London: Tavistock, 1987.

Freud, S. (1910). Leonardo da Vinci and a Memory of his Childhood. *SE 11.*

Freud, S. (1912–13). Totem and Taboo. *SE 13.*

Freud, S. (1914). On Narcissism: an Introduction. *SE 14.*

Freud, S. (1923). The Ego and the Id. *SE 19.*

Freud, S. (1926). Inhibitions, Symptoms and Anxiety. *SE 20.*

Gaddini, E. (1969). On Imitation. *Int. J. Psychoanal. 50*: 475–84.

Gomberoff, M. (1988). El Método Psicoanalítico. Comentario sobre los Relatos de Luiz Mayer y Benzion Winograd. Sao Paulo: XVII Congreso Latinoamericano de Psicoanálisis (unpublished).

Gomberoff, M., Noemi, C. & Pualuan, L. (1987). Algunas Aplicaciones Clínicas del Objeto Autista. Buenos Aires: IX Simposio y Congreso Interno (AP de BA) II (pp. 234–263).

Hermann, I. (1929). Das Ich und das Denken. Vienna: Internationaler Psychoanalytischer Verlag. Cited by F. Tustin in *Autistic States in Children*, London: Routledge & Kegan Paul, 1981.

Innes-Smith, J. (1987). Pre-Oedipal Identification and the Cathexis of Autistic Objects in the Aertiology of Adult Psychopathology *Int. J. Psychoanal. 68*: 405–413.

Jacobson, E. (1964a). Narcissism, Masochism and the Concepts of Self and Self Representations. In: *The Self and the Object World* (pp. 3–23). New York: Int. Univ. Press.

Jacobson, E. (1964b). The Fusions between Self and Object Images and the Earliest Types of Identifications. In: *The Self and the Object World* (pp. 33–48). New York: Int. Univ. Press.

Kernberg, O. (1976). *Object Relations Theory and Clinical Psychoanalysis.* New York: Jason Aronson.

Klein, M. (1952a). Some Theoretical Conclusions Regarding the Emotional Life of the Infant. In: *Developments in Psychoanalysis* (pp. 198–236). London: Hogarth.

Klein, M. (1952b). On Observing the Behaviour of Young Infants. In: *Developments in Psychoanalysis* (pp. 237–270). London: Hogarth.

Liberman, D. (1958). Autismo Transferencial: Narcisismo, el Mito de Eco y Narciso. In: *Conflictos Psicologicas del Niño y la Familia* (pp. 135–163). Buenos Aires: Rodolfo Alonso Editor, 1973.

McDougall, J. (1978). The Anti-Analysand in Analysis. In: *Plea for a Measure of Abnormality* (pp. 213–246). New York: Int. Univ. Press, 1980.

McDougall, J. 1984 The "Dis-Affected" Patient: Reflections on Affect Pathology. *Psychoanal. Q. 53*: 386–409.

Mahler, M. (1960). Perceptual Dedifferentiation and Psychotic Object Relationship. In: *The Selected Papers of Margaret S. Mahler, Volume 1* (pp. 183–192). New York: Jason Aronson, 1979.

Mahler, M. (1975). *The Psychological Birth of the Human Infant.* London: Hutchinson.

Meltzer, D., Bremner, J., Hoxter, S., Weddell, D. & Wittenberg, I. (1975). *Explorations in Autism: A Psycho-Analytical Study.* Strathtay: Clunie Press.

Oelsner, R. (1986). Alicia a través del Espejo y lo que Contó del Otro Lado. Paper given at Buenos Aires: VIII Simposio y Congreso Interno (AP de BA).

Oelsner, R. (1987a). Variaciones sobre el Tema del Autismo: "El Paciente Nonato". Paper given at the 35th Congress of the Internatioanl Psychoanalytical Association, Montreal.

Oelsner, R. (1987b). Vulnerabilidad y Fenómenos Autistas. Paper given at Buenos Aires: IX Simposio y Congreso Interno (AP de BA).

Pualuan, L. (1979). Autismo Transferencial en el Comienzo de un Análisis. Paper given at Asociación Psicoanalítica Chilena.

Rodrigué, E. (1966). Autismo Transferencial. In: *El Contexto del Proceso Psicoanalítico* (pp. 151–179). Buenos Aires: Paidos.

Rosenfeld, H. (1987). Projective Identification in Clinical Practice. In: *Impasse and Interpretation* (pp. 157–190). London: Tavistock.

Schumacher Finnell, J. (1985). Narcissistic Problems in Analysis. *Int. J. Psychoanal. 66*: 413–445.

Steiner, R. (1982). Intonation and Osmotic Communication. Unpublished paper cited by H. Rosenfeld in *Impasse and Interpretation*, London: Tavistock, 1987.

Tustin, F. (1972). *Autism and Childhood Psychosis*. London: Hogarth.

Tustin, F. (1981). *Autistic States in Children*. London: Routledge & Kegan Paul.

Tustin, F. (1986). *Autistic Barriers in Neurotic Patients*. London: Karnac.

Winnicott, D.W. (1951). Transitional Objects and Transitional Phenomena. In: *Playing and Reality*. London: Tavistock, 1971.

CHAPTER ELEVEN

Working analytically with autistic-contiguous aspects of experience[1]

Thomas H. Ogden

In this chapter, I will attempt to convey aspects of my thinking about the way I work both with patients who are living in the solipsistic world of pathological autism and with patients who are experiencing the world in terms of normal early infantile experience of a sensation-based sort. The earliest sensation-based experience of the infant—and possibly of the foetus—can devolve into pathological autism as a consequence of a combination of constitutional and environmental problems. The constitutional hypersensitivity to stimuli (i.e. an inadequate capacity for filtering and ordering stimuli) may in some cases be so severe that even good mothering is not sufficient to supplement the infant's capacity to filter and organise his experience. The infant is so "raw" (metaphorically skinless) psychically that he cannot tolerate the unexpected. Consequently, human interaction, with all of its inherent unpredictability, is unbearably painful and leads the infant or child to withdraw into an inner, lifeless, mechanical world governed by autistic defences (forms of psychic self-protection that I will be describing in the course of this chapter).

I should explain at the outset what I mean by the *autistic-contiguous position*. It is a concept I have introduced which refers to the most primitive, healthy psychic organisation (see Ogden, 1989, for more detailed discussions of this concept as well as many of the other concepts introduced in this chapter). It involves a sensation-dominated way of organising experience. One might think of it as a psychic perspective or vantage point from which earliest experience is viewed by the infant and which continues as a dimension of all subsequent experience at every stage of life. Of course, everything one says about the infant's experience is a speculation. I think of such speculations as metaphors which I may find useful in working with the patient who is in my consulting room with me.

I will begin by describing the shapes the world may take from the perspective of the autistic-contiguous position and pathological autism. I will then discuss the experiential differences between the world of autistic-contiguous and pathological autism; the experience of anxiety from an autistic-contiguous perspective; forms of self-protection (modes of defence) against danger in the psychological world of autistic-contiguous experience; and finally, the ways one is shaped by experience at the autistic-contiguous level of the personality. I will offer clinical examples at each step along the way.

Autistic shapes and objects

Tustin (1980, 1984) has described two types of experience with objects which constitute important means of ordering and defining experience in the autistic-contiguous position. The first of these forms of relatedness to objects (which only an outside observer would recognise as a relationship to an external object) is the creation of "autistic shapes" (1984). Shapes generated in an autistic-contiguous mode must be distinguished from what we ordinarily think of as the shape of an object. These early shapes are "felt shapes" (Tustin, 1986, p. 280) arising from the experience of soft touching of surfaces, which makes a sensory impression. The experience of shape in an autistic-contiguous mode does not involve the conception of the "objectness" or "thingness" of what is being felt. As Tustin (1984) describes it, we can attempt to create for ourselves the experience of an autistic shape if we reduce the chair we are sitting on to the sensation it makes on our buttocks. From this perspective there is no sense of the chair as an object aside from the sensation that is generated. The "shape" of that impression is idiosyncratic to each of us, and changes as we shift in our seats.

For the infant, the objects generating shapes in an autistic-contiguous mode include the soft parts of his own body and the body of the mother as well as soft bodily substances (including saliva, urine and faeces). Experiences of shape in an autistic-contiguous mode contribute to the sense of cohesion of self and also to the experience of perception of what is becoming the object. Much later in development, words like "comfort", "soothing", "safety", "connectedness", "cuddling", and "gentleness" will be attached to the experience of shapes in an autistic-contiguous mode.

A second form of very early definition of sensory experience described by Tustin (1980), the experience of "autistic objects," stands in marked contrast to the experience of autistic shapes. An autistic object is the experience of a hard, angular sensory surface that is created when an object is pressed hard against the infant's skin. In this form of experience, the individual experiences his surface (which in a sense is all there is of him) as a hard crust or armour protecting him against unspeakable dangers that only later will be given names. An autistic object is a safety-generating sensory impression of "edgedness" that defines, delineates and protects one's otherwise exposed and vulnerable surface. As experience is increasingly generated in paranoid-schizoid and depressive modes (see Ogden, 1986, for a discussion of Melanie Klein's conception of the paranoid-schizoid and depressive positions), words like "armour", "shell", "crust", "danger", "attach", "separateness", "otherness", "invasion", "rigidity", "impenetrability", and "repulsion" are attached to the quality of sensory impressions created by autistic objects.

I worked for many years in intensive psychotherapy with a congenitally blind schizophrenic adolescent named Robert. In the initial years of this work, which began when the patient was 19 years old, he spoke very little. The patient said that he was terrified of the millions of spiders that were all over the floor, his food, and his body. He felt that they were crawling in and out of all his bodily openings, including his eyes, mouth, ears, nose, anus and penis, as well as the pores of his skin. He would sit in my office trembling with his eyes rolled back into their sockets so that only the sclerae were visible.

According to the history given by the patient's parents, siblings and other relatives, Robert's mother's handling of him as an infant was characterised by unpredictable shifts from smothering over-involvement to extremes of hatred for him. He was left alone in a mobile crib for hours. Robert would stand up in the crib, holding on to the bar forming its upper edge, and would propel himself around the room by rhythmically banging his head against the bar. His mother told me that he had seemed oblivious to the pain and that she had been horrified by his "demoniacal wilfulness".

In the period of treatment on which I will be focusing here, Robert refused to bathe despite every act of prodding, cajoling, bribing and threatening that the nursing staff could devise. (He was hospitalised for the initial year of treatment.) He rarely changed his clothes even to sleep, and his hair was a mass of greasy clumps.

Robert developed an intense body odour which silently accompanied him and lingered for hours following his departure from my office. He would lie back in the soft chair in my consulting room with his greasy hair on the hard, padded back of the chair. The aspect of the transference-countertransference interaction I was most aware of at the time was the way in which I felt invaded by this patient. When he left my office, I could not feel that I had a respite from him. I felt as if he had managed, in a literal way, to get inside me—to get under my skin—by means of his odour which was saturating my furniture (with which I had become closely identified). I eventually understood these feelings as my response to (unconscious participation in) a projective identification in which the patient was engendering in me his own feelings of being painfully and unwillingly infiltrated by his internal object mother.

In retrospect I feel that I did not give sufficient weight to an aspect of the experience to which the patient was unconsciously directing my attention. When I asked Robert what it was about showering that most frightened him, he said "the drain". I now feel that I understand in a fuller way than I did at the time that Robert was terrified of dissolving and literally going down the drain. Thus he attempted to ground himself in the sensation of his own distinct body odour, which was of particular importance to him in the absence of the capacity to form well-defined visual images. His odour constituted a comforting autistic shape that helped him to create a place in which he could feel (through his bodily sensations) that he existed. His trembling gave him a heightened sense of his skin; his rolling of his eyes back into the vault of his skull insulated him from the blurred, edgeless shadows that he perceived visually. (Years later he told me that these shadows were "worse than seeing nothing at all" because they made him feel as if he were drowning.)

The patient's insistence on holding his head against the back edge of my chair served to provide some degree of boundedness for him. In early childhood, Robert had in a similar way desperately attempted to repair a failing sense of cohesiveness through banging his head against the hard edge of his crib in response to the disintegrative effect of long periods of disconnectedness from his mother. This early "relationship" to hardness represents a form of pathological use of an autistic object as a substitute for a healing relationship with an actual person. The rhythmic component of the head-banging and of the crib's motion can be viewed as an effort at self-soothing through the use of an autistic shape.

From this perspective, Robert's insistence on not bathing is more fully understandable. The loss of his odour would have been equivalent to the loss of himself. His odour provided the rudiments of being someone (someone who had a particular odour), being somewhere (somewhere in which he could perceive his odour), and being something for another person (a person who could smell him, be infused by him, and remember him). The use of odour as an autistic shape can in this case be viewed as non-pathological to the extent that it existed as part of the transference-countertransference relationship that was to a large degree aimed at the establishment of an object relationship of contiguity (the "touch" of odour), and was not simply an effort at creating a substitute for the object.

Autistic-contiguous experience and pathological autism

Although pathological autism can be thought of as constituting an "asymbolic" realm, the normal autistic-contiguous mode is "presymbolic" in that the sensory-based units of experience being organised are preparatory for the creation of symbols mediated by experience of transitional phenomena (Winnicott, 1951). The developmental directionality of this process stands in contrast to the static nature of asymbolic experience in pathological autism, wherein the effort is to maintain a perfectly insulated closed system (in which sensory experience does not lead anywhere except back to itself). Pathological autism aims at the absolute elimination of the unknown and the unpredictable.

The machine-like predictability of experiences with pathological autistic shapes and objects substitutes for experiences with inevitably imperfect and not entirely predictable human beings. No person can compete with the capacity of never-changing autistic shapes and objects to provide absolutely reliable comfort and protection.

Experience at the skin surface is critically important during infancy in that it constitutes an arena where there is a convergence of the infant's idiosyncratic, pre-symbolic world of sensory impressions and the interpersonal world made up of objects which—as viewed by an outside observer—have an existence separate from the infant and outside his omnipotent control. It is on this stage that the infant will either elaborate a way of being in the world in relation to the mother and the rest of the object world, or will elaborate sensory-dominated ways of being (more accurately a way of *not-being*) which are designed to insulate a potential self (which never comes into being) from all that lies outside his sensory-dominated world. To the extent that the bodily system is closed off from mutually transforming experiences with human beings, there is an absence of "potential space" (Winnicott, 1971) between oneself and the other (a potential psychological space between self-experience and sensory perception). This closed bodily world is a world without room in which to create a distinction between symbol and symbolised, and therefore a world in which there is no psychological space between the infant and the mother in which transitional phenomena might be created or discovered.

The syndrome of pathological infantile rumination is paradigmatic of the self-enclosed circularity of the pathological autistic process:

> Rumination or merycism . . . [is] the active bringing into the mouth of swallowed food which has already reached the stomach and which may have started to undergo the process of digestion . . . The food may be partially re-swallowed, partially lost, with serious consequences for the infant's nutrition. Unlike regurgitation, where the food runs out of the infant's mouth without any effort, in

rumination there are complex and purposeful preparatory movements particularly of the tongue and of the abdominal muscles. In
some cases the hard palate is stimulated by fingers in the mouth.
When the efforts become successful and the milk appears on the back
of the pharynx, the child's face is pervaded by an ecstatic expression.
[Gaddini & Gaddini, 1959, p. 166]

In infantile rumination, the beginnings of the awareness of otherness
(through the feeding interaction) is short-circuited by the infant's
appropriating to himself the entire feeding situation and then
engaging in a tightly closed auto-sensory cycle of creating his food
(more accurately, creating his autistic shapes). These autistic shapes
then substitute for the mother, thus transforming the feeding
experience from an avenue towards increasingly mature object
relatedness, into a pathway leading to objectless "self-sufficiency"
(in which there is no self or other person).

In the analytic setting, one form of equivalent to merycism can
be seen in patients who take the analysis into themselves. Instead of
internalising an analytic space in which one thinks and feels one's
thoughts, feelings and sensations, such patients present a caricature
of analysis in which rumination and imitation substitute for an
analytic process. The analyst's role has been entirely co-opted. Such
patients often present the unconscious phantasy of having "raised
themselves" by taking into themselves the functions of both parent
and child, thus replacing genuine object relatedness with an inner
world of phantasied object relations and experiences with autistic
shapes and objects.

Mrs M, a 62-year-old widow whom I saw in intensive psychotherapy for eight years, had originally been referred to me by her
internist after a suicide attempt. She had used a razor to carefully
make deep incisions across her wrists, arms, legs, and ankles. She
then got into a tub filled with warm water and patiently waited for
over three hours to bleed to death. After lapsing into a coma, she
was discovered by a cleaning-woman. While waiting to die, she had
felt the relief of the end of decades of oppressive obsessive-
compulsive rituals.

Speaking in clipped sentences and almost exclusively in response
to direct questions, Mrs M told me that she would stand for hours
in front of one door or another in her apartment before she would

allow herself to go through it while she attempted to "get a thought right". "Getting a thought right" involved generating for herself a perfect mental re-creation of some experience from her past, including all of its sensory features. For years (including the initial years of the therapy), this effort was focused on an attempt to re-experience the taste of the first sip of a cold glass of wine which the patient had tasted early in the relationship with her husband some thirty-eight years before. She could not allow herself to open any door of her apartment, whether to go into the next room or out into the hallway, until she had successfully completed this task. She compared getting a thought right to having an orgasm; it was a fitting together of different sensations and rhythms in a very specific way. For years, such obsessive-compulsive activity filled virtually every moment of Mrs M's life. This activity was understood in the course of the therapy as providing a form of comfort which was nightmarishly tyrannising and yet life-sustaining.

The patient was terrified of the disruption of her bodily rhythms, particularly her breathing. During her obsessional marathons, Mrs M felt terrified of suffocating and felt she would not be able to resume breathing until she "got the thought right". In the meantime, she felt that she had to take over the process of breathing with conscious control; she could never feel that her breathing was natural, automatic and sufficient. The patient was convinced that if she forgot to breathe she would suffocate.

Although Mrs M highly valued the therapy and was never late to her daily meetings with me, she found it extremely painful when I spoke because this interfered with her ability to concentrate. The experience of being with this patient was quite different from that of being with a silent patient for whom one feels one is providing a "holding environment" (Winnicott, 1960a). Instead, I generally felt useless. Mrs M could and did ruminate at home in precisely the way she was doing with me. If anything, I seemed to make things worse for her by placing an additional demand on her—the demand she felt from me to be acknowledged and made use of as a human being and as a therapist. I said to her in small bits in the second year of our work that I assumed that my own wishes to be experienced by her as human were a reflection of an aspect of herself, but she did not at the moment feel she could afford this complicated luxury since she was so fully involved in fighting for her life. She would look at me and nod as if to say "I understand what you said, but I'm too busy to talk now", and then would continue with her task.

Occasionally she would breathe a sigh of relief, glance at me, nod her head and smile in a joyless way, saying "I got it right". She would then seem to relax and stare at me as if she were coming out of anaesthesia, looking to see who it was that had been with her during her ordeal. She would then begin to brace herself for the inevitable recurrence of the need to chase another thought so that even these interim periods were far from relaxed.

Mrs M was able to offer fragments of history during the brief periods of respite before becoming fully re-immersed in her rumination. I learned that she had deeply loved and admired her husband, a professor twenty years her senior, and that they had lived very happily together during their twenty-two years of marriage. It was eight years after his death that the patient attempted suicide.

Dr and Mrs M had had a large photograph collection of their lives together which the patient impulsively threw out after Dr M died, "because it was too much at loose ends to pack". (It pained me to hear her speak of this since it felt as if she had brutally sliced out a terribly important part of herself in this impulsive act.) Mrs M had saved only one picture from that collection, a photo of herself and her husband with a "real lion" between whose open jaws her husband was holding his hand.

Mrs M's mother had been a psychotic actress who believed that she could read her daughter's mind and knew what she was thinking better than her daughter herself did. Mrs M as a child was used as a prop in her mother's delusional dramas. The child kept important trinkets and ticket stubs in a Chinese box given to her by her grandmother. In a fit of rage about the secretive nature of this child, the mother (when the patient was 10 years old) threw the box away while the patient was at school. When Mrs M told me this, I said that I thought I was finally beginning to understand something of the meaning of her throwing her photographs away; your most precious possessions are only safe if they are inside you.

Over time, I realised that this interpretation was incomplete in an important way. Mrs M often indicated that she had practically no sense of an internal space within which to keep anything. She told me: "I have no insides. I had a hysterectomy when I was 45."

I later said to her that I thought when she felt she had no safe place in her to keep the people and things that were most important to her, she felt she had to find a way to freeze time. "Getting a thought right" about the taste of the wine was not an attempt to remember something. To remember would be much too painful because she would then know that the moment was over. I said she gave me the feeling that she was attempting to become timeless and placeless— that she could enter the sensation, the taste, and become it. Everything she needed would be there. It was only there that she could relax. (The photograph of her husband holding his hand between the lion's open jaws must also have captured for Mrs M a feeling that time could really be frozen.)

Mrs M's ruminative symptoms had not begun with her husband's death. From adolescence and before, she had devoted her life to endless attempts at living in a realm of timeless sensations. In the therapy, I initially attempted to understand the meaning of the choice of each sensation, but over time I realised that this patient's psychological world was not composed of accretions of meaning; rather, she lived in a world of timeless sensory experience that was neither internal nor external. The ruminative activity was the essence of pure, unchanging sensation. Mrs M's suicide attempt and her longing for death represented her hope that if this timeless state could not be achieved in life, perhaps it could be achieved in death.

The early relationship between Mrs M and her mother had not resulted in the creation of a gradual internalisation of a holding environment. Instead, Mrs M had defensively attempted to create a substitute for such an environment. She could not take for granted that the rhythm of her breathing would sustain itself and her without her consciously willing it. The patient's life was devoted to creating a substitute for the space between mother and infant in which the infant ordinarily finds a place to live between self and other. In the absence of such a space (symbolised by the box in which the patient had attempted to store precious bits of herself and her relations to external objects), Mrs M attempted to become sensation itself.

In the course of eight years of therapy, Mrs M began to be able to live for extended periods of time in a state of mind relatively free of her obsessive ruminations. While this was occurring, I increasingly felt that I was perceiving the faint glimmer of a living human being in the room with me. At times I saw brief glimpses of a little girl capable of some joy as Mrs M laughed about some humorous event in her life with her husband, or about something I had said that she found funny. It was with a mixture of sadness and a vicarious sense of relief that I received a phone call I had been half expecting from the moment I met Mrs M: she had been brought to the hospital after a massive stroke and died soon afterwards.

I view the autistic-contiguous mode as an important dimension of all obsessive-compulsive defences, and believe that these defences always entail the construction of a tightly ordered sensory containment of experience that is never simply a symbolic, ideational ordering of experience designed to ward off, control, and express conflicted unconscious anal-erotic wishes and fears. This form of defence regularly serves to plug sensorially experienced holes in the individual's sense of self through which the patient fears and *feels* (in the most concrete sensory way) that not only ideas, but actual bodily contents, will leak. Obsessive-compulsive symptoms and defences have their origins in the infant's earliest efforts at ordering and creating a sense of boundedness for his sensory experience. Very early on, such efforts at organisation and definition come to be utilised in the service of warding off anxiety related to the disruption of the sensory-dominated, rudimentary sense of self.

The nature of autistic-contiguous anxiety

Each of the three basic psychological organisations (the autistic-contiguous, the paranoid-schizoid and the depressive) is associated with its own characteristic form of anxiety. In each case, the nature of the anxiety is related to the experience of disconnectedness (dis-integration) within that mode of experience, whether it be the disruption of whole object relations in the depressive position, the fragmentation of parts of self and object in the paranoid-schizoid position, or the disruption of sensory cohesion and boundedness in the autistic-contiguous position.

Depressive anxiety involves the fear that one has in fact or in fantasy harmed or driven away a person whom one loves; anxiety in a paranoid-schizoid mode is at its core a sense of impending annihilation which is experienced in the form of fragmenting attacks on the self and on one's objects; autistic-contiguous anxiety involves the experience of impending disintegration of one's sensory surface or one's "rhythm of safety" (Tustin, 1986), resulting in the feeling of leaking, dissolving, disappearing, or falling into shapeless unbounded space (Bick, 1968).

Common manifestations of autistic-contiguous anxiety include terrifying feelings that one is rotting; the sensation that one's sphincters and other means of containing bodily contents are failing and that one's saliva, tears, urine, faeces, blood, menstrual fluids, and so forth are leaking; fear that one is falling—for example, anxiety connected with falling asleep for fear that one will fall into endless, shapeless space. Patients experiencing this form of insomnia often attempt to relieve their anxiety (their fear of "falling asleep") by tightly surrounding themselves with blankets and pillows, keeping bright lights on in their bedrooms or playing familiar music all night.

> Ms K, a 25-year-old graduate student, began therapy because of her terror of the fog and of the sound of the ocean. The fog was frighteningly suffocating: "You can't see the horizon". The patient was terrified of "going crazy" and of being unaware that it was happening; she frequently begged the therapist to inform her if the therapist should sense that the patient was losing touch with reality.
>
> When Ms K was four months old, her mother contracted spinal meningitis and was hospitalised for fourteen months. From the time her mother returned home, she tyrannically ruled the house from the metal wheelchair to which she was confined. The patient's earliest memory (which seemed to her as much a dream as a memory) was of reaching out to her mother in the wheelchair and being pushed away by her. At the same moment, the patient, in this memory, looked out of the window and saw a small girl falling through the ice on the pond that was located just behind the patient's house. Mrs K said to her daughter: "You'd better go save her."

I view this "memory" as a vivid representation of the patient's experience of falling through the containing surface of self (initially created in the interaction of mother and infant). Ms K is both the small child falling through the ice and the older child who must try to pull the younger one out of the hole before she drowns. The metallic, wheelchair-mother is felt to be incapable of saving the child and in fact seems to be the one who is unconsciously being blamed for the little girl's fall through the hole (the mother's pushing Ms K away).

The ocean and the fog came to be experienced by Ms K as the ever-present danger of annihilating shapelessness into which she might fall. Because of the tenuousness of the patient's sense of cohesiveness of self, she lived in constant fear of "going crazy" (losing "touch" with reality in a literal, sensory way). The patient lacked the feeling of sensory groundedness that is ordinarily provided by the interpersonal "touch" of our shared sensory experience of the world, which contributes heavily to our sense of being sane.

Autistic-contiguous modes of defence

Defences generated in an autistic-contiguous mode are directed at re-establishment of the continuity of the bounded sensory surface and of the ordered rhythmicity upon which the early integrity of self rests. Within the analytic hour, patients spanning the full range of psychological maturity commonly attempt to reconstitute a sensory "floor" of experience by means of activities like hair twirling or foot tapping (even while lying on the couch); stroking of the lips, cheek or ear lobe; humming, intoning, picturing or repeating series of numbers; focusing on symmetrical geometric shapes on the ceiling or wall; or using a finger to trace shapes on the wall next to the couch. Such activities can be thought of as self-soothing uses of autistic shapes.

Between analytic hours, patients commonly attempt to maintain or re-establish a failing sense of bodily cohesion by means of rhythmic muscular activities including long periods of bicycle riding, jogging, lap swimming and the like; eating and purging rituals; rocking (sometimes in a rocking chair); head banging (often against a pillow); riding buses and subways or driving a car for hours; maintaining (and continually working on "perfecting") a system of numbers or geometric shapes in one's head or in computer programs; and so on. The absolute regularity of these activities is so essential to the process of allaying anxiety that the individual cannot or will not allow any other activity to take precedence over them.

Bick (1968) uses the phrase "second skin formation" to describe the way in which the individual attempts to create a substitute for a deteriorating sense of the cohesiveness of skin surface. Often the individual attempts to use the sensory experience of adhering to the surface of the object in order to resurrect the integrity of his own surface.

Meltzer and colleagues (1975) have introduced the term *adhesive identification* to refer to the defensive adherence to the object in the service of allaying the anxiety of disintegration. Imitation and mimicry, for instance, are utilised in an effort to make use of the surface of the object as if it were one's own. In an autistic-contiguous mode, one attempts to defend against the anxiety of disintegration by sticking bits of the surface of the object to one's own failing surface.

> Mrs R, in a regressed phase of her analysis, would spend hours at a time picking at her face. She suffered from severe insomnia in large part due to a fear of nightmares that she could not recall. Over time her face became covered with scabs, and she picked at these. As this "picking" was occurring in the analytic hours, the patient was clearly in a painfully anxious state, although she said that she had "absolutely no thoughts".
>
> Mrs R took bits of tissue from the Kleenex box next to the couch and stuck them to the lesions she was creating on her face. (She would also take extra pieces of these tissues home with her at the end of the hour.) It did not seem to me that either self-destructive wishes or displaced hostility towards me was at the core of this activity at this point in the analysis. I told her that I thought she must feel as if she were without skin; that she did not sleep because when she was asleep she must feel psychologically defenceless to the danger of nightmares. I said that I could understand her attempt to cover herself with my skin (tissues) since this seemed to make her feel a little less raw.
>
> In the hour following this intervention, Mrs R fell asleep and slept for almost the entire session until I woke her to tell her that our time was up. During the next meeting, the patient said that even though she had not had a blanket while sleeping in my office, she had the distinct feeling when recalling that session that she had been sleeping under some sort of cover. Mrs R's capacity to sleep during her session represented an expanded and more fully symbolic use of me as a second skin. She had utilised me and the analytic setting as a symbolic and yet tangibly felt medium in which to wrap herself. She had thus felt sufficiently covered and held together to sleep safely.

Before concluding this section, I would like to briefly mention two forms of symptomatology in which the concept of autistic-contiguous modes of defence must supplement understandings formulated in terms of defences erected to deal with anxiety resulting from conflicted sexual and aggressive wishes. First, compulsive masturbation often serves the purpose of creating a heightened experience of a sensory surface in order to ward off feelings of loss of sensory cohesion. For example, a female patient would masturbate for hours each day without conscious sexual fantasy. Orgasm was not the goal. When orgasm did occur, it was experienced as an unwelcome "anticlimax" which ended the only part of the patient's day during which she felt "alive and in one piece".

Secondly, painful, anxiety-producing procrastination also often serves the purpose of generating a palpable sensory edge against which the patient attempts to define himself. The "deadline" is elevated to the position of a continually felt pressure in the patient's emotional life which can be a felt presence at every moment, whether or not the patient is consciously focused upon it. These patients describe the anxiety of the approaching deadline as a pressure they hate, and yet at the same time continually seem to create for themselves: "A due date is something to push up against like a wall in front of me."

Under such circumstances, a deadline that is finally met does not usually produce more than a sense of momentary relief, and instead often throws the patient into a state of panic. Very frequently such patients become physically ill once the task has been completed (usually at the last possible moment prior to the deadline), experiencing such symptoms as migraine headaches, dermatitis, or somatic delusions. Such symptoms can be understood as substitute efforts at maintaining a sensory surface in the absence of the containing pressure of the deadline.

Internalisation in the autistic-contiguous position

As previously mentioned, in a psychological field in which the individual has little if any sense of internal space, the concept of internalisation becomes virtually meaningless; this is especially true when the idea of internalisation (including identification and introjection) is linked to the notion of conscious and unconscious fantasies about taking parts or all of another person into oneself. Nonetheless, psychological change can result from experience with external objects in an autistic-contiguous mode; such change is mediated in part by the process of imitation. In autistic-contiguous forms of imitation, the individual experiences a change in the shape of his surface as a result of the influence of his relations with external objects. At times, imitation is one of the few ways the individual has of holding on to attributes of the object, in the absence of the experience of having an inner space in which the other person's qualities or parts can in phantasy be stored (E. Gaddini, 1969). Since in an autistic-contiguous mode the feeling and phantasy of being entered is synonymous with being torn or punctured, imitation allows the influence of the other to be carried on one's surface. In pathological autism this sometimes manifests itself as echolalia or as an endless repetition of a phrase or a word uttered by another person.

Imitation as a method of achieving a degree of cohesiveness of self must be distinguished from Winnicott's (1963) concept of a False Self personality organisation. There is nothing false about autistic-contiguous imitation in that it does not stand in contrast to, or serve to disguise or protect, something truer or more genuine within: there *is* no within or without. In an autistic-contiguous mode, one is one's surface, and therefore the act of imitation is an effort to become or repair a cohesive surface on which a locus of self can develop. Imitation serves not only as a form of perception, a defence, and a way of "holding on to" (being shaped by) the other, it serves also as an important form of object relatedness in an autistic-contiguous mode.

In a previous paper (1980), I described aspects of my work with a hospitalised chronically schizophrenic patient who for years lived in a world so stripped of meaning that people and things were treated by him as completely interchangeable. Phil seemed psychologically dead as he lay on the floor of my office or was escorted from one hospital "activity" to another. The initial form of contact he made with me in the therapy was by imitating my posture, my tone of voice, my every gesture, every word I spoke, and every facial expression I made. Rather than celebrating this as his entry into the land of the living, I experienced it at the time as an attack on my ability to feel alive. I felt as if my spontaneity was being tyrannically drained out of me. Nothing I did felt natural.

At that time I understood this as a form of projective identification in which the patient was engendering in me (communicating to me) his own feelings of lifelessness and incapacity for spontaneity as well as his inability to feel alive in any way. However, I did not at the time understand the phenomena I am describing here as autistic-contiguous sufficiently to appreciate the nature of the affection in the patient's imitation of me. He was using me as a second skin or container within which he was experimenting in a primitive way with what it might feel like to be alive. He was paying me a very great compliment indeed by indicating that it was to be my skin in which he would conduct this experiment.

In a letter to Michael Fordham, Winnicott addressed—from the perspective of the treatment of an autistic child—the role of imitation as a primitive form of object relatedness:

> I know an autistic child who is treated by very clever interpretations and who has done moderately well. What started off the treatment was, however, something which the first analyst did, and it is strange that I have never been able to get the second analyst to acknowledge the importance of what I will describe. The first analyst, Dr Mida Hall, died. Dr Hall found this boy who had gone autistic after being normal and sat in the room with him and established a communication by doing everything that this boy did. He would sit still for a quarter of an hour and then move his foot a little; she would move her foot. His finger would move and she would imitate, and this went on for a long time. Out of these beginnings everything showed signs of developing until she died. If I could have got the clever analyst to join on to all this I think we might by now have had something like a cure instead of having to put up with one of those maddening cases where a lot of good work has been done and everybody is very pleased but the child is not satisfactory. [1965, pp. 150–151]

Imitation in an autistic-contiguous mode is by no means restricted to patients suffering from pathological childhood autism, borderline conditions and schizophrenia. It is very common for a therapist early in training to attempt to imitate his superiors or his own therapist in an attempt to hide from himself the absence of his own identity as a therapist. One such therapist described this experience as "using the skin of the supervisor" when he was with his patients. This "skin" was felt to be "stripped off" when a second supervisor was critical of this student's work, leading the trainee to feel painfully "raw". He would then immediately attempt to "take on the skin of the second supervisor". In therapy, this patient imitated his own patients by presenting their difficulties as his own, thus defending against his awareness of the feeling that he did not have a voice of his own with which to speak. Instead, the patient desperately attempted to get the therapist to make interpretations and give advice which would serve as substitutes for the patient's own thoughts and feelings, as well as a substitute for a voice that he could feel was his own.

Many years ago, I inadvertently stumbled upon a way of creating for oneself this type of disconnection of language from meaning, leading to the experience of no longer having a voice or language of one's own. After dinner one night, while I was still sitting at the dining-room table, it suddenly occurred to me how strange it was that the thing called a napkin was named by the conjunction of the sounds "nap" and "kin". I repeated the two sounds over and over until I began to get the very frightening feeling that these sounds had no connection at all with this thing I was looking at. I could not get these sounds to naturally "mean" the thing they had meant only minutes before. The link was broken, and, to my horror, could not be mended simply by an act of will. I imagined that I could, if I chose to, destroy the power of any and all words to "mean" something if I thought about them one at a time in this way. At that point, I had the very disturbing feeling that I had discovered a way to drive myself crazy. I imagined that all things in the world could come to feel as disconnected as the napkin had become for me now that it had been disconnected from the word which had formerly named it. Further, I felt that I could become utterly disconnected from the rest of the world because all other people would still share in a "natural" (i.e. a still meaningful) system of words. Such is the nature of the beginnings of a collapse of the dialectic of experience in the direction of sensation-dominated experience that is unmediated by the use of symbols. It took some years before the word "napkin" re-entered my vocabulary in a fully unselfconscious way.

The fact that one's experience of self is powerfully rooted in the dialectical interplay of the sensory and the symbolic is often highly visible in psychoanalytic work with teachers and students of linguistics. These patients often experience anxiety states bordering on panic in association with the feeling that they are dissolving as they dismantle the binding power of language. This has in each case I have encountered led to the patient's need to leave the field of linguistics at least temporarily.

Summary

In this chapter, the idea of an autistic-contiguous position has been used as a way of conceptualising the perspective from which the world is viewed in earliest infancy and as a part of all subsequent human development. The autistic-contiguous mode is conceptualised as a sensory-dominated, pre-symbolic way of generating experience which provides a good measure of the boundedness of human experience, and the beginnings of a sense of the place where one's experience occurs. Anxiety in this mode consists of an unspeakable terror of the dissolution of boundedness resulting in feelings of leaking, falling, or dissolving into endless, shapeless space. I have described principal forms of defence, ways of organising and defining experience, types of relatedness to objects, and avenues to psychological change in the autistic-contiguous position. These forms of experience have been contrasted with the far more impenetrable states to be found in pathological autism.

Note

1. This chapter is a modified version of a paper which originally appeared in the *International Journal of Psychoanalysis*, 1989: 70.

References

Bick, E. (1968). The Experience of the Skin in Early Object Relations. *Int. J. Psychoanal. 49*: 484–486.

Gaddini, E. (1969). On Imitation. *Int. J. Psychoanal. 50*: 475–484.

Gaddini, R. & Gaddini, E. (1959). Rumination in Infancy. In: L. Jessner & E. Pavenstedt (Eds.), *Dynamic Psychopathology in Childhood* (pp. 166–185). New York: Grune & Stratton.

Meltzer, D., Bremner, J., Hoxter, S., Weddell, D. & Wittenberg, I. (1975). *Explorations in Autism: A Psycho-Analytical Study*. Strathtay: Clunie Press.

Ogden, T. (1980). On the Nature of Schizophrenic Conflict. *Int. J. Psychoanal. 61*:513–533.

Ogden, T, (1986). *The Matrix of the Mind: Object Relations and the Psychoanalytic Dialogue*. London: Karnac.

Ogden, T. (1989). *The Primitive Edge of Experience*. London: Karnac.

Tustin, F. (1980). Autistic Objects. *Int. Rev. Psychoanal. 7*: 27–40.

Tustin, F. (1984). Autistic Shapes. *Int. Rev. Psychoanal. 11*: 279–290.

Tustin, F. (1986). *Autistic Barriers in Neurotic Patients*. London: Karnac.

Winnicott, D. W. (1951).Transitional Objects and Transitional Phenomena. In: *Playing and Reality* (pp. 1–25). London: Tavistock, 1971.

Winnicott, D.W. (1960). The Theory of the Parent-Infant Relationship. In: *The Maturational Processes and the Facilitating Environment* (pp. 37–55). London: Hogarth, 1965.

Winnicott, D.W. (1963). Communicating and Not Communicating Leading to a Study of Certain Opposites. In: *The Maturational Processes and the Facilitating Environment* (pp. 179–192). London: Hogarth, 1965.

Winnicott, D.W. (1965). Letter to Michael Fordham, 15 July 1965. In: R. Rodman (Ed.), *The Spontaneous Gesture: Selected Letters of D.W. Winnicott* (pp. 150–151). Cambridge, MA: Harvard Univ. Press, 1987.

Winnicott, D.W. (1971). *Playing and Reality*. London: Tavistock.

CHAPTER TWELVE

On the survival function of autistic manoeuvres in adult patients[1]

Judith Mitrani

Frances Tustin (1972, 1981, 1986, 1990) devoted her life's work to the psychoanalytic understanding of the bewildering elemental world of the autistic child. Her realisation that some of our more neurotic adult patients are haunted by these same primeval forces which constitute an enclave of autism has been profound. The notion that autistic manoeuvres serve as a protective shell against the terrifying awareness of bodily separateness and dissolution into nothingness has had a substantial impact upon the rethinking of such notable analysts as Boyer (1990), Grotstein (1983), D. Rosenfeld (1984) and H.A. Rosenfeld (1987).

In the last decade several other authors have taken up Tustin's work to expand our understanding of certain personality organisations which impede development in our adult patients and which constitute an impenetrable resistance within the analytic relationship, leading to unresolvable impasse and interminable treatment. For example, Sydney Klein (Chapter Eight) described those patients who, despite the appearance of progress in the analysis, remain untouched in some essential way due to encapsulating forces which cut the patient off from the analyst as well as from the rest of the personality.

Klein posited that walled off in these cystic areas of the mind are intense and unbearable fears of "pain, and of death, disintegration or breakdown" related to unmentalised separation experiences of early infancy. And he suggested that such phenomena "are strikingly similar to those observed in so-called autistic children" (*ibid*).

Innes-Smith (1987) has eloquently discussed the over-investment in sensation objects as a factor in the aetiology of adult psychopathology. He emphasised the importance of attending to that pre-oedipal state of mind in which dyadic communication is achieved on a nonverbal level, and those moments in the analysis when such states predominate.

Ogden proposed a primitive mental organisation prefacing those of the paranoid-schizoid and depressive positions, which he termed the "autistic-contiguous position" (this volume, Chapter Eleven). He suggested that, like the two aforementioned positions, the latter constitutes an ongoing state of mind—a way of being and experiencing with its own set of defences, anxieties, and a mode of object relating which persists throughout life and which may be mobilised in the transference at times in the analytic process.

Most recently, Gomberoff *et al.* (this volume, Chapter Ten) have focused upon certain aspects of the transference-countertransference interaction wherein a collusive tendency develops in the analytic couple to transform the analysis, particularly some aspects of verbal language, into an autistic object which wards off anxiety over twoness for both analyst and analysand.

In this chapter I will first highlight some of the main features of Tustin's work, particularly those which pertain to the analysis of adult patients, as a prelude to several clinical illustrations which, it is hoped, will emphasise the survival function of autistic shapes (Tustin, 1984), autistic objects (Tustin, 1980) and other sensation-dominated delusions.[2] These may be understood as serving to contain unmentalised experiences[3] protecting the patient from unbearable feelings of the catastrophic loss of and painful longing for the primary object, which threaten the subject with overwhelming anxiety. Finally, I will suggest that further discrimination is necessary in our work to distinguish between the analysis of these autistic mental states which are related to the threat of unintegration, and those still primitive, yet more organised states of mind which involve anxieties of a paranoid-schizoid or depressive nature (M. Klein, 1948; 1975).

In her most recent work, Tustin (1986, 1990) demonstrates the important link between autistic pathology in children and such autistic states of mind in adult neurotic patients seen in analysis. Her capacity for observation and self-reflection has enabled her to describe in an evocative way some of the most elemental human fears and anxieties which are alive and active in each of us, as well as the specialised protective forms which our patients create for purposes of survival. Throughout her work, Tustin describes the sensations of mutilation, of spilling and falling, of dissolving and evaporating which characterise the intolerable terror of two-ness.

Tustin (1986, 1990) helps us to understand how autism acts as a protective shell made up of what she terms "sensation-dominated delusions" which serve to block out the unbearable "agony of awareness of two-ness" and the threat which such awareness represents to a sense of personal continuity and integrity. She uses the term "delusion" not in the common psychiatric sense, which implies some symbolic process and thought, but in a very concrete sense on the level of what Segal (1957) called "symbolic equation". These delusions are the thing-in-itself, not to be confused with a representation.

Tustin also demonstrates how this protective barrier acts as an impediment to the healing effects of the relationship with the therapist. Her pioneering work within the primordial territory of autistic states of consciousness has enabled psychoanalytic therapists to proceed where our work with such patients had previously been stopped. She has given us a key with which we may gain entry into the once-forbidden and foreboding area of our patients' earliest experiences.

She draws our attention to her observation that certain neurotic adults have much in common with autistic children, in that both share a sense of tentativeness in their existence as persons. In these adults, mental growth has taken place by circumventing an area of truncated development which is calloused over or encapsulated. As one patient explained: "I have this hole—an empty spot deep inside me—maybe I'm just afraid to find that nothing is there." He seemed to cover over the hole with a "chip on his shoulder".

Eventually we came to understand this "chip" or calloused, cynical attitude as a "chip off the old block", which referred to his feelings about his father. "He protected me," my patient said one day. "But he just didn't seem to know what to do with me when I couldn't throw the ball right. He thought I was a sissy—I threw the ball like a girl." This man was perhaps also telling me about a growing awareness that, like his father, he could protect the soft, tender part of his experience by covering it over with a hard "daddy chip", but that he was frightened of, and did not know how to help or handle, the baby-him with the soft spot on his head, the soft skin which was easily bruised, and the tender, loving feelings he had for the mummy-me.

As this patient demonstrates, some of our analysands struggle courageously in analysis to give verbal expression to those primitive states in which development has been impaired. Their symptoms and actions are often valiant attempts to give expression to their bodily experiences and to communicate their terrors so that we may lend meaning to them through our interpretive work. Many of our patients are moved to communicate their states of terror as they are re-experienced in the transference situation, provoked by the in-numerable separations engendered in the analytic frame at the end of the analytic hour, the analytic week, and around vacations.

In my own experience with patients, I have found that Tustin's model of understanding is far more applicable to adults in psycho-analytic treatment than I had first imagined possible. As exemplified in the following clinical vignettes, *autistic-like shapes, hard objects, and delusions function to contain the unmentalised experience of the catastrophic loss of and painful longing for the primary object.*

Hope

Hope, a woman in her early thirties, came to analysis after many years of therapy. Having recently lost her father after nursing him through a painful illness, she moved to this city to be closer to an aged mother who she feared was needy and infirm. Hope thought her own depression attributable to a recent abortion she had had, and complained of her relationship with the father of the aborted baby, a man she described as unprepared for the responsibilities of marriage and children.

As she was predisposed to see almost all those around her as needy and dependent upon her, it seemed there was ample evidence that much of my patient's suffering was a result of excessive intolerance towards a needy baby part of herself, and the tendency to handle this painful aspect of her experience through excessive splitting and projective identification. However, the handling of this over time, as it appeared in the transference, seemed to result in only a limited measure of relief, and it soon became apparent that Hope had hidden away in an enclave of autism a very dependent, sick and dying baby part of herself, and that this encapsulation was interfering with her relationships as well as with her work.

Relevant to the material which I present here, I will give a bit of Hope's history. Hope's mother had been severely depressed after the death of her own mother, and just six weeks after the birth of my patient, her milk suddenly dried up. Around this time, it seems that the father dropped the baby Hope while holding her in his arms, and her lip was painfully split open in the fall, the scar remaining to this day.

In this session, the first of the week, which took place in the third year of the analysis, Hope began with a long silence characteristic of her re-entry on Monday after the three-day break. During this silence, which lasted several minutes, I had the unsettling sensation of falling, as if my chair were being progressively lowered into the floor beneath me. When finally I broke the silence by asking what she had been thinking, she began by telling me that over the weekend her boyfriend had gone out with friends, and that she had awakened at 3 a.m. to find that she was still alone in their bed. She said that she could not fall asleep, as she was hurt and angry at the boyfriend and fearful of being alone, thinking she heard noises outside as if someone were trying to break in.

Immobilised in her fear of intruders, she told me that she had lain very still looking up at the ceiling, concentrating upon one single spot. She felt physically that she was being lifted up into a soft, pink cloud as she spread her tongue between her teeth, filling her mouth from corner to corner, touching her lips with her own fleshy organ. She reported how soothing the sensation was of uniting with this soft, pink cloud, and how she soon drifted off to sleep. In fact, she said she had been doing that same thing—trying to get back there—when I interrupted her silence.

She then went on to tell how, on the previous morning, she had made love with her boyfriend, and how delicious this had been, but that he had immediately jumped out of bed to prepare for work, leaving her feeling as if her heart had been "torn out of her chest". I told Hope that she seemed also to be telling me about how it felt to be deeply touched and fed by me throughout the last analytic week, only to feel me wrenched painfully away from her at the weekend, as if a vital part of her had been torn away, as if I had dropped her, just as she may have felt her mother's nipple torn out of her mouth, leaving a terrible wound in its place.

As Hope's hand went to her mouth and she began to weep, I told her that she also seemed to be saying something about how she experienced me on Monday as transformed into a dangerous predator-intruder; how this betrayal of her trust paralysed her capacity to allow me to help her with these feelings of being dropped and wounded. By filling the space between us with these soft sensations of her own tongue in her mouth, I believe Hope gave herself a continuous comfort which I failed to offer. However, this also seemed to stop up the analytic work, interfering with the kind of healing which comes through interaction with a caring human being.

Hope went on in the session to say that she had often taken refuge in the pink cloud as a child, feeling its suffocating sweetness, getting lost in the pinkness of it all, as if this pink were the soft, wet and full sensation of her own tongue in her mouth. This feeling filled her mind at times when she felt unbearably disappointed and alone. Tustin reminds us that we must be able to bear these lonely and disillusioned states for our patients for quite some time, so that we may be better equipped to weave, out of the threads of our own experience, a blanket of understanding which may adequately hold and warm them, if we are to expect them to relinquish the self-soothing protections they have come to rely upon so heavily.

Bill

In contrast to Hope, who used soft sensation shapes to protect against unbearable feelings of falling and emptiness, Bill, a professional man in his forties, seemed to rely more upon the hard autistic objects Tustin tells us about. Bill's mother had a history of clinical depression which predated his birth. A peculiar characteristic of this patient was manifest in his lack of verbal expression for any feelings such as sadness, anger, or even pleasurable excitement. These emotional states were instead expressed in terms of substances, movements and physical sensations in various parts of his or others' bodies. He spoke of his tears as moisture, without reference to feeling sad; his nostrils twitching, without the notion of anxiety; his feet moving, without the experience of arousal; and I struggled to decode this idiosyncratic mode of expression for over a year.

He seemed to feel always at risk of having his feelings spilled out through what he referred to as "the hole in his body" or "the hole in his head" which constituted the deep emotional wounds which impacted both his physical and intellectual functioning.

He often spoke of masturbation as a means of stopping the twitching nostrils and the wiggling feet in a rhythmic way, and he referred to this as "getting rid of sex". Quickly and controllably by his own hand, he would have his "little death". Earplugs were also used to keep him from spilling, frightened, out of bed, and often in the sessions he would present an impermeable hostility towards me, or a stone wall of silence, or he would bite his fingers mercilessly in a desperate attempt to ward off contact with the more vulnerable soft centre of his experience.

By the beginning of the third year of his analysis, Bill had revealed much of surprise to both of us. For example, murderous jealousy and paralysing guilt experienced towards a child patient he had encountered in the waiting room led to the unearthing of a long-buried memory of a baby sister, Kathleen, who had died of pneumonia when Bill was just two years old. Such memories would come in spurts, as though these moments in his history had leaked out in times of intense affect; and then, just as quickly, these would be sealed off during subsequent weekend or holiday breaks in the treatment, leaving us to contend with many mysterious gaps in his experience. Often I felt certain that these surprise revelations had leaked out, like some vital substance from deep within an inner capsule, when the emotional contact between us was such that he could be certain I would retain and contain for him in my consciousness this precious, if painful, overflow.

In the twenty-ninth month of analysis, Bill was able to tell me more about the nature of this deeply hidden reservoir to which those painfully traumatic and unbearably pleasurable early experiences were relegated for safe keeping, albeit out of reach of his awareness and the analytic process.

One Monday Bill had returned from a horseback-packing trip to the mountains, where he had experienced some sense of progress. He felt proud to tell me that he had ridden a horse up and down miles of narrow switchback trails without fear of tumbling to his death, since he had faith that his mount had been along these same trails before, and that she seemed surefooted and confident. He felt that perhaps his lifelong fear of heights had been somehow overcome, and he was quite pleased and encouraged by this accomplishment, which he connected with the work of the analysis. He spoke of how gratifying it was for him to tell his colleagues at work about his weekend, and noticed this as a deviation from the usual feeling that he had nothing to share with others of his personal life, which felt so dead and empty, especially after a weekend away.

In the Tuesday hour, Bill was quite sullen and sarcastic, and spent a good portion of the session in a customary mute silence which I felt to be impenetrable. I found myself falling into a state of despair, feeling him lost to me—unreachable and almost dead—followed by the feeling that he was punishing me for some heinous crime which I had unwittingly committed. When asked about his silence, he would simply reply "I'm empty".

On Wednesday, we came to understand that he had felt lost and alone at the end of the Monday hour, when I became transformed first into a deadly, depressed mother who had left him alone spilling over with excitement, and then, on Tuesday, into a mean, withholding and envious mother who would take from him all that of which he was proud. It seemed his impermeable muteness was employed primarily as a primitive survival tactic to stem the flow of disillusionment into nothingness, and secondarily as a means of preserving his good objects from attack.

Having somewhat mitigated his disillusionment in the Wednesday hour, I found Bill in the waiting room on Thursday, socks and shoes off, stretched like a hammock between the two benches which he referred to as "love seats". "I wouldn't have thought I could do this," he exclaimed when I invited him in. "But it wasn't as uncomfortable as I thought"—referring to his new position. I said that I thought he was telling me something of how he felt after the Wednesday hour—that the two of us were somehow linked together —connected in a comfortable if awkward way between the sessions, and that he felt it was unnecessary to hide his tender parts from me today.

Seemingly touched by my remarks, Bill then recalled how he had felt on Monday with Sarah, his supervisor, when she seemed to reach out to him in a personal way, asking how his holiday had been. He said: "I was afraid—no one wants to get into that shit—my loneliness. I guess I felt that she was like my mother. I called Mother over the weekend, finally asking her about Kathleen [the dead baby sister he had resurrected some months before in the analysis]. But she seemed too busy, superficial with me, and preoccupied with others, and I felt so disappointed. I guess I just felt that I had nothing personal to share with Sarah."

When I observed how curious it was that with Sarah he had felt empty, and seemed to have forgotten his experience of the weekend trip of which he had been so proud, just as he had felt empty with me in the Tuesday hour, he fell suddenly silent. When he finally spoke, it was only to utter "Four worn-out tyres".

I had come to know such utterances as his attempt to share with me various pictographs which flashed across his mind. These flashes of his experiences seemed often to startle him, and rarely could he comment on them. However, this time he seemed physically to struggle in his prone position as if to give birth to some thought, and he added: "I'm wondering if they have inner tubes or not." I replied that it appeared that it might be important to know. "Yes," he explained, "an inner tube is for protection—in case of blow-out, it would be less dangerous." I then said: "I think these four worn-out tyres are the analysis, felt perhaps like the mummy-me on the week-end, when you experience me as too worn-out to get excited about you and your progress, or too preoccupied with my other children to help you bear your dreadful losses, fears and loneliness. This must feel like some kind of dangerous blow-out—like going mad or exploding to pieces, or leaking out everywhere."

His nodding response to this urged me on to tell him that I thought of the inner tube as a way to protect himself from the feeling of losing everything. "You keep all these personal experiences sealed up in this tube for safety. But it's so tightly sealed that you become cut off from the very things you feel you need in order to have a relationship with Sarah and also with me, which is like forgetting—this leaves you feeling empty inside."

Perhaps this patient's material speaks to the notion that the body image as a system of tubes (D. Rosenfeld, 1984; Tustin, 1986) is one which is even more elemental than that of the whole body being contained by a skin (Bick, 1968). For Bill, the skin, or "four worn-out tyres", representing the experience of the four analytic hours during the break (the "blow-out") must be fortified by the "inner tube" or the encapsulation of experience during felt absences and loss.

I believe the use made of the autistic encapsulating manoeuvres throughout this analysis is apparent in the material presented. In his muteness, the patient was indeed sealed off from his experiences, past and present, and future contact was in jeopardy as well. Going forward in an imaginative way, rather than giving in to our despair, distinguishes the analyst from objects in the patient's past, who perhaps could not tolerate such narcissistic wounds, or the feelings of abject loneliness which these patients engender in us.

Carla

Like autistic objects and shapes, psychosomatic representations seem to take the place of unconscious phantasies, and are not mentational processes. Tustin (1987) calls these "innate forms" and sees them as innate biological predispositions with psychic overtones. In psycho-somatic patients, as with autistic patients, these have been untrans-formed by reciprocal interactions with the attentive thinking mother, and find expression in physical illness, in which the symptoms may act as bodily containers or a second skin—depositories for unmentalised experiences which ensure survival but which further block development and transformation.

Like Bill, my patient Carla, who was asthmatic, seemed to rely upon a hard, impermeable object to protect her from spilling uncontrollably. However, this hard object took the form of a hard mucous plug in her bronchial tubes. Having lost her mother at a very early age shortly after she, her four sisters and her mother were all abandoned by her father, Carla presented herself mostly as a tough, sassy, streetwise kid whose toughness served as a second skin resembling the tight leather clothing she often wore, and which we eventually traced to her image of the father's erect penis and the paternal function of protection.

In the second year of her analysis, however, a fragile baby part of her began to emerge, crying out to be born and to be allowed contact with the caring presence of the mother-analyst. In one session, Carla began to cry in a way we had not heard before, a cry which penetrated me to a depth as no other, and I felt this corresponded to the strata from which it emanated, as from her deepest and earliest experience of infancy. When I told her as much, she said: "I feel like something terrible wants out of me. I can't let myself breathe. I don't want it to come out. I'm afraid I'll never stop crying." She seemed to be saying that she would spill out and be gone, unable to collect herself at the end of the hour as she experienced once again the father's abandonment and the loss of a sense of security.

Robert

Many patients, like Carla, lacking the mental containment necessary to catch the unbearable overflow of their painful experiences, take refuge within areas of their own body, just as they had once been protected deep inside the recesses of the body of the mother. Others substitute the delusions of being inside the body of the analyst. Such was the case for Robert, a 34-year-old man who had been referred for analysis after a series of hospitalisations following the suicidal death of his mother. His history and his lack of a sense of continuity were so extreme that I felt he should be seen six times a week. Even so, he suffered extreme despair and anxiety between the analytic hours and during the Sunday break.

It was in the seventh month of treatment that Robert was reminded of the events surrounding his actual birth. The doctor was unavailable when his mother commenced labour, and thus the delivery was effected by his father, resulting in trauma for both mother and infant. The grief, rage and terror of this event were re-experienced by my patient in the transference, provoked by my moving office.

From a quiet, dark brown panelled room which he described as "humming", and in which we spent the first few months of the treatment, he suddenly found himself in what he felt to be a sunny environment, with light-coloured walls and carpeting. The catastrophe was felt in a thoroughly sensation-dominated way, as though the sounds, sights and textures were painful in unmitigated form, leading to an experience of physical pain.

He often cried out from such painful assaults, and could not open his eyes for many months while on the couch in this new office. Every sound precipitated a bodily start, and he longed for the feel of the wooded wall next to the couch in my old consulting room, which he had often stroked as a soothing presence in times of extreme distress, just as he had stroked and been stroked by his mother in her bed throughout childhood and early adolescence, to soothe both of them in their seemingly shared and undifferentiated depression.

Not unlike patients described by Tustin (1986, 1990), my patient too had an unduly close relationship to his mother which had fostered false hopes that his body was one with an ever-present immortal being, and so could never come to an end. When Robert's mother died, he was forced to become aware of his bodily separateness. She had jumped from a tenth-storey window to her death, but he was left falling forever—out of windows, out of spaces and absences.

Unable to cope with such terrors, Robert was tenaciously insistent that I was the reincarnation of this immortal mother, and he attempted to manoeuvre me in ways which would give credence to his belief, since he felt certain that his life depended upon physical continuity with me. The loss of my old consulting room, as the womb-mother, re-evoked in him the earliest experiences of being barbarically torn from the mother's body, and the later versions of this event, which were numerous, all leading to the mother's suicide as the final straw which toppled what he called his "house of cards".

In the following session, occurring mid-way between the move to my new office and the Spring break, Robert demonstrated one of the numerous ways in which he attempted to reinstate some sense of safety by reconstituting a concrete delusion of bodily continuity with me. In this session, Robert began by telling me about a woman who had just had a spontaneous abortion, a miscarriage, and of how sad he felt as she appeared to him like a wounded animal. He told me how desperately he felt the need to take photographs of various scenes which came into view during his day in order to bring these to my attention in palpable form. I told Robert about the unspeakable frustration of his separateness from me between the hours and his desire to have me know what he experienced; but to tell me about these experiences only attested to the harsh, cruel fact of our separateness, and added to his frustration and grief.

Though somewhat grudgingly, he then told me about having come upon a shop which sold large statues, displayed in great numbers in front of it. He described the atmosphere of the day as grey and gloomy, the same colour as the plaster from which the statues were made. He said that although the figures were of varying styles, shapes and sizes, some replicating ancient works of art, others more contemporary, arranged with some in the foreground and others behind, he could envision in his mind's eye the composition of a photograph in which all discrimination between background and foreground, old and new, large and small, would be lost. As there was no sun, there would be no shadow; all would appear as one. Time would be compressed and spaces would be obliterated, as would any distinction between these varied objects.

I said that he seemed to be telling me about a state of pristine at-one-ness which could be frozen in time with the click of his camera shutter, providing the concrete proof of this blissful state of affairs. I also called his attention to the urgency of such proof positive at night and on Sundays, when the separation between us became unbearable to him. His response was to tell me that the pronoun "I" was the thing he hated most in all the world. He recalled the first time he knew the "awful truth", as he watched his own hand reach out to grasp his coat in his teens, when he was sent away for the first time. He felt then, for the first time, alone inside his skin. He said: "It was the first time I knew. It wasn't 'I think, therefore I am', a sense of being, but just 'I am alone'."

The solution Robert proposed to "the problem of this analysis" which made him be an "I" was the phantasy of placing his camera on a tripod in my consulting room, setting it for a 30-minute exposure, blurring the two of us into a state of one-ness with no space between and no distinction of sex, age or position in the relationship, the resultant photograph being a "souvenir": a concrete memory of this perfect state, as well as a guarantee of his existence, without which he seemed to feel ever at risk.

Such autistic delusions have permeated the analysis of this young man, and he often yearns for the safe, if constricting, enclosure of the hospital and the four-point restraints he had known many times prior to the beginning of treatment. Perhaps the unthinkable, uncontrollable overspill of emotions which threatens Robert with dissolution is what we call madness, and the straitjacket and four-point restraints are, like the autistic shell, a defence against this madness. However, like the locked ward of a mental hospital, such delusions disallow the establishment of caring connections with the therapist—the "gentle straitjacket" to which Tustin (1986) referred.

Literary after-thoughts

I believe that Mrs Tustin not only helps us with her insights to open ourselves up to fresh perspectives on our patients' communications, but she also encourages us to attend to the poets and artists who can further help us to develop an even greater understanding of the experience of breakdown which most of our patients fear, and which some may already have encountered. For example, in *Celestial Navigations*, Anne Tyler (1974) describes one character who lives in a fragile, yet impermeable world created as a variation on a design by his mother. Tyler describes the constant terror which threatens to overwhelm her hero should he emerge from his self-made fortress. I believe she describes Jeremy's experience of the "black hole" in a most sensitive way:

> These are some of the things that Jeremy Pauling dreaded: using the telephone, answering the doorbell, opening mail, leaving his house, making purchases. Also wearing new clothes, standing in open spaces, meeting the eyes of a stranger, eating in the presence of others, turning on electrical appliances. Some days, he awoke to find the weather sunny and his health adequate, and his work progressing beautifully; yet there would be a nagging hole of uneasiness deep inside him, some flaw in the centre of his well-being, steadily corroding around the edges and widening until he could not manage to lift his head from the pillow. Then he would have to go over every possibility. Was it something he had to do? Somewhere to go? Someone to see? Until the answer came: Oh yes! Today he had to call the Gas Company about the oven. A two-minute chore, nothing to worry about. He knew that. HE KNEW. Yet he lay on his bed feeling flattened and defeated, and it seemed to him that life was a series of hurdles that he had been tripping over for decades, with the end nowhere in sight.

On the Fourth of July, in a magazine article about famous Americans, he read that a man could develop character by doing one thing he disliked every day of his life. Did that mean that all these hurdles might have some value? Jeremy copied the quotation on an index card and tacked it to the window sill beside his bed. It was his hope that the card would remove half of every pain by pointing out its purpose, like a mother telling her child, "This is good for you. Believe me." But in fact, all it did was depress him, for it made him conscious of the number of times each day he had to steel himself for something. Why, nine-tenths of his life consisted of doing things he disliked! Even getting up in the morning! He had already overcome a dread before he was even dressed! If that quotation was right, shouldn't he have the strongest character imaginable? Yet he didn't. He had become aware lately that other people seemed to possess an inner core of hardness that they took for granted. They hardly seemed to notice it was there; they had come by it naturally. Jeremy had been born without it. [Tyler, 1974, pp. 76–7]

Tyler also tells us something of the nature of Jeremy's survival tactics: what it feels like inside his protective shell—the price he pays for protection.

Jeremy Pauling saw life in a series of flashes, startling moments so brief that they could arrest motion in mid-air. Like photographs, they were handed to him at unexpected times, introduced by a neutral voice: here is where you are now. Take a look. Between flashes, he sank into darkness. He drifted into a daze, studying what he had seen. Wondering if he HAD seen it. Forgetting finally, what it was that he was wondering about, and floating off into numbness again. [ibid., p. 37]

Conclusion

Like Jeremy Pauling, the patients discussed in this paper frequently experience, and often attempt to describe, the numbness resulting from the use of autistic protections. There is a certain quality of poignancy conveyed as they complain of isolation from their own internal experiences and objects, as well as from the potential healing effects of contact with the analyst. I believe this must be distinguished from the triumphant pleasure of manic flight from depressive anxiety which we often observe in these very same patients who, while on another track, evade and avoid the shame and guilt of the depressive position or the persecutory feelings associated with the paranoid-schizoid position.

Like Jeremy Pauling, Bill often experiences his life in flashes; Carla calls this "checking out" on herself; Hope refers to these states as "losing" herself; while Robert describes this as "falling through windows". When we as analysts listen carefully to our patients, I believe we can detect their desperate appeals for our help in finding a way out of the autistic tomb—this numbness which incarcerates them. Just as the analyst must discriminate between unintegration and disintegration; between paranoid-schizoid and depressive; between internal and external; between "attacks on linking" and links which have yet to be formed, or which are at best tenuous in nature; between active and passive; between words as communication and words used defensively as action; between the varying dimensions and geoanatomical locations of mental experience—so we must make the fine discriminations between these various primitive states of mind in order to be maximally responsive to our patients in the analytic relationship.

Notes

1. This is a slightly modified version of an article published in the *International Journal of Psychoanalysis* 1992: 549–559.
2. Tustin distinguishes "autistic objects" from objects (inanimate or animate) in the ordinary sense, in that the former are not related to as objects, but rather used for the tactile sensations which they engender upon the surface of the skin of the subject. Autistic shapes may be differentiated from objective shapes (such as a square or a circle), in that they are idiosyncratic, endogenous swirls of sensation produced upon the surface of the skin or internally with the aid of bodily substances or objects. These distinctions, first based upon observations with autistic children, are now widely extended to include numerous other behaviours observable in adults and children with an enclave of autism, which may be conceived of as "sensation-dominated delusions". The key word is "sensation". Such sensations either serve to distract one's attention away from anxiety, providing an illusion of safety, strength and impermeability, or they may have a numbing or tranquillising effect upon the individual which blocks out terrifying awareness.

3. I utilise the term "unmentalised experience" to denote elemental sense data, internal or external, which have failed to be transformed into symbols (mental representations, organised and integrated) or signal affects (anxiety which serves as a signal of impending danger, requiring thoughtful action), but which are instead perceived as concrete objects in the psyche or as bodily states which are reacted to in corporeal fashion (e.g. somatic symptoms or actions). Such experiences are merely "accretions of stimuli" which can neither be used as food for thought nor stored as memories in the mind. Bianchedi calls these "the 'unthoughts' ... perceptions and sensations, not yet subjected to 'alpha function' (Bion, 1962) ... " (1991, p. 11). I believe Freud's notion of the "anxiety equivalent" (1895, p. 94) in the actual neurosis was the first attempt to characterise this phenomenon in psychoanalysis.

References

Bianchedi, E. (1991). Psychic Change: the "Becoming" of an Inquiry *Int. J. Psychoanal.* 72: 6–15.

Bick, E. (1968). The Experience of the Skin in Early Object Relations. *Int. J. Psychoanal.* 49: 484–6.

Bion, W.R. (1962). *Learning from Experience*. London: Heinemann. Reprinted London: Karnac, 1984.

Boyer, L.B. (1990). Countertransference and Technique. In: *Master Clinicians on Treating the Regressed Patient*. New Jersey: Jason Aronson.

Freud, S. (1895). On the Grounds for Detaching a Particular Syndrome from Neurasthenia under the Description "Anxiety Neurosis". *SE 3.*

Grotstein, J.S. (1983). A Proposed Revision of the Psychoanalytic Concept of Primitive Mental States: Part II. The Borderline Syndrome. Section I: The Disorders of Autistic Safety and Symbiotic Relatedness. *Contemp. Psychoanal.* 19: 571–609.

Innes-Smith, J. (1987). Pre-Oedipal Identification and the Cathexis of Autistic Objects in the Aertiology of Adult Psychopathology *Int. J. Psychoanal.* 68: 405–413.

Klein, M. (1948). *Contributions to Psycho-Analysis, 1921–1945.* London: Hogarth.

Klein, M. (1975). *Envy and Gratitude and Other Works.* London: Hogarth.

Ogden, T. (1989). *The Primitive Edge of Experience.* London: Karnac.

Rosenfeld, D. (1984). Hypochondriasis, Somatic Delusions and Body Scheme in Psychoanalytic Practice. *Int. J. Psychoanal.* 65: 377–388.

Rosenfeld, H.A. (1987). *Impasse and Interpretation*. London: Tavistock.

Segal, H. (1957). Notes on Symbol Formation. *Int. J. Psychoanal. 38*:391–7.

Symington, J. (1985). The Survival Function of Primitive Omnipotence. *Int. J. Psychoanal. 66*: 481–488.

Tustin, F. (1972). *Autism and Childhood Psychosis*. London: Hogarth.

Tustin, F. (1980). Autistic Objects. *Int. Rev. Psychoanal. 7*: 27–40.

Tustin, F. (1981). *Autistic States in Children*. London: Routledge & Kegan Paul.

Tustin, F. (1984). Autistic Shapes. *Int. Rev. Psychoanal. 11*: 279–290.

Tustin, F. (1986). *Autistic Barriers in Neurotic Patients*. London: Karnac.

Tustin, F. (1987). Personal communication.

Tustin, F. (1990). *The Protective Shell in Children and Adults*. London: Karnac.

Tyler, A. (1974). *Celestial Navigations*. New York: Berkeley Books.

Winnicott, D.W. (1956). Primary Maternal Preoccupation. In: *The Child, the Family, and the Outside World*. London: Penguin, 1964.

CHAPTER THIRTEEN

Keeping the ghosts at bay: an autistic retreat and its relationship to parental losses[1]

Kate Barrows

In "Mourning and Melancholia" (1917), Freud described how inadequate mourning could lead to a pathological identification with the person who is absent or lost. Instead of missing them and letting them go, the melancholic acts as though he has become them. His repetitive self-reproaches may actually represent reproaches towards the person by whom he feels abandoned and with whom he has unconsciously identified. Freud hauntingly and memorably stated: "Thus the shadow of the object fell upon the ego . . . as though it [the ego] were an object, the forsaken object" (p. 249). This conceptualisation was a major step forward and laid the basis for further investigation of forms of identification which have proved central to the development of psychoanalysis. However, in the clinical material which I will present in this chapter, we can see a situation in which it is rather the shadow inside the object, the shadow of the object's internal object, which falls upon the ego. The patient whom I shall describe spontaneously used the same image when she said that she felt she only had a "shadow life".

In infancy and childhood, when things are going well enough, the child's development of a reasonably secure sense of identity and sufficient confidence in his own goodness and that of his caregivers requires parental containment of the wide range of feelings intrinsic to the development of personality. The mother takes in the infant's extremes of feelings—love and excitement as well as anger and distress—and digests them emotionally. She feeds them back to the infant, as it were, confirming that they are bearable and can be thought about and can gradually become securely integrated into his personality (Bion, 1967, p. 114). The father or other caregiver does the same, and the parents support each other in their capacity to respond adequately to their baby's emotional needs.

However, there may be many obstacles to this process, and in this chapter I shall be describing one such obstacle. I suggest that when parents have particular difficulty in performing this function because they not been able to come to terms adequately with their own bereavements, the child may experience the parent as pre-occupied by a dead internal object. This may be represented by a shadow or ghost, a concrete phantasy with which the child comes to identify and which impedes his development as an individual in his own right, with a life and personality of his own. The presence of the ghost means that there is no room for the lively ambivalence which is essential to separation and emotional growth. The child then identifies not with the object *per se* but with the object's un-mourned internal object; thus an incapacity to mourn can lead to generations shadowed by loss. There may also be factors in the child's personality which make him particularly vulnerable to this kind of identification.

I have found that coming to understand the patient's relation-ship to his parents' internal ghosts can significantly free him to feel able to enter into life more fully and to experience a wider range of feelings, both positive and negative, in his own right. However, for this sort of change to take place, the situation needs to be re-experienced within the analytic relationship. Through dreams or relevant material, the patient is then able to express the phantasy that the analyst is pre-occupied by ghosts or other deathly figures which threaten his life. Recognition of this fear can lead to him having the experience of feeling safe enough to get in touch with his own emotions and make fuller use of the analysis. The patient may then talk in terms of becoming a member of the human race or having a personality of his own, as did the young woman whom I shall describe in this chapter. Having their fears accepted and understood in their analysis is, I think, what leads these patients to move from a state of isolated withdrawal to a sense of shared humanity (see also Rhode, this volume, Chapter Seven).

The importance of these parental ghosts was initially described by Fraiberg *et al* (1975). They described as "ghosts in the nursery" the frightening figures—remembered or unremembered—from the parents' childhoods who take up residence in the nursery of their own children and dominate their current relationships. The influence of the ghosts is determined by the extent to which the feelings associated with difficult experiences have been repressed and the children—now parents—have dealt with their pain by unconsciously passing on the suffering to the new generation (see also Fonagy *et al*, 1993, 1995).

When these "ghosts in the nursery" are too terrifying, the children may deal with their fear of them in various ways. One of these is to resort to autistic defences of the kind that have been described by Tustin (Chapter Two). She described the contrast between a hard, protective shell and a hypersensitive, vulnerable part of the personality and suggested that autistic children hide behind their shell or cling to their bodily sensations in order to prevent or to shut out potentially catastrophic feelings. I would suggest that in situations where there are "ghosts in the nursery", the minds of the parents and others may be experienced as threatening and potentially overwhelming. The child will then not feel safe to express and to become aware of his own ambivalent feelings about, for instance, being separate from the mother, or having to share her with the father or his siblings. He may resort to autistic defences as a denial of separateness, experiencing the mother as if she were part of his own body, thereby turning away from the experience of having a mind or even a body of his own.

Adults with marked autistic features may employ similar defences, but sometimes in more subtle or hidden ways. They may hide behind their shell, or cling tenaciously to an idealised relationship with the analyst, while persecutory fears are denied. The idealised relationship masks the fact that the analyst is not experienced as separate and that fears are being kept at bay. While adult patients may not be immersed in a world of physical sensations to the same extent as autistic children, they may nonetheless stick to the presence of the analyst or to their ideas in a way that suggests a concrete type of attachment rather than actual digestion or integration of the analysis. This can lie behind the wish for an interminable analysis. Despite being highly articulate, they may also use speech "to maintain a link with the analyst or to avoid the link, rather than as a means of communication" (S. Klein, this volume, Chapter Eight). The young woman whom I shall describe used not only speech but also reading and the television to block out awareness of her terrors, to keep ghosts and monsters at bay.

The analysis

Miss Y was in her mid-twenties at the time of her referral. I describe some central aspects of the first three years of her analysis. At first she attempts to maintain an autistic type of retreat where she starves herself of food and contact with life and fills herself up with books and television. She uses the retreat to foster a kind of psychic materialism, which I have called "materialism of sense-impressions", taking things in but not digesting them. She is in charge of her own supplies. The clinging to sensory functioning corresponds to Tustin's descriptions of autistic, concrete modes of operating which can be used to forestall the possibility of unbearable emotions. Then, as she begins to emerge from her retreat, she clings desperately to an adhesive relationship to her boyfriend, her work and her analysis, whose loss she feels would leave her utterly bereft. This protects her from a persecutory relationship, where a damaged object full of ghosts is felt to be pulling her back from her attempts to develop her life. When this becomes clear in the analysis, she does then become more able to have a life and a mind of her own. She begins to be able to own and tolerate her own ambivalence and feelings of loss, emotions essential to her own development.

Miss Y was referred for five times weekly psychoanalysis in her late twenties after she had tried several other forms of therapeutic treatment. These had not managed to shift her presenting symptoms of bulimia, chronic withdrawal from life and escalating suicidal thoughts. I was asked if I would consider seeing her as an alternative to much more costly long-term hospital in-patient treatment. She had to travel over an hour on trains and buses to get to her sessions, and attended very regularly. She felt that her analysis was her last chance.

Miss Y was the second of several children born in quick succession in a large family where there seemed to be little space for her feelings and where important things were not talked about. She had turned to an idealised relationship with her somewhat withdrawn father to avoid a difficult relationship with her mother, whom she felt to be intrusive and hysterical. Her father died in her teens, and the whole family clearly had great difficulty in mourning his loss.

When I first met Miss Y, I was struck by how pale she was, almost ghostly. She was later to describe herself as a "shadow person". Her eyes moved constantly, sliding over the contents of the room and myself as if I were another piece of furniture, a feature I had only seen previously in an autistic child. Her neck also moved from side to side, giving an impression of avoidance and inability to settle. Her clothes were like a conglomeration of opposites: pretty, white feminine blouse and big dirty men's shoes, carefully matched colours and neglected, badly chewed cardigan cuffs.

Her periods stopped when she was 21. Much later, she connected this to her weight loss. She had been overweight at university. She dropped out of college and developed anorexia and then bulimia, which she had had for several years at the time of the referral. Her teeth had been damaged and she was having hormone treatment to prevent bone damage. She was told that so many years of eating disorders and of hormone treatment might have affected her possibilities of restarting her periods and of conceiving children.

She would often say that she felt that she was not meant to have a life like other people, that she thought she was destined in particular never to marry and have children, as though any possibilities of a fulfilling sexual or family life were blighted from early on. She saw no point in living and resented the fact that her breath carried on, regardless of her wish to die.

Although Miss Y expressed her desperation about herself when she came for her initial consultation, when her analysis started it soon became clear that she was entrenched in a retreat which she was terrified of leaving, and which at times she felt to be far superior to other modes of existence. She talked about how bad she felt about having thrown away all her opportunities, particularly in her education and her social relationships, but then went on to describe dieting and filling herself up with books. As she spoke she took on an arrogant tone, saying how she couldn't see how people bear to live their boring lives, with mortgages, children and jobs, although there must be some "compensations". Her retreat was a place which seemed to her to be superior to the realities of life, including the life of her analyst, which she was looking down on as though she now had no needs of her own and nothing to lose. She would talk of how important she felt it was for things to be "pleasant", "comfortable" and "peaceful". This had a deathly quality—her "pleasure principle" was laden with qualities of the "death instinct" (Freud, 1920).

Autistic features soon came to the fore, with images familiar from work with autistic children. Early on she described feeling as though she were spinning round and round in a dark blue sky with twinkling stars far away. This made her feel calmer. She described spinning and spinning when she was a child. Gradually, as she began to emerge from her retreat, her primitive terrors became clearer. There was an image of her whole self bleeding out, of having a vital bit missing. There was a feeling of being like a tortoise without its shell, or of living at the bottom of a dark well and only occasionally daring to come out.

She was thought to be less intelligent than her siblings, and felt very aware that her younger brothers and sister could read and write before she could. "What were you doing while they were learning?" I asked. "Looking on," she replied. (I am reminded of Tustin having pointed out how children with autistic features were often thought to be lacking in intelligence. I did not find her unintelligent; it seemed more a question of whether she would be able to use the untapped resources that were indicated, for instance, in her good ability to find images to express her feelings.) She described much of her childhood as having been spent listening or looking on rather than joining in with others or getting on with things independently. There was a dream of a fish with huge eyes, in a tank too small for it and unable to grow; and a dream that *she was looking after a little silver-grey rabbit with large ears and neglecting it. She put it in a brown paper bag in a drawer and asked someone how to look after it. They told her that she was starving it and that it needed to be taken out and fed properly and allowed to run around.* She said that this dream was like others she used to have as a child, except this time she was asking someone to help her understand so that she could know what to do. The rabbit was like the rabbits which she had had as a child, and she felt guilty because although she remembered being upset about them dying she couldn't remember why they had died, and she suspected that she had actually let them starve.

This material illustrates the split which she effected between the sensory and the psychic, in that her ears or eyes could be used or even over-used, but she could not link what she saw and heard to her feelings or her experience. The part played by her perceptions had become enlarged, as represented by the large ears of the rabbit or the huge eyes of the fish. However, in the dream about the rabbit, she recognised that she needed understanding to free herself from this state of passive perception so that she could be "fed properly and run around", which implied awareness of the need to digest her experiences and to feel free to move and to engage with life. She felt responsible for the neglect of her needy aspects. The paper bag and the small tank also suggested an internal container which constricts her emotional growth.

These dreams can also be seen to be connected to her eating difficulties. When she was anorexic she did starve herself, like the rabbit. The overuse of her perceptual apparatus in both dreams is in some ways similar to the overeating in her bulimia, where she took in too much but could not allow herself to digest it. Williams (1997) reflects on the use of a "no entry system of defences" (p. 115) by some individuals with eating disorders. She describes a reversal of the container-contained relationship, in which the child has been used by the parents to contain their projections. The child becomes a receptacle for the parents' internal objects and anxieties, which are experienced as "foreign bodies"; he develops strategies to keep these out or to get rid of them. Miss Y's split between sensory perceptions on the one hand and thoughts and feelings on the other can be seen as part of her "no entry system". She responded with relief to the containment provided by the analysis, in that her symptom of bulimia disappeared within a few weeks of her starting her sessions, though there were, as far as I know, two occasions prior to holidays when she made herself vomit.

The split between sensory and psychic modes of functioning described above was not immediately apparent, as Miss Y ostensibly had all the asceticism which is more typical of the anorexic than the bulimic patient. Her asceticism was expressed though repudiation of instinctual life and of obvious forms of materialism. (See Kestemberg *et al* [1972], as well as A. Freud's [1966] discussion of asceticism as a repudiation of instinct.) Yet, paradoxically, her intake of intellectual fodder was performed in a materialistic way, to fill herself up but not to change or nourish herself. Her reading or television-watching was an escape into a vicarious world which left her completely unaltered. She would say in an off-hand way that she did not want to get to know people—she could get to know them by watching the television. She spoke as though getting to know had nothing to do with a relationship but was simply an accumulation of material facts. Yet it became clear, for instance from the dreams described above, that her overuse of her perceptions did not lead to development. Her kind of materialism might be termed materialism of sense impressions. It served to protect her from frightening objects as well as from her own feelings, which she felt were too dangerous to experience. She told me on one occasion that she felt like a child in a Japanese legend who kept reading and reading to keep monsters, terrors and ghosts at bay. This psychic materialism can be linked to Tustin's discussion of autistic objects. The object no longer has meaning in its own right, but serves to protect the individual from terrors of death and disintegration.

Miss Y's fear that there was no-one who could really stand her feelings of ambivalence and loss seemed of central importance in her withdrawal from contact. For instance there were several sessions which seemed helpful, following which she was able to have a meal and socialise with people, something which she had previously been unable to do. She seemed heartened but then feelings of exclusion came up and she felt that her positive feelings were getting lost. She told me that she used to love animals as a child and wanted to keep all sorts of pets. Her first pets were goldfish but they developed a fungus; two of them died. She remembered "screaming with terror and a sort of frustration" when she discovered that two of them had fin-rot, and her father said that she shouldn't keep pets if she was that upset before they even died. In the light of her new-found positive feelings getting lost, I interpreted her fear that I might not stand her feelings about things getting killed off inside her. She then remembered moving house aged ten, and going back to stay with her best friend. When she came home she missed her friend and was terribly upset, crying a lot. Her father said that she shouldn't go any more if she was that upset when she came home, so she tried to shut out her feelings and bury herself in books. She did not have any more close friends until after her father died, when she formed an intense friendship with another girl at school. However she could not stand her friend's other attachments (even to the friend's own parents), so she broke off the friendship.

I commented on her fear that I would not stand her upset feelings about missing me between the sessions, or her feelings about my other attachments to my family and other people. She agreed, and then described her father as finding her upset feelings "irritating and annoying", as though he had no place for them. He was a very "moral" person and could not tolerate any jealousy or squabbling; Miss Y said that it "made him go all sad". She felt inadequate and despairing because she knew that she could not be "mature" enough to please him. This was something she also feared in relation to me. She initially assumed that my idea of maturity meant not having any jealous, rivalrous or possessive feelings or any feelings of loss. So it was also unsafe to be lively: if she was lively, she would also risk coming into contact with the ambivalent feelings which might meet with rejection.

The persistent impression of her father as being unable to tolerate feelings, particularly feelings of loss, made sense several months later, in Miss Y's third year of analysis. She told me that when her father was eight years old he was looking after his younger sister in the garden, and she fell into the pond and was drowned. His sister's death was never talked about. He felt that his father never forgave him and his mother never recovered. These grandparents seemed to Miss Y frighteningly stern and disapproving. She used to dread visiting them and felt that she should sit still *as though she didn't exist*. A couple of months after she had told me about her father's sister, she told me that her mother had a younger sister who had a chronic illness throughout her childhood, which was spent in and out of hospital. Her mother referred to her as "pathetic", and she never managed to join in life like other people, remaining a misfit in her adult life. Miss Y seems to have identified with her parents' dead or damaged younger siblings. She frequently expressed this in terms of feeling that she was not meant to have a life like other people: on one occasion she thought of hermit crabs who lay their eggs in the sand, and when the young hatch out they have to get to the sea. Only one or two survive out of thousands, and she felt that she was one of the ones who were not meant to survive.

Miss Y was very sensitive to my tolerance or intolerance of her feelings, and often seemed to be listening out for signs of experiences inside me which might make it hard for me to deal with her feelings: it was as though she was listening out for my ghosts. Her sensitivity was also extended to my relationship to my ideas. It was at times a struggle to keep my thinking alive and to deal with the feeling of being inhabited by dead ideas or hollow theories. While it was sometimes possible to see that this deadness was related to attacks on my thinking, I also formed the impression that she was afraid that I harboured something frightening. I felt it important to be aware of my ghosts, for instance of archaic internal figures who fear or disapprove of emotions and whom she might experience as making her feel, as her grandparents did, that she shouldn't exist emotionally.

Notwithstanding Miss Y's attempts to protect herself from human relationships, fears of loss and rejection often came up before my holiday breaks. When I first met Miss Y, she told me that she had never had a boyfriend. Shortly before the first summer holiday, she told me that she had in fact had one brief sexual relationship. She had always felt that she was destined not to have a sexual relationship or to marry, but curiosity got the better of her and she had a brief relationship with a passing stranger, in order not to get too involved. She was surprised that she felt devastated when he moved on after a few weeks, although she had known that he would. She said that she felt as though she had lost everything, had lost a part of herself. It was after this that she became anorexic and amenorrhoeic, determining never to have a sexual relationship again. It seems to me that there was a link between her autistic fear of loss of "everything"—a vital part of herself—and her subsequent eating difficulties.

She was very thin and seemed initially resigned to, or even relieved by, her probable infertility. However, she gradually became terrified of the damage she might have done to herself and her chances of child-bearing. She managed to put on some weight, and after a year of psychoanalysis had her first period for ten years.

During the next year she did make considerable strides in her analysis as well as in terms of external achievements and some social life. She managed to undertake a university course. She gradually developed a friendship with a young man and became sexually involved with him. At first she felt scornful of him for caring for her, but felt that this was a mad response and wanted to understand it. I interpreted this in terms of her scorn of a part of herself which could care for someone or desire them. Then other anxieties came to light: sexual revulsion, fears of engulfment and abandonment, loss of her splendid isolation. But she also felt heartened at this stage, saying that she had never thought she would feel like being with another person. She was grateful to be wanted sexually and socially and, notwithstanding her many anxieties, began to enjoy her relationships with enormous surprise at beginning to feel so much more alive. She felt grateful to me and to her analysis for having helped her thus far.

These feelings of relief and gratitude contrasted strongly with resentful feelings about being encouraged out of her hide, and fears about how vulnerable she could become. Her fear of being awakened from her shadow life to a life of intense feelings and sensations only to lose everything often put me in mind of Oliver Sacks' (1973) account of the short-lived "Awakenings" of patients who had been asleep for twenty years. They experienced a heightened intensity of emotions, sensations and gratitude for being alive, as well as the almost unbearable poignancy that all this would be lost if they were to fall once more into a sleep from which they could never be woken. Miss Y saw her boyfriend, her work, her analysis as being irreplaceable. If she lost them she would have to go back to her withdrawn state (her autistic retreat), but now she would no longer be able to tolerate that way of life. She still seemed to feel that she had very little inside her which would help to sustain loss or change, as though it could all be swept away in a moment. I felt puzzled as to why her fear of loss was so acute.

After two and a half years of her analysis, her boyfriend went away for a year. This plunged her into a very difficult period as she seemed to have partially lost her old defences without yet having secure enough internal or external objects. The period of "awakening" gave way to a time of great anxiety. She became obsessed with possible losses. A dream from this period in her analysis threw some light on the precariousness of her hold on life and its relationship to parental ghosts. She had agreed to go away to see her boyfriend for a long weekend, which would mean missing a few sessions of her analysis. This was unusual as she attended very regularly.

She arrived in a fluster for her session and apologised for being a few minutes late. She talked at first about having been to the doctor's surgery and having found it hard to leave in case he might think her ungrateful. I linked this to her feelings about missing some sessions and suggested that she was afraid I might think her ungrateful. She said with relief that she had been feeling really awkward and could hardly bear to talk about it, yet there was such a lot to say. She told me the day of her return. She added that the doctor had been talking with her about the possibility of her having children at some point in the future. She also spoke about her regrets at missing her sessions next week and seemed apologetic about her need to see her boyfriend. I interpreted that she seemed to think I might not realise that she felt she needed to see him and to talk to the doctor about the possibility of having children.

She seemed again relieved by this interpretation and went on to tell me a dream which she had had the night before last. She was stuck in a sort of swamp, trying desperately to get out. There were some figures who were like ghosts or corpses, she didn't know which. They were trying to get her, to kill her. She was absolutely terrified that she would be dragged back and killed. Her sister, Z, was helping her. Z wasn't affected and could survive this and help her out of it; her sister was managing to pull her out. Miss Y was so frightened that when she woke up she had to have the light on all night. It reminded her of the dreams she used to have about a dead town, but in those dreams she used to be attracted to and interested in the dead places and to like wandering round them, whereas this time she was terrified.

I commented on her having left it until today to tell me about the dream and wondered aloud whether perhaps it felt too real. She said that it was terribly frightening; she woke up but felt that it could really be happening. She had always been terrified of ghosts and even recently had to have her light on all night after her mother told her and her sister about ghosts.

I understood this dream in terms of Miss Y's relationship to me both as a helpful sister and as a swamp-like mother full of ghosts. She said that she thought of me as being like her helpful sister, helping her out of the swamp: "You wouldn't hold me back!" However, it seemed to me that her relief when I addressed her fear of telling me about going to see her boyfriend also implied that she was also afraid of my pulling her back from her relationship and the prospect of having a family. When I suggested this she replied: "But I have to have a life, it can't be helped!" She went on to describe an anxious couple who held her back from going to a talk that she wanted to hear. This seemed to express her fear of my anxieties, my ghosts holding her back from getting the most out of her analysis and her life.

It seemed to me important to be open to taking seriously her thoughts about her analyst as an anxious parent or part of an anxious couple and not to swamp her with interpretations relating to her own aggression and possessiveness, for instance, which would have been to identify her with the ghosts, to confirm her idea that she could only have a shadow-life. This dream vividly illustrates Miss Y's fears about having a life of her own, of emerging from her autistic retreat. One might see her previous withdrawn way of life, her retreat, as having protected her from the swamp of ghosts, the deathly place which she has been trying to avoid. It is significant that she has the dream at a time when she is taking important steps to develop her own life and future as someone with a sexual relationship and the possibility of having children.

When this problem of her relationship to her objects' internal ghosts had been to some extent worked through, she did gradually become more able to take responsibility for her own negative feelings, without feeling that they made her into someone unfit to have a life. Her ventures became more rooted in the real world.

The split shown in Miss Y's dream between a helper and a frightening object also affected her view of the parental couple who were split along similar lines: father-helper and damaged mother. Material from a session several months later showed this split particularly clearly. In this session the idealisation of the helping object is more pronounced, as is the part played by Miss Y's resentment of the parental couple. Miss Y talked of her confusion between Kew Gardens and the burned down Crystal Palace. At Kew she had been taken by her father to see some statues, and she particularly liked the griffin because it is made up of different animals, not conceived and born like others. She also remembered her father's magic stories which she liked to escape into. It seemed that she was turning to a magic father to help her to get away from her burning attacks upon her fragile mother (the Crystal Palace) and on the parental couple who conceive babies in the normal way. She also turned to a magic, patched-together object—the griffin—to avoid her ambivalence. This threw light upon the fact that when I first met Miss Y, her appearance struck me as somehow patched together, a "conglomeration of opposites". Likewise, her internal objects had not been conceived or put together properly, so they could not be assimilated into her personality and her inner life was not free to develop. In the griffin session Miss Y also became painfully aware of the way in which her resentment of the parental intercourse extended to resentment of my capacity to think fruitfully about her, hence affecting her own thinking capacities.

Her capacity to recognise her own feelings and to think her own thoughts developed considerably after the part played by the parental ghosts had been understood and to some extent worked through in the analysis. She could then begin to take responsibility for her own ambivalence without feeling that this made her unfit to have a life. She also developed a greater capacity to take an interest in other people, and began to see her analyst as a human being rather than as ideal or terrifying. Despite her remaining difficulties, I felt that her life was now launched and was a going concern rather than an awakening which might not last. She said that she felt she had become a member of the human race.

Discussion

Although Miss Y had had created an autistic retreat to protect herself from her fear of the ghosts inside her parents, she had not managed to avoid identification with them. It was as though, like the ghosts, she was fated not to have a life or personality of her own. When she exclaimed "But I have to have a life, it can't be helped!" this seemed a startling revelation, a spontaneous affirmation of life.

A feature of Miss Y's retreat was that she turned to a material relationship to her objects when thought and feelings became too threatening (Bion, 1962, p. 10). As she described, she used reading to fill herself up and to "keep the ghosts and monsters at bay". It seems to me that this material use of objects or language is similar to the autistic child's physical clutching of a toy as if it were part of himself, to keep away fears of catastrophic feelings. Her personality lacked the cohesiveness that is based on taking in a good object (Klein, 1946, p. 9) instead being tacked together like the griffin, or hidden behind a protective carapace like the shell of the hermit crab.

It was helpful to Miss Y that there was also a healthier part of her that was at times well aware that she starved herself of interests and of a capacity to think. A large part of her motivation for getting better consisted of her awareness of the deathly quality of her retreat and her wish to be able to keep alive feelings of interest in things and people outside herself.

While at the start of her analysis she was in the grip of something so life-destroying that she was actually at risk of suicide or of starvation, I felt that it was important to keep an open mind about the location and the nature of the deadliness. Initially she was all too ready to see herself as deadly and destructive—"a bad lot"—and it seemed to make a difference to her that I didn't accept this as the whole picture. This might have felt like a confirmation that she was indeed so negative that she could not hope to have a life like other people. Recognition of the ghosts in her dream and in the transference relationship to me seemed to lessen her feeling of being swamped by negativity and hopelessness. This in turn made it gradually become possible for her to become more aware of the conflict between her own positive feelings and her destructive ones. Her responsiveness to her analysis suggests to me that her destructiveness was not the main factor which had driven her to a standstill, but that this had as much to do with her fear of, and identification with, parental damaged objects. She had turned to her retreat in an attempt to avoid these feelings of damage.

The fact Miss Y was so withdrawn as a child, and seems to have felt that it was unsafe to be in touch with her ambivalent feelings, may have contributed to their very raw and visceral nature when they did begin to surface in her analysis. Tustin (1972) has suggested that both in autistic children and in an anorexic patient, at the point when the patient is beginning to be able to think for himself, feelings of intense rivalry often appear, accompanied by a phantasy which

Tustin calls the "nest of babies" (p. 177–8): the therapist/mother is felt to be occupied by predatory rivals who are given special food and a privileged place in the mother's mind (see also Houzel, this volume, Chapter Six). This phantasy is accompanied by visceral feelings of jealousy. When Miss Y's jealousy did surface, it had the same intense, raw quality. For instance, she once expressed a grim and shocking pleasure that a group of young children in a nursery school were being held hostage and might be shot. Miss Y's anger and upset about the births of her younger siblings had not been worked through, her sister being idealised while intense feelings of hostility were experienced in relation to her other siblings as well as to other sibling figures like the children in the nursery, representing, I think, my internal children.

It seems likely that there was a connection between Miss Y's raw hatred of the "nest of babies" and her sensitivity to her parents' internal dead or damaged siblings. She seems to have suffered from hypersensitivity to siblings, her own and her parents'. She felt that her jealous and possessive feelings were intolerable, and it seems likely that at some level she felt that her feelings were responsible for the ghosts inside her parents (a confusion between her murderous feelings towards the children in the nursery school described above, for instance, and the parental "ghosts in the nursery"). She gradually became able to acknowledge the way in which her jealousy and envy entered into her analysis and affected her ability to use her mind constructively. In the session where she preferred to turn to the griffin or to her father's magic stories, she became aware of resenting her analyst's thinking capacities and her parents' creativity. It seemed a relief to her when I was able to address her resentment, since this showed that I could recognise her feelings without collapsing like the Crystal Palace or retaliating like the ghosts in the swamp. Until then it seems that Miss Y had felt that the feelings of jealousy evoked by three-person relationships were beyond the pale. She now began to feel that rather than being catastrophic and unmanageable, jealousy and envy are emotions which one is bound to experience as a member of the human race, and that the way one deals with such feelings is part of one's individual personality.

When Miss Y was in her withdrawn state she was unable to develop her potential for work and for human relationships. The effect of her retreat was to isolate her not only from life but from her own better qualities and capacities, such as her sensitivity and her gift for expressing herself in language. These seem to have been part of a healthier inheritance from her relationship with her parents which her fear of the "ghosts in the swamp" had prevented her from developing. She was able to find a profession in which she could utilise her gifts, and her sensitivity eventually found its place in a capacity for human relationships. After three years of analysis, as she emerged from her shadow-life, Miss Y was able to say that she felt that she was beginning to have a personality of her own.

Note

1. This chapter is a modified version of a paper which appeared in the *International Journal of Psychoanalysis* 1989, 70.

References

Bion, W.R. (1962). *Learning from Experience*. London: Heinemann. Reprinted London: Karnac, 1984.

Bion, W.R. (1967). A Theory of Thinking. In: *Second Thoughts*. London: Karnac, 1984.

Fonagy P., Steele, M., Moran, G., Steele, H., & Higgitt A. (1993). Measuring the Ghost in the Nursery: an Empirical Study of the Relationship Between Parents' Mental Representations of Childhood Experiences and their Infants' Security of Attachment. *Journal of the American Psychoanalytic Association* 41: 957–989.

Fonagy, P., Steele, M., Steele, H., Leigh, T., Kennedy, R., Mattoon, G. & Target, M. (1995). Attachment, the Reflective Self, and Borderline States. In: S. Goldberg, R. Muir, & J. Kerr (Eds.), *Attachment Theory: Social Developmental and Clinical Perspectives*. Hillsdale, NJ & London: The Analytic Press.

Fraiberg, S., Adelson, E. & Shapiro, V. (1975). Ghosts in the Nursery: a Psychoanalytic Approach to the Problems of Impaired Infant-Mother Relationships. In: *Clinical Studies in Infant Mental Health*. London: Tavistock, 1980.

Freud, A. (1936). *The Ego and the Mechanisms of Defence*. London: Hogarth.

Freud, S. (1917). Mourning and Melanchlia. *SE 14*.

Freud, S. (1920). Beyond the Pleasure Principle. *SE 18*.

Kestemberg, E., Kestemberg D. & Decobert, S. (1972). *La Faim et le Corps*. Paris: P.U.F.

Klein, M. (1946). Notes on some Schizoid Mechanisms. In: *Envy and Gratitude and Other Works*. London: Hogarth (1975).

Sacks, O. (1973). *Awakenings*. London: Duckworth.

Tustin, F. (1972). *Autism and Childhood Psychosis*. London: Hogarth.

Tustin, F. (1981). *Autistic States in Children*. London: Routledge & Kegan Paul.

Williams, G. (1997). *Internal Landscapes and Foreign Bodies*. London: Duckworth.

CHAPTER FOURTEEN

Finding the bridge: psychoanalysis with two adults with autistic features[1]

Caroline Polmear

Zara came to her session one Friday morning in July exactly on time. She had been in analysis for nearly nine years. Her barely audible double ring of the bell alerted me to the fact that she was feeling particularly raw. She had perfected a technique whereby she could make the bell vibrate just enough to let me know she was there without making it utter its harsh, shrill sound, which could completely annihilate her fragile sense of self. I tried to respond to her two short rings with a response played on my door buzzer that followed the *allegro con vivo* beat she had established. Her appearance confirmed my suspicions that today was a difficult day for her. She came into the consulting room with her pillow clutched tightly to her front, her clear nail varnish bottle in one clenched fist and her "see-through" key ring in the other. After taking up a position on the floor to the side of my desk, she began to gather herself. With her compelling wish to communicate however difficult it might be, she told me that she wasn't normal today and that she had a list of items to talk about.

We worked together for half an hour or so, going through the degrees of hopelessness, helplessness, hope and despair which characterised our work together, and eventually managed the contact we were striving for. Zara relaxed and began to speak directly, with an arresting purity. She said that now, just from this term, she had started to feel what it was like to be "normal"; not all the time, but sometimes. For the first time in her life, she had a sense that she was like other people some of the time, not an alien species. She said she didn't know how this had come about, but thought it was because I had found a bridge between our two worlds. She didn't know how I knew what she felt, because I was "normal", not like her. But when I found the bridge, she felt more "normal".

I t has been my privilege to work with two adults with autistic features. Zara, a young woman lawyer, completed a ten-year psychoanalysis five sessions a week. Catherine, a woman in her late forties, an archaeologist interested in the very earliest civilisations, completed a twice-weekly psychotherapy, which lasted for four years. Both women might be described either as having Asperger's syndrome or as being high functioning autists.

My patients were able to convey to me their experience of a world constantly threatening to overwhelm and annihilate them with unmoderated sensory experience. It is a world where perceptions are as sharp as raw nerve endings; where broken-off body parts and violent explosions can erupt at any time; where rigidity and ritual offer only a partial protection, and autistic retreats afford the only peace and respite from unmitigated and exhausting terror. Small wonder that such retreats feel infinitely preferable to the painfully assaulting world of "reality".

Adults such as those I treated are seldom referred for intensive treatment. They may function well enough with a false self (Winnicott, 1960), relying on a meticulous attention to detail, a capacity for mimicking relationships and an occupational setting which is syntonic with their condition. In many cases they function extremely well.

People such as Zara and Catherine may seek help when they change jobs and the people and activities holding projected aspects of themselves and providing a kind of exoskeleton are lost. Alternatively they may feel troubled by their difficulty in relating, or a relative or friend may suggest they need support. A sense of feeling different, alien, of not fitting, may lead to a search for help, although without a well-developed sense of self it can be difficult for the person in this situation to want or need anything for themselves. They may accept help if it is seen as helping others.

Patients describe the feeling of being different. As I will show, the work requires something subtly different from the analyst too. I hope it will become clear that while retaining a firmly analytic attitude, the analyst has to go beyond what is usually required of her in understanding and responding to the experience of another.

From my limited experience I recommend psychoanalytic treatment if both parties feel they can manage it. Intensive treatment gives patient and analyst the opportunity to experience the encapsulated terror of traumatic contact and separation many times, and hopefully to work towards understanding and containing this. The process is testing and demanding for both parties, and I have been impressed by, and grateful for, the courage and tenacity of both my patients.

This chapter is in two parts. In the first, I will give clinical examples to convey the patients' subjective experience. In the second part I will discuss the treatment of adults through psychoanalysis and psychoanalytic psychotherapy.

The subjective experience

Contact and avoidance of contact

Ordinary human contact, which warms and gratifies and gives meaning to life, was experienced by my patients as a threat to their and my survival. They might yearn for a soft contact but then feel the need for hard contact to maintain the shell of self which saved them from annihilation, from non-existence or from their insides spilling out. Besides, loving contact could feel ferocious and devouring, and had to be avoided in order to protect the loved one.

Saying "Good morning" at the door or looking at me on entering the room felt to Zara like lasering me with such an intensely focused beam that I would be dispersed into fragments, vaporised or burned up. Catherine described in vivid detail car crashes in which death was instant, violent and gory and the bodies were splattered around the scene of the accident. I soon came to respect the fact that contact meant impact and violent death by explosion. The two of us were indistinguishable at the moment of impact and neither survived. On other days I was warned that if I came too near at the door I risked death from the fallout of the explosion of a nuclear bomb.

In the early days of treatment, the experience of feeling under-stood by me also felt like unbearable contact. It was immediately dispersed in a range of ingenious ways. Zara would typically whizz off into a flurry of cartoon images of me as a Monty Pythonesque person made up of human-like machinery bits, with no meaning or purpose. She laughed uproariously at the mental image of me on ritual tramlines, moving backwards and forwards day and night between my chair and the door, dehumanised and safe and yet, sadly, utterly useless to her of course. Sometimes when something I said made real and helpful sense, she would instantly tell me of herself in the helping role doing for someone else a version of what I had just done for her. She could preserve something of the learning by removing from it any knowledge of me as a separate alive person, and thus removing the element of contact which so terrified her.

Helpful contact could also be experienced as unbearably exciting and overwhelming. In this state, Zara found herself speaking in a robotic, computerised voice while trying to hold on to what I'd said. The words within the sentence were detached from each other and the experience of being understood, longed-for but overwhelming, was stripped away from the intellectual content. That way the thought could be preserved while the emotional experience of it was neutral-ised. It would be tempting to see these defences as envious and destructive, yet it was clear to me that they were efforts at preserving rather than destroying. If Zara's experience of me could be split up like this, then at least some of me could be retained at this stage.

While emotional contact felt like dangerous physical contact, actual physical contact, for example in the moment of taking the bill from me, was almost impossible. Catherine would hold her breath in panic and turn her face away, flapping one hand and arm franti-cally to rid herself of overwhelming anxiety and a physical feeling of being invaded. All openings in the face: eyes, ears and mouth, had to be shut tight. Even so, Catherine shuddered involuntarily as she grabbed the envelope and rushed for the door.

It became clear that contact could mean the coming together in an instant of primitive ferocious, biting love and ruthless, violent hatred, with very little ego to moderate the impact of the hatred with something more loving. As both patients gained in ego strength, new ways emerged of managing this seemingly impossible situation. One day, Zara, eager to take in what I was saying because we were well in contact that day and the session was feeling fruitful, listened intensely to what I was saying while giving a complete simultaneous translation into German. This seemed to lessen what could have felt like the penetrating physical attack of my words by discharging them through her mouth while she retained the understanding.

The fear of being touched or physically impinged upon was always present. On one occasion, Zara recalled the fear of being cuddled by her mother, which she said physically hurt her and made her feel evil. When contact was not mutually destructive, it was feared as a dangerous merger. Zara accused me in patent terror of "locking on" to her so that I took over her mind, leaving her "brain dead".

Identity, self and self experience

I think that before treatment my patients had little sense of self as it is ordinarily understood. When I spoke about "doing something to yourself", Zara replied incredulously: "I don't have a self!" In fact my suggestion put her in a panic, which I later understood to be related to the dangers of having a self. The unconscious fantasy which emerged in numerous different ways was that as soon as one came into existence as a self, one would be destroyed. If I thought she had a self then I must be about to annihilate her. Ringing the doorbell proved that she existed, and she expected its harsh, shrill sound to shatter her at the moment of existing if it rang fully.

Such experiences seem to me to link with a severe problem about being recognised. I imagine an infant whose basic primitive communication with its mother or carer fails for some reason. It cannot recognise itself in the other, or perhaps cannot bear the contact enough to feel held and contained. When this is repeated during treatment, the analyst experiences it as a failure to communicate emotion. The patient, on the other hand, feels she is communicating powerful emotions but getting back no feeling reaction. The analyst receives a communication from the patient of something either dead and empty or "otherwise engaged" and self-sufficient. This failure of fundamental recognition and of communication with the analyst at first feels irreparable and devastating to the patient, as I assume it must have been in her early experience. The whole enterprise feels doomed, and failure seems to stare both patient and analyst in the face.

While these patients feel "selfless", in fact they exist inside others. My patients projected their whole selves into me where I could begin to learn about them. They described me as dead, as "brain dead" or "brain damaged". They said that I was someone deeply split within myself, that my mind was out of touch with my emotions. I was someone from another species, an "alien form", unrecognisable as human, cut off, unfeeling and mechanical in all my interactions with other people. I was psychopathic and had no conscience; I had an empty mind, was unable to think for myself, someone who mouthed psychoanalytic theory without understanding and without concern for my patient. Equally important was my quality of wrongness. I was the wrong shape, an uncomfortable angular shape. Catherine said that I made her feel sick in her stomach and that she wanted to sick me up. I was of the wrong culture and of the wrong theoretical persuasion. All this was pushed into me with a violence and primitive hatred that made it hard to bear.

My sense was that I was being made to experience how it felt to be Catherine and Zara; I was also learning about their expectation that a significant person wouldn't really take them in, couldn't bear them or stand them, perhaps even wanted to kill them. Zara in fact believed that when her mother was pregnant with her, she had starved herself in an attempt to deny the pregnancy. Catherine thought that her mother had nearly miscarried her (both women's mothers had in fact suffered more than one miscarriage). In between bouts of violent attack on me, I felt I was sometimes being offered a lifeless "baby" to treat, perhaps in the mistaken belief that that was what I wanted. Perhaps my patients unconsciously wished to restore the dead babies to their mothers.

Gradually a sense of a deep internal split emerged in both patients. It seemed like an experience of traumatic and unmetabolised rupture at the very heart of the self. I am struck by the similarity with those patients described by Balint in *The Basic Fault* (1968), and assume that as Stewart suggests, Balint's patients brought a borderline psychotic transference to analysis, and in addition to this they were to varying degrees autistic or during treatment they hit upon autistic "pockets" (Tustin, 1981, 1986; S. Klein, this volume, Chapter Eight). Zara described a chasm of unbridgeable proportions that could suddenly open up. The floor of the consulting room became plates in the Earth's surface, and she was convinced that I had only put a rug there to hide the fault line. It was as if the internal experience of rift was mirrored in the outside world. The space between us was frequently an infinitely deep hole, and she could not trust me to want to reach across the chasm and make contact with her. If she risked it herself, she might fall into the death gap to annihilation. Better not to want contact.

> At a time when Zara's anxiety was at its height and she was beginning to experience a wish to make contact with me, she arrived for a session in a panic, flapping her arm to get rid of some of it and blowing out as she entered the consulting room. "Big, enormous hole outside," she gasped, tapping the surface of my desk to hear the hard sound with hollow tones in it. "It wasn't there yesterday." (I realised she must have been talking about some road works she'd passed.) "You pulled up that plant; there's an enormous gap in the garden; there's nothing there. Oh no! Where is that book? There's a gap on the bookshelf". Now quite frantic, she tried to look at me, and as she did so she threw her head from side to side, scanning me as a way of reducing the impact of taking me in through her eyes. She began repeating something over and over, getting more and more anxious as I failed to grasp what was terrifying her. Finally I got it. "Dead budgerigar; dead budgerigar, dead budgerigar. Why would anyone wear a dead budgerigar on their suit?" I realised that she saw my ellipse-shaped, plastic tortoiseshell brooch as a dead bird, perching on my jacket lapel. The gap between the sessions, the terror of not being able to trust that one or other of us could get safely across the gap to make contact with the other, the near-certainty that she'd look at me for life and contact only to find a dead hole, and a belief that I'd uprooted our connection, miscarried her and left a yawning chasm for her to disappear into, fell into place in my mind.

Though I am describing the lack of an integral sense of self, my patients did have various identities. At one level there was the professional person, renowned for her exceptional intelligence, diligence, wacky sense of humour and absolute integrity. The capacity for detail and the degree of focus of people such as Zara and Catherine means that in good conditions they do very well in certain professions, particularly the more academic ones. At a deeper level, though, there is a more painful identity as "alien". In Oliver Sacks' account of his meeting with Temple Grandin, he captures this alien feeling in the title: *An Anthropologist on Mars* (1995). I wonder whether part of this lies in the feeling of being unrecognised and in the lack of a feeling of physical fit with others. I certainly found in my patients a yearning for body moulding and fit with another. But as our work progressed the identity as alien seemed to recede, until Zara could describe feeling "normal" when I found the bridge between our two worlds.

Another feature, which seems to contribute to the identity as alien, is a sense of living in a primitive part of the brain. Any sophisticated thinking feels like something learned, or grafted on, false and not to be trusted. Primitive experience of a sensation world is the "truth" while the world of people interacting with a mixture of self-interest and interest in others is the world of "lies". What is felt in the body is real. In my patients' material there were numerous images of damaged babies; babies born with the front part of their brain missing, their foreheads short and sloping backwards; and of primitive forms of humankind. Both Zara and Catherine felt more related to animals than to people; Catherine was sure that she was descended from a different evolutionary branch. In the early years, I often felt that Zara's analysis was dominated simply by fight-or-flight reactions. The first dream she brought concerned a homunculus with its eyes wide open left on a shelf to die. I think she felt at that point that she hadn't even reached conception. I have already mentioned that both patients' mothers had suffered several miscarriages. Perhaps unconsciously conception itself was felt as the first destructive contact.

This profound sense of alienation—in the early days, when she was in a dispersed state of "selflessness", Zara described herself as a hologram—suggests another perspective on the continuing attacks on me. Zara might have felt compelled to provoke and attack me in order to elicit a "real" reaction, and in that way feel real herself. If she failed to throw me off track, she would go off on a manic flight of violent "cartooned" attacks on me, describing with glee how she was picking me up by the legs and banging me rhythmically against the wall—bang, bang, bang—then swinging me around her head before letting go and sending me off to outer space. My task was to find ways of containing the excitement of all this before she crashed into the alternative state, which she experienced as having "flopped". Both Catherine and Zara explained to me, and showed me, the problem of swinging between two extreme states: one over-reactive, over-active, too excited and "hyped up", too focused, "like someone with all the dials on the radio receiver turned up too high"; and the other a flopped, turned away, timeless sleep state.

Shells, wrappings and retreats

Much has been written about the autistic shell, notably by Frances Tustin (1972, 1981, 1986, 1990). What I became most aware of with my patients was the dual function of the "shells" they used. They served both to keep *in* the psychopathic, pre-ruth (Winnicott) violence and to keep *out* the annihilating, penetrating other. Equally the shell was both to avoid contact and, in its choice of medium, to communicate and make contact. It was to control the intrusion of external stimuli like light, noise and smell, then playfully, taking that same stimulus, to turn it into a barrier to further intrusion.

For example, a troubling light shining into the consulting room unusually brightly was at first hated, as was I for allowing it, then turned into a delightful ritual light show for the patient's benefit, created by moving her head around in a fast circular motion to play with and control the way the light fell on her face. The shell preserves a liveliness, a fast-moving flapping and tapping world full of humour and connections, yet paradoxically in its very use it creates deadness. At times it can feel imperative to the patient to keep the shell going when the alternative might be either the deathliness or the deadness of contact. In so doing, the possibility of contact and real life is lost. Anything can be used as a barrier: autistic hard objects (Tustin, 1981) such as nail varnish bottles, jangling sets of keys, coloured glass bottles, shiny pens, rubbish bins; more or less anything which comes to hand, and the more glittery and shiny, the better. Something which catches the light and plays tunes at the same time, like a bunch of keys which jingle at different frequencies, on a see-through key ring which reflects then refracts the light and offers wonderful patterns in a kaleidoscope effect, is sheer joy! Herein lies an important aspect of the barrier. It is created as a defensive, protective shell, but becomes a retreat of sheer pleasure. My ordinary world could scarcely compete with such a multimedia experience.

On the soft side, a pillow into which one can press one's shape and have it mould reflectively to one's face feels receptive and comforting; as do soft padded jackets and big soft toys.

"Shells" based less on sensation do of course exist. Gomberoff and Gomberoff (Chapter Ten) describe a way of using language as an insulating wrapping. My patients used language in various ways, but usually with the dual aim of communicating and hiding. The pace of most sessions was hectic. Masses of detailed descriptions half finished, interrupted by two or three more descriptions, raced by. Sometimes it seemed as if I was being given a complete account of all the meetings and interactions, the papers read, the lectures given, of the few days since we'd last met. All this was delivered in about five minutes, in a tone which implied "I'm just getting rid of all this, take no notice!" Yet taking notice always helped. There were always important communications in the content and level of anxiety, and if I could find a way to speak about them, the patient could be helped towards contact and out of the ritualistic recitation. Sometimes this happened several times in one session as we dipped in and out of being in touch. At other times it was necessary to bring my patient back from a very deeply turned-away and cut-off place where she felt utterly alone and helpless, "left for dead". It was an important moment in Zara's analysis when she conveyed to me just what this felt like.

> Shortly after we had revisited the encapsulated trauma of rupture, she repeatedly berated me for my failure to empathise. She was absolutely sure now that there was something completely missing in me: the "missing link". Things had gone badly wrong here because of my utter failure to empathise and now she was damaged. I'd made her ill, so much worse. Everything I said was simply defensive, just self protection. Now she had to do it all on her own, had to try and keep her baby self from dying. She then told me that she'd had a consultation and taken full recordings of some of our sessions to a senior analyst to discuss. He'd said it looked as if I were completely out of touch. She reiterated how greatly I'd harmed her. I went through a range of feelings but most particularly felt a devastating hurt of an almost physical quality as if she'd stuck a dagger into me. I felt something in me begin to disintegrate as if all my professional foundations were crumbling. It was as though I were abandoned and defenceless against an ultimate catastrophe. I knew in my guts what Zara meant when she talked about her baby self dying. In the silence that followed, heavy with failure, I felt shocked and shaken. Zara began making agitated, rustling and flapping noises under the

blanket, which she now had over her head covering her face. My silence was clearly making her anxious. I said that I thought that if I spoke, my words and voice might feel unbearable, like a dagger going into her, and yet if I were silent that felt dangerous and bad also. She lay quietly and very alert. Emboldened, I continued that I thought her rustling sounds in the warm air around her head were the only protection she felt she had from me annihilating her altogether. After a silence she said, "Well that's good, at least you're trying to understand. You've taken in what I've said and made an effort."

Rhythm and music can form another barrier-retreat-shell-communication: contact could sometimes be made without some of the violence. In a turned-away state, Zara often tapped on my desk. If she was just "ticking over", staying alive, possibly imagining that she was providing for herself inside my space, there would be a gentle andante heartbeat rhythm. It felt calming, though sad, like keeping something going without coming dangerously to life. On other days the tapping would be less regular. After a missed session, Zara began with a list of the all holes she had circumnavigated in getting to me. There followed stories of people who had lost limbs, or died, or been irrevocably separated. She seemed to experience each story in her own body as she sped through them. She brought the terror of the gap into the room. Her drumming on the desk became recognisable: the heavy slow rhythm of the Death March. Dum, dum, de-dum, dum, de-dum, de-dum, de-dum. The "rag and bone" man went past in the street outside, ringing his bell. "Bring out your dead, bring out your dead!" she called.

Separation

As all this implies, the developmental step of separation has not been achieved. Instead, separation feels like a sudden shocking rift (Tustin, 1972). I think the example above in which the Death March was tapped out illustrates this to some extent.

Holidays and weekend breaks were always difficult. Early in treatment the defence of being one's own carer (Winnicott, 1960) could take over, but after a while this no longer worked. Both patients noticed that for a time they became ill, or injured themselves, during holidays. The difficulty lies in not being able to symbolise feelings when these are equated with body parts. An example might be helpful:

> Zara's anxiety was palpable as she entered the consulting room on a Friday shortly before a holiday break. In response to my "Good morning", she rejoined, "Bad morning; bad, bad, bad." She did not look at me, and held a favourite little glass bottle pressed into the ear nearest to me. "A broken arm and crushed finger! Ugh!" she continued, shuddering. "I see the break, the fracture, broken bones everywhere and he didn't look well, it's a shock for him. And I didn't know. I didn't see it in your face. You're all cool and calm. You don't realise a break is serious. And now I think of Gerry's arm broken" (a loved and loving member of her family). "Broken bones—break, break, break. Gerry drives at night. How did your husband do it? A car accident, a crash? I can't bear to think about it; and you didn't tell me it had happened." (Shuddering and flapping frantically). "You're not distressed; you should be looking after him. He probably shouldn't be working, you know."

Zara had seen my husband leaving the house with his arm in a sling and a bandaged finger. I spoke of the shock of suddenly seeing something of my world which she didn't know about, of my reality; of her panic about not being able to control the breaks, and her experience of the break as a physical fracture which was not happening to her, but to people she and I loved. I addressed her fear that she should be able to control it but couldn't, and her lack of hope that I, or anyone, could protect her from breaking. I said that she felt afraid I was careless, and unaware of the terrible danger that I put her in and that she put the world in. Earlier in the analysis it would have been impossible to speak about a "break", since all separation was denied along with any attachment. But at this point, my talking calmed her, and she responded by saying that she thought it probably was "the break" that was distressing her, clearly meaning now the break in our continuity.

Discussing holiday dates was always difficult. My patients became watchful for any sign that I was about to mention them. It seemed vital for them at least to feel in control of what they expected to be a shocking experience. Catherine learned to sense exactly the day I would raise it, and would come in with studied nonchalance saying: "It would probably be a good time to give me the holiday dates." The underlying terror remained palpable. For Zara, the shape of the break was important. It had to be exactly a full week, ending on a Friday and beginning on a Monday. Another shape would unleash a torrent of abuse about my irresponsibility and carelessness, putting people's lives at risk. I can only think that it was my failure to ritualise the separation which was so unforgivable. In knowing that I really was separate and could leave at times she had not defined, she seemed to feel open to the frightening experience of being unable to protect herself or those around her.

In the context of separation, it is interesting that both Catherine and Zara experienced difficulties in moving on from one activity to the next. It seemed that an awareness of time meant being aware of loss and separation too. They would "get stuck" in an activity and find it almost impossible to change to another. This made it hard to keep to times and arrangements. Catherine said that in order to get to her evening appointment with me she had to ask the secretary at work to tell her to leave the building: if she became engrossed in her work, she might be hours late.

The treatment process

Most of the examples in this section are drawn from Zara's analysis, since daily sessions offer the opportunity to work at greater depth. However, the phases I shall discuss were recognisable in Catherine's psychotherapy too.

Following the collapse of the "false self" (Winnicott, 1960), I think there are two phases in treatment, not following exactly one upon the other, but often contiguous and overlapping. Gradually one becomes aware that the first phase has more or less given way to the second. I think of these phases as the "contact containment" phase and the "developmental thrust" phase.

Contact containment phase

From my description of the patients' subjective experience, it will be clear that the first hurdle for patient and analyst is to establish a way of making and retaining contact that does not obliterate them both. Add to this the fact that the retreats are not only essential to the patient's survival but often feel so good, so amusing and so far superior to anything the analyst has to offer, and you have a problem! Since contact can feel so painful, it can unleash violent primitive hatred. Catherine described her feelings as "primitive savagery", and reported images of her as a lion holding me in her mouth as she growled and ripped me to bits with the blood dripping down her chops. The analyst has to be able to bear a seemingly never-ending amount of attack without being destroyed as an analyst. When I could understand that the attacks felt to my patients to be coming from an uncontrolled, primitive part of the brain, ruled by fight-or-flight mechanisms and unmoderated by passage through the ego, then I could join with them in trying to understand and moderate the fear of annihilation and the need to destroy me in order to survive. Late on in her analysis, Zara could warn me with a mixture of glee and dismay: "Oh no! They're at it again! Now I'm chopping you up into little bits and turning you into a meat loaf. That's horrible!"

I was helped, too, when I realised that all that I was being subjected to day after day, was but a taster of my patients' experience of me, and their world, day after day and year after year. If I felt assaulted, what must they feel like? I could see the attacks as both a way of surviving and a way of communicating to me their overwhelming experience.

In the light of this, I find Meltzer's description of autism as a failure to attach, a failure to feel, a condition of "autistic mindlessness" (Meltzer, 1975), a description which stresses the absence of ordinary human qualities, does not fit with my experience with Zara and Catherine. Rather, the attachment is enormous; too overwhelmingly intense, too possessive to be bearable to the patient, too greedy and oral to be manageable, too ferocious to be survived. Equally the so-called failure to empathise or feel human feelings seems to me to be more like its opposite. The experience of others' feelings as if they were in one's own body is so strong, so overwhelming that it must be evacuated or dissociated if the patient is not to be assaulted by feelings which cannot be moderated or contained. So for "mindless-ness" I would say "mind over-fullness" or perhaps more accurately "mind body over-fullness".

This shift in thinking is important because it allows the analyst to be ready to catch the wish to make contact, or to recognise the need for the retreats for a recovery period at a particular moment in the session; to realise when language and action are being used not simply as a barrier but as a communication too. Without this state of mind in the analyst, communication could be experienced and understood simply as destructive attacks. For example, for months Zara "cartooned" scenes in which she sprayed me with bullets. She described how my body jumped from the impact of the bullets and fell into lifelessness between shots. At last, one day, into my own thoughts came my three failed attempts to sit through the whole of the film *Apocolypse Now*. Each time I had had to give up and leave the room, sick and faint with the unremitting impact of the violence, the music, the spray of bullets and the unmoderated brutality. Meanwhile, Zara seemed to feel engaged in an amusing, though worrying activity. "Oh no!" she said. "I'm doing it again! Spraying you with bullets. There are bloody holes all over your jumper," and so on. The feelings were dissociated by turning the violence into a "cartoon". Over time we were able to understand many aspects of this activity. The spraying action of the bullets conveyed the danger of her looking at me and dispersing herself, in bits, violently into me. At the same time it expressed her wish to make contact with me—with the real inside of me—as well as the danger of doing so. Would I be able to stand it, to see it through? In conjuring up my own private memories and feelings, Zara did manage to get through to me by non-verbal communication, which was an enormous step forward. Usually I was left "cold" and puzzled by these attacks. There was communication too in the image of my lifeless body coming alive in "contact" with the bullet. Our contact brought us both to life, but was bound up with instantaneous death. Between moments of violent contact she, or I in the cartoon, fell back into lifelessness.

There is another important "mind shift" for psychoanalysts working with these patients. Sandler wrote of the analyst's collection of theories and part theories, which he holds in his pre-conscious mind and around which he organises the patient's material (1983). We call them up as required to help us make sense of our experience and observations. At the beginning of my work with Zara, I lacked a theory, or even a description, in my pre-conscious collection that could help me make sense of the roller-coaster of intense physical and emotional experience which characterised the work with her. To think in terms of defences seemed to deny the raw undefended quality of our contact. I think we both longed for "defences" but could find them nowhere. Her turned-away, flapping and tapping retreats were the only place she appeared to be able to go for any relief and protection against overwhelming experience. The dissociation and concreteness seemed psychotic, yet here was a fine mind in some intellectual areas, in someone holding down a tough job.

When I read Oliver Sacks' essay *An Anthropologist on Mars* (1995), I was able to recognise a similarity in the experience of my patient and his. With a neuropsychology view added to my armoury of theories, I felt freer to "believe" my patient's communications as fact, not fantasy. When she talked of being "brain damaged" or "brain dead", I had assumed she was telling me about an unconscious fantasy of what she had done to her mind. Actually she was telling me that she experienced herself as brain damaged, and in fact she was (however this might have come about). I think that this shift in me must have helped her feel better understood and known by me. I can only guess at how often in the early part of the analysis my communications had felt subtly wrong and like foreign bodies being put into her.[2]

Recognising the non-verbal communication is essential. Flapping and tapping are never quite as ritualistic as they might seem. Each instance will express a different rhythm or a different quality of panic. At this point, skills derived from infant observation are the most useful ones. It is not always possible to go on thinking while under attack, or being rejected and ignored. Concentrating on observing and thinking about one's observations, sometimes out loud if the atmosphere permits, sometimes quietly to oneself, keeps the process going and counters the patient's compulsion to turn the analytic process into one of her own rituals.

While retaining a separate mind in this way, one needs at the same time to join the patient's world. Cecchi (Chapter Five) describes beautifully how the analyst joins the alien world of Mariela, a little girl with autistic syndrome, as a step towards greater separateness. The examples I gave earlier of listening out for musical rhythms, or responding to the rhythm of the bell with the rhythm of my buzzer, were attempts to do this. Sometimes, however, there is a force that works against this empathy. A powerful countertransference can arise, matching and mirroring the patient's own hatred of being invaded or intruded upon. Catherine, for instance, shuddered and flapped away contact, saying: "Get out of me; come near me and you're dead meat!" The countertransference equivalent is: "No! I'm separate; I'm not part of this mad world of yours!" I can only understand this as part of the traumatic rupture of separation and the failure of pre-verbal communication as a developmental stage in attachment and early containment. The pressure on the analyst is to get rid of—abort—the patient. Staying with my patients' experience moment by moment seemed to help them to feel more contained.

Developmental thrust phase

It seems to me that when there is good enough containment, an internally driven developmental push comes into play. Perhaps it owes something to the tenacity and courage of these patients; perhaps it is common to all of us. Once we could establish a working relationship enough of the time, my patients set about trying to make up on the developmental steps which they had missed.

For Zara, this phase began after a holiday break. She entered without acknowledging me and looked anxiously around, flapping one arm and hand in a panicky, evacuating movement. Instead of going to the couch she sat on the floor beside my desk. She was very still and mostly hidden from view. I thought of a child playing dead. Inevitably she was afraid that I would object. In fact it felt like an act of freedom, which suggested she now inhabited herself. I was allowed to witness her terror and to talk to her about it in a different way. Her courage and determination to pursue the truth were our allies. She set us on a path of trying to understand her feeling that she was of a different species, and of searching for developmental stages that she felt she had not achieved. Her terror of contact was palpable, and she had to gather herself together before each session. She often bought reading material, drawing paper or puzzle books to hold her attention in case I failed her. She communicated conflicting messages to me: "Go away!" on the one hand, and on the other a desperation to be able to make contact, and a fear that if we failed she could die.

Though sometimes she continued to provoke me, she increasingly recognised how much this was meant to create an excitement that made her feel real. This was her dilemma: contact of that kind offered only momentary triumph and was followed by hopelessness. Getting in touch less violently was harder.

Drawing became helpful. When I first commented that in her drawings she was showing me how she thought in pictures, she was excited that I could know, and suspicious that I might use the knowledge to intrude. But soon she used drawing as a way of expressing what she could not say in words.

The drawings showed her inside various sorts of steel casings, or in thick padded spacesuits and impermeable protective shells. She might be a dot inside a steel box, safe but still dying from lack of oxygen. The steel box could swiftly become a coffin. Gradually she began to represent herself and me, usually separated by a brick wall or by something even safer and stronger. Then a drawbridge appeared in the wall, or grids, which could be opened or shut as necessary. It seemed that the need for a feed or for "oxygen" could be contemplated so long as she controlled the amount of opening time. We came to think of this as the need for a concrete regulator, or moderator, of a blast from the outside world, in the absence of an adequate internal cushion or filter.

Sometimes Zara dispensed with drawing and experimented with objects to hand. She placed the rubbish bin and her legal briefcase in front of herself as a barrier against me, and gingerly moved a little away from the desk so that I could see her and, on days when she felt able to look, she could see me. Sometimes a movement which looked like grasping and pulling the door handle of a heavy safe let me know that she was trying to open a little crack for me; though she might immediately shut it again to make sure she could. When I said I understood that she wanted to let me in and needed to be able to control my invasiveness at the same time, she readily agreed.

She was sure that it was important to try and look at me, but this was really difficult. She felt that she had lost an important part of her development through her terror of looking into dead eyes, and summoned up her courage to try. Often she threw her head from side to side while flapping or tapping away her anxiety; this was the scanning I mentioned earlier. She could manage catching sight of me in passing if at the same time she provided herself with muscular stimulation and sensations to counteract the potentially annihilating effect of taking me in through the eyes. If she was really anxious when arriving in the consulting room, she would say "dead eyes;

dead eyes; dead eyes" as if this mantra could keep them at bay. Any changes in my appearance, or in the consulting room or house, heralded the opening of a dead and empty chasm into which she might fall.

Zara's wish to look at me persisted. She explored various ways of "logging on", or "docking", or "plugging in". My desk was the medium, the control panel that she could link up with. From the beginning of the analysis my desk had fascinated her, with its numerous little drawers which could hide everything away and keep things organised and separate. Well before she could have acknowledged any relationship with me, she joked that she was having "a long-term relationship" with my desk. It seemed odd to her at first when I spoke of the desk as a safer representation of me: solid and enduring. (I quote: "This desk is older than you and will be here when you are dead.") But this idea seemed to fit the facts over time, and became acceptable as a way of thinking about her attachment to the desk. Sometimes when she felt suicidal she would move up very close to the desk and silently rest her head against it.

One way of trying to come in to land was to "dock" or "log on" to me by means of a visual image, which she enacted, of tuning in her radar, getting me on her screen and attaching to me. What surface I seemed to offer her depended on her state of mind. As she imagined herself attached by a cord, gradually being pulled in to land, my surface might feel jagged and inhospitable, and landing seemed as dangerous as running a ship onto the rocks in a heavy sea. On easier days, when the fit seemed better, my surface might feel smooth to her, more malleable and receptive. When I appeared smooth there was another danger: that I might turn glassy and she might slip off.

As she became able to look at me and talk directly to me at the same time, she would check my clothes, then shudder as though she herself were wearing them. Rubbing her neck, she told me that my sweaters were too itchy on her skin, my collars too hard. She felt the discomfort of my clothes on her own skinless surface. Getting inside my clothes seemed to be a vital part of reconnecting. It did not feel intrusive, and I wondered if this was an attempt to get inside as a baby does when it pushes its hand inside its mother's mouth to explore. I did not experience the old countertransference wish to evacuate her. Sometimes it felt quite playful.

Separations clearly disturbed Zara, but now it was possible to talk more about them. Although the repeated traumatic ruptures of the early part of the analysis were revisited many times, these episodes were shorter and contact was never completely and devastatingly severed. She often described an experience of being attached to the desk/me by a lifeline, and would make brave attempts to move a little out into the room, or look around it from a different perspective. She was terrified that the lifeline might detach, leaving her to float off. Neither of us would be able to do anything about this catastrophe. It brought to mind Piontelli's work on the ultrasound observation of foetuses (1992), and I wished we could see a video of her life in the womb to see if there had been a dangerous rupture and near-miscarriage. Perhaps a partial detachment of the umbilical cord had led to a temporary shortage of blood supply to part of her brain.

As our work progressed, Zara began to experience existing. Perhaps a new feeling of having the right to exist came together with the emergence of a stronger ego. However, with each experience of existing came the conviction that she would be destroyed almost immediately, either by her colleagues or by me. There were periods when she seemed to be exploring a split in her mind. She was ambidextrous, and if she was struggling to communicate something too frightening and found that her words were becoming disjointed and unavailable to her, she would occasionally change hands and see if she could draw or write it with the other hand. She explained to me that by using the other side of her brain she could maintain a bit more distance from the overwhelming emotions that stopped her functioning. While she could move between sides like this, she still lacked the flexibility to use her whole self, to integrate thinking with action, or to look at me at the same time as feeling and relating. She had experienced me as unable to integrate my thoughts with my feelings in the earlier part of the analysis. Now she knew it in herself. She thought of this difficulty as lack of communication between the left and right hemispheres of her brain.

Both of us wondered whether we were seeing an ego and sense of self which had been traumatically obliterated, or which had never developed properly because the capacity for ego development had not been "wired in" in the first place (Alvarez, 1999). My patient felt more drawn to the theory that the wiring wasn't right. I do not feel

I know. I thought that the world-view Zara showed me was one created by an intelligence and inventiveness without a strong enough ego (for whatever reason) and without a sense of self. Developmentally, in analysis she seemed to be trying to move from Body Ego (Freud, 1923) and brain to mind and psyche, with internal representations that promote the development of a containing and moderating ego.

Imperceptibly, Zara's sense of herself grew. Despite her despair at recognising her autistic features, she felt the beginnings of a sense of identity through getting to know herself with me. She reported situations at work in which she could hold to her own point of view with less fear of being wiped out. She even began to trust that her clear-sighted intelligence and heightened sensitivity to people's moods and feelings could be precious capacities if she could find ways to filter their overwhelming quality. She could notice when she was being what she called "Aspergersy" and when she was more "normal".

The development of this more observing and judging ego function was supported by our work. She came to sessions brimming full of all that had happened since she'd last spoken to me. Everything was reported fully and at great speed. Various anxieties would emerge. If I took up the anxieties before she had reported in full, we might get somewhere in understanding them, but she would return to her account, to the uncompleted list of events. I learnt to wait and hear the whole list through. At first it was hard to understand my role in this. I didn't feel that I was offering anything much. Then it became clear that if she put everything that had happened into me, she could feel less overwhelmed by it and still hold on to it in her own mind. She realised that she had always let anything overwhelming drop out of her mind up to this point, so much so that she lived in dread of completely forgetting vital meetings. Having emptied her mind, she would fill it up with the next focus of attention. The new procedure, which involved using me as auxiliary ego, allowed her to feel that I was looking after the overwhelming aspect, so that she could go away and deal with what needed to be dealt with. Even so, she could be suddenly panicked by the thought that I had been overwhelmed by all that she had put into me, and had died. It was as if she could still not rely on my having a living mind of my own which could survive her use of it. It was a relief to find that I could go on thinking and feeling. Perhaps because of these anxieties, she was very sensitive to my mind wandering and watched my face carefully to see if it suddenly went dead. It seemed as though she had the burdensome task of keeping me alive while needing to use me for something which, in her experience, killed or annihilated.

Some concluding remarks

The achievement of contact—first bearable, later enriching—seems to have been the significant breakthrough in these treatments. With this came the possibility of restarting the development of some of the most fundamental of ego functions.

What is particularly hard to bear, however, is the fact that despite fundamental improvement the autistic features do not go away. There is real ego damage, and concreteness of thinking, which does not change, and sensory experience can continue to be overwhelming. The difference, by the end of treatment, was that these were not the only features. They became features within a person who for the first time feels that she exists and is human and loveable, and that those autistic aspects of her personality can be included and thought about.

Notes

1. A version of this paper was first published in *The Many Faces of Asperger's Syndrome* (ed. Rhode & Klauber), London: Karnac, 2004.
2. I am grateful to Dr John Steiner for the illuminating suggestion that the patient could have experienced me in the transference as a demanding parental object who constantly hoped for their child to grow out of their autism. My mind shift could have been experienced by the patient as the removal of that enactment of the transference.

References

Alvarez, A. (1999). Addressing the Deficit: Developmentally Informed Psychotherapy with Passive Undrawn Children. In: A. Alvarez & S. Reid (Eds.), *Autism and Personality*. London: Routledge.

Balint, M. (1968). *The Basic Fault: Therapeutic Aspects of Regression.* London, Tavistock.

Freud, S. (1923). The Ego and the Id. *SE 19.*

Meltzer, D., Bremner, J., Hoxter, S., Weddell, D. & Wittenberg, I. (1975). *Explorations in Autism: A Psycho-Analytical Study.* Strathtay: Clunie Press.

Piontelli, M.E. (1992). *From Foetus to Child.* London: Routledge.

Rhode, M. & Klauber, T. (2004). *The Many Faces of Asperger's Syndrome.* London: Karnac.

Sacks, O. (1995). *An Anthrolpologist on Mars.* London: Picador.

Sandler, J. (1983). Reflections on some Relations between Psychoanalytic Concepts and Psychoanalytic Practice. *Int. J. Psychoanal.* 64: 33–45.

Shuttleworth, J. (1999). The Suffering of Asperger Children and the Challenge they Present to Psychoanalytic Thinking. *Journal of Child Psychotherapy* 25: 239–265.

Stewart, H. (1996). *Michael Balint: Object Relations Pure and Applied.* London: Routledge.

Tustin, F. (1972). *Autism and Childhood Psychosis.* London: Hogarth.

Tustin, F. (1981). *Autistic States in Children.* London: Routledge & Kegan Paul.

Tustin, F. (1986). *Autistic Barriers in Neurotic Patients.* London: Karnac.

Tustin, F. (1990). *The Protective Shell in Children and Adults.* London: Karnac.

Winnicott, D.W. (1960). Ego Distortion in Terms of True and False Self. In: *The Maturational Processes and the Facilitating Environment.* London: Hogarth, 1965.

Index